The Whaling People

of the West Coast of Vancouver Island and Cape Flattery

Eugene Arima and Alan Hoover

ROYAL **BC** MUSEUM
Victoria, Canada

Preface

Eugene Arima wrote the original edition of this book, entitled *The West Coast (Nootka) People*, published by the British Columbia Provincial Museum (now Royal BC Museum) in 1983. This new edition has been substantially revised and updated and includes five more narratives. It addresses a misconception about the economic importance of whaling to the Whaling People, noting the relationship between whale hunting and drift whaling. And it includes information on treaty negotiations between the Nuu-chah-nulth and the governments of British Columbia and Canada.

In this edition we use the term "Whaling People" to include the Nuu-chah-nulth proper, the Ditidaht and Makah. Although the Whaling People of Vancouver Island now refer to themselves as Nuu-chah-nulth or West Coast People, they formerly had no overall name because they comprised about two dozen independent groups named separately in the 19th century. The name for each group was taken from the name of the place where it lived or a descriptive term with the suffix *ʔatḥ* or *'atḥ* in Nuu-chah-nulth proper or *ʔaꞏʔtx̱* in the related but different Ditidaht and Makah languages (see page 248 for a spelling key). These suffixes can be translated as "residing at", "belonging to", or "people of". Consequently, Gilbert Malcolm Sproat, who settled in Alberni in 1860, called them the "Ahts" in his book on the Whaling People (1868), mistaking the origin of the suffix to be from the mythic character *kwatyat*, whose name he wrote "Quawteaht". Other early writings about the Whaling People refer to them as "Aht", "Aht Indians" or "Ahts".

"Nootka" and "Nootkans" are the most common identifying names for the Nuu-chah-nulth, still widely used in ethnology and linguistics (e.g., Suttles 1990), but they arise from Captain James Cook mistakenly thinking that the large inlet he visited in 1778 was called "Nootka". Gesturing, he asked some native men what the place was called. The men did not understand him, but guessed that he wanted to know if the inlet continued around the large island (Brabant 1926:160), and with a circling gesture supposedly replied "*no·tka·*", noted as "Nookka" in Cook's journal (Beaglehole 1967:308). But according to Chief Kwi·sto<u>x</u> (Charles Jones Sr) of Port Renfrew, the men said, "*No·tkshe···! No·tkshi?e·! Ch'a?ak?e·!*", meaning "Get 'round! Get around! The island!", warning Cook about the reefs he was approaching at Yuquot village (Arima et al. 1991:6).

Although the geographical names Nootka Sound and Nootka Island continue, the people of this region never liked being called "Nootka" or "Nootkans". In 1978 the Allied Tribes of the West Coast (established in 1958), changed its name to Nuu-chah-nulth Tribal Council. The term Nuu-chah-nulth was suggested by Mowachaht elder Abel John (*Ha-Shilth-Sa* 1978:5:5:4): "He explained that this word best described the west coast and how all our tribes are tied together through the mountains."

Attempts to make "Nuu-chah-nulth" the name for all Whaling People ran into a linguistic problem: in the languages of the Ditidaht and Makah peoples, to the south, the term for "all along the mountains" is *do·cha·?dł*, which sounds quite different. Some political distances also make the name difficult to use for the southern groups. In this light, the common English term "West Coast" (sometimes "Westcoast") was proposed in the first edition of this book as an appropriate term for the people: it alludes to the open-ocean side of Vancouver Island and its extension to the people of Cape Flattery was ethnically appropriate. There is a Nuu-chah-nulth counterpart in *Hitistis?at<u>h</u>*, meaning "West-side People". In this edition of the book we use "west coast" to refer to the geographical area on the west coast of Vancouver Island that is the traditional territory of the Nuu-chah-nulth, Ditidaht and Pacheedaht peoples.

Captain Cook proposed another name for the people: "Wakashian", from the applauding shouts he received when he went ashore. "*Wa·ka·sh!*", "*Wayke·sh!*" and "*Ka·ha· wa·ka·ah!*", the people cried, translated as "Bravo! Bravo!" (Beaglehole 1967:323, Sapir and Swadesh 1939:258). This name survives in linguistics as "Wakashan" to designate the language family embracing the languages of the Nuu-chah-nulth, Ditidaht and Makah and another related branch, the so-called "Kwakiutl" (Kwagu'ł) languages of northeast Vancouver Island and neighbouring mainland.

In summary, we use the term Whaling People to include all groups of the Nuu-chah-nulth, Ditidaht, Pacheedaht and Makah. We also maintain the three-part geographic division to distinguish certain words: the northern and central groups, who speak the Nuu-chah-nulth language, though some words differ between the regions, and the southern groups, the Ditidaht, Pacheedaht and Makah, who speak the two closely related languages Ditidaht and Makah. Unless otherwise indicated the terms are in the Nuu-

Where the Whales Used to Dig Clams. Tim Paul drawing, 2008.

when whaling while being unmanly. That is the reason he said that he found what was now given to him light and that the situation made him brave and unafraid. Even when it was cold he was not afraid to go out. A weak-minded person, a chicken-heart, was afraid: one reason the whales had no respect and did not become tame to him.

Tłan'iqoł began getting ready from then on, from the time he was formally given the spear. It was winter when this happened. He continued to bathe ritually from then right up to summer. He shopped around to buy harpoon heads and sealskin floats, and started making twisted rope. Many people were helping him twist up cedar branch rope. At the same time he was bathing, for he was bathing and praying ritually for whales, the rascal Tłan'iqoł! He had everything ready by the time the next winter was coming – as much equipment as was required for those who go out whale-hunting. He also bought a whaling canoe when he had all the required gear as winter came along.

He began bathing and praying ritually in earnest when it turned into winter. By the time it became another year he had all his crew gathered together. The one who was going to be at the right-hand side of the canoe was always bathing to death, also the one who was going to be steering. There are three who work hard at bathing: the one at the bow, the one next to him and the steersman. It would cause bad luck, they say, if one was not ritually prepared like that when he took hold and pulled on the line. He prayed ritually that he would cause it to become good and free of bad luck whenever he touched the line, when the whale was there on it. For it causes the whale to be in great pain, they say, if one was not ritually prepared like that when he took hold and pulled on the line. For that reason the whale would then run, and the bowman would not get another chance to spear.

The steersman was also praying that the Humpback or Grey Whale would become tame and not shy away, that he would cause it to become glad when it looked into his face. He was standing against the sternpiece stooped over, the steersman, watching for signals from the bowman who would wave, "Head that way." The paddle was put on the other side and the canoe was turned by drawing in. He didn't alter course when they were trying to spear. He would put his paddle to one side of the canoe to make it go the other way where the bowman waved. He switched his paddle from side to side over his head. He did not point his paddle towards the bow, fearful lest it create delay and slow the canoe. He did not only steer by drawing, for as soon as the sea became calm they paddled up to the whale, all working together when it came up.

Then the harpooner and the one next to him let their paddles go at the same time, whereupon the one sitting before the steersman on the right-hand side grabbed both paddles and put them in the canoe. Now they found themselves to be in position alongside the whale when it surfaced at the same moment the harpoon struck. Then the one on the left side backpaddled, also the one behind him, and the one on the right, too, backpaddled to make the canoe back up. They all backpaddled, the whole crew. Only three were idle in the canoe not doing anything at this time: the harpooner and the ones behind him. The line was being looked after, the one tending it using a paddle. The other three were still all busy backing the canoe away, which is why they were quickly far behind, out of danger of the beating tail of the whale.

When the warm weather peeked through the winter cold and spring was arriving, the Tla-o-qui-aht moved. The Grey Whales began sounding in the water. Tłan'iqoł got ready. He set out on the ocean at dawn, went around the point at Tin'im'a [Whetstone Place (Portland Point, west of Long Beach by Schooner Cove)] and anchored there. Well now, the Greys appeared. They say that they used to travel in great numbers, many to-gether, sometimes ten going along together, sometimes five. And then one was blowing close to Tłan'iqoł, where he was waiting in ambush on the rocks! Tłan'iqoł paddled hard away from the rocks where he was hiding. He went towards the whale and started chasing, going after it, the rascal! Right away they were side by side with it. It had now happened the way he wanted it to, the way he prayed it would happen: that it would come alongside his canoe, that it would not run away from him, that it would become tame and not be afraid of him. He speared while it was alongside, the whale, that rascal Tłan'iqoł! Now he was using that which was given to him at the potlatch. He hit a vital spot, causing it to die instantly, the rascal! His whaling spear was still in the whale, right there on the ocean. At once they started towing it for him. They arrived at ʔIch'a·chisht [a

"Tłan'iqoł Becomes a Whaler." Tim Paul drawing, 2008.

small bay on southeastern Echachis Island], tied it up on the beach and began to butcher it for him. Tłan'iqoł had fulfilled his obligation to the one who had said, "You be the one to make use of this."

Tłan'iqoł stayed home for two days, then went out once more. He lay in ambush on Tin'im'a again where the Tla-o-qui-aht had their place for ambushing passing whales. Grey Whales appeared, two of them going along together. He came out of his hiding place, the rascal, and went after the whales again. Once more they were side by side like that, and he speared, the rascal! The whale ran off. His line was not yet all out of the canoe when it leaped out of the water with mouth wide open and died, the Grey. The mother came up on the surface of the sea and lay face down alongside.

"Ha! All right! Spear the mother too," his crew began to say together.

Tłan'iqoł fixed a line onto his spare harpoon, speared again and hit the other one. Then many harpooned his whale, for there were numerous whalers out, and again it died right there on the ocean. And Tłan'iqoł was towing the whales around the point at ʔIch'a·chisht.

A spokesman for Tłan'iqoł said, "Here you are, Sit'aqinim, here it is, what you told me to make use of. I now have made use of your former whaling spear. Come then, down the beach, for here are two Grey Whales! I am now returning a gift for the gift you gave to me."

So he had his speaker say. Our tribe heard about this. "Tłan'iqoł has captured," they said. It was not long before everyone started to say that Tlan'iqol had two whales behind him. Sit'aqinim came down the beach and started butchering the whales. Tłan'iqoł made him have the two dorsal saddles on his head face down, the one who had given him the gift of a whaling spear. Those were all he caught: three Greys – that many. They got jealous of him, it is said, and made Tłan'iqoł eat his own blubber [taboo for whalers]. But no one knew who did this to him; we only heard that it was done to him. All right, that is how long this story is. It happened but a little while ago. I was a boy at the time; I was quite a big boy.

This account (Sapir and Swadesh et al. 2004:88-91), taken down from dictation by Alex Thomas, was mailed in 1916 to Edward Sapir who headed Anthropology at the new museum in Ottawa. The typed copy available to us lacked the name of the teller, but he might have been Thomas's greatest source, his grandfather, Sa·ya·ch'apis, who was old and blind. If so, the events described may be from about the mid 19th century.

THE COUNTRY

The territories of the Whaling People stretch over roughly 300 kilometres along most of the Pacific side of Vancouver Island from Cape Cook to Glacier Point, with a southward spur of about 50 kilometres across Juan de Fuca Strait that takes in the Cape Flattery region as far south as Ozette. Their country is a rugged coastal strip dominated by the Pacific Ocean and backed by the steep peaks of the Island Range. Along the major inlets the people range far inland, particularly on the Alberni Canal, which extends well over half way across Vancouver Island. With the great warm Black (Japan) Current flowing by offshore, the climate is mild for the latitude, but the water, even inshore, is very cold. When the warm air blowing off the Pacific from the west meets this cold current and the high coast, its heavy charge of moisture condenses into fog, cloud and rain – constant features of west-coast weather. Annual precipitation is commonly 300 centimetres or more, producing a luxuriant northern rain forest. Dense growth on land makes travel on foot difficult; it is much easier to travel by water. On the other hand the forest provides ample wood, including the exceptionally useful Western Redcedar, for human uses.

The country of the Whaling People, previous to the environmental degradation that resulted from 20th-century industrial practices, was rich in fish, shellfish, mammals, birds, berries, shoots and roots. By hunting, fishing and gathering, the people lived well with no need for agriculture. Although land resources were important, the once bountiful sea provided most of the food. Salmon, herring, cod and halibut were the main fish caught.

From the tidal shore, the Whaling People harvested clams, cockles, mussels, oysters, barnacles, chitons and sea urchins. The Nuu-chah-nulth were the only groups on the Northwest Coast to harvest dentalia, a tusk-shaped univalve mollusc, from beds near Tachu Point in Ehattesaht territory (Drucker 1951:111). Dentalia are an important ornamentation for headdresses, earrings and other ceremonial clothing. The Nuu-chah-nulth traded dentalia to many of their neighbours. For example, Sarah Olabar in the 1930s recounted that people used dentalia shells to buy Yellow-cedar-

The tip of a dentalia spear (model). RBCM 2232.

bark blankets and "kelps" (long bull-kelp tubes filled with Eulachon oil) from Kwakwala speaking groups. Fifteen large or thirty small dentalia shells would buy one "kelp" (Drucker n.d., vol. 10, p. 93).

Whales, porpoises, sea-lions and seals are the big game of the sea, along with the Sea Otter, hunted for its precious pelt. Ducks, geese, swans, albatrosses, gulls, loons and cormorants are among the aquatic birds hunted, while in the forest grouse are easy to approach. On land, the main game animals are Columbian Black-tail Deer, Elk and Black Bear, and the smaller mammals taken include Mink, Marten, River Otter and Raccoon. Grey Wolves and Cougars are more important in mythology than as food. Commonly eaten plant foods include the berries and tender spring shoots of Salmonberry and Thimbleberry, the berries of Salal, blackberries, cranberries, gooseberries and huckleberries, the roots of clover and Skunk Cabbage, the rhizomes and fiddleheads of ferns, the bulbs of Blue Camas, and the inner bark of Western Hemlock, all harvested mainly in spring and summer.

In winter, the Whaling People tended to concentrate in villages on the more sheltered shores of bays and inlets or behind islands; and in summer, when it was relatively calm, they moved to smaller camps on the more open coast. They formed villages near the salmon streams running into the protected inlets, which tended to be natural geographical units for further association into tribes and even confederate alliances of tribes under the pressures of warfare (see Drucker 1951:6 and Sproat 1868:10, 303).

Radiocarbon dating reveals that the Whaling People have occupied their land for at least 4,000 years (Dewhirst 1978, McMillan 1999:104, 109). Archaeological evidence suggests that, over this time, their tools and presumed ways of living changed very slowly. Fishing has probably always been the primary livelihood. Woodworking was likely well developed early, judging by the chisel and adze blades, wedges, hammer stones and abraders found in a strata dated 2200-1000 BC that are remarkably similar to recent ones (Dewhirst 1978:13-17). Whaling People always hunted both sea and land mammals, but they exploited more over time as they improved their hunting gear.

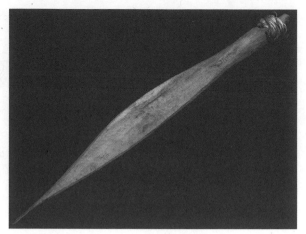

Wood-working tools: a stone hand maul (left) and a yew wedge.
RBCM 14202 and 2237.

THE WHALING PEOPLE

Although the Whaling People of the distant and recent past shared a common way of life, they were not united as one nation but divided into major groups that may be called "tribes" and "confederacies" of tribes. Each tribe was made up of one or more smaller "local groups" centred around chiefs and their extended families. The local group is the basic autonomous political unit and thus the real "First Nation". There is no overall Nootka, Aht, Nuu-chah-nulth or Westcoast "nation", such blanket names being merely general ethnic labels. They are recent terms originating from European need for simplistic categorization and ignore the true political realities with their long histories.

Over time, tribes changed as all human groups do – forming, growing or shrinking, and lasting for various periods. Traditional memories take some groups back perhaps two or three centuries, or further, but more-or-less full knowledge of all Whaling People's tribes and confederacies dates from about the mid 19th century. Records from the late 18th century mention many of them. The coming of western civilization with its guns seems to have made warfare more intense, increasing the formation of confederations by alliance and conquest. More than 20 major groups existed in the first half of the 19th century, but only 16 have survived into the second half of the 20th century as politically separate, officially recognized "bands". Through diseases and warfare the Nuu-chah-nulth and Ditidaht population fell from about 30,000, late in the 18th century when Europeans arrived, to a low in the 1930s of about 2,000. Since then, the population has been increasing,

Early 20th-century whaler Do·kmi·s (Wilson Parker) from the Cape Flattery area. He wears a bear-skin cloak, holds a whaling harpoon and has two inflated seal-skin floats at his feet. (See also Savard 2010:112.)
Edward S. Curtis photograph; RBCM PN-4980.

passing 4,000 in the 1970s and 8,500 in 2006 (Canada 2007:71-87). Catastrophic as the population crash after European arrival seems from these figures, the drop was greater still, for the pre-contact population may have been twice as much as the roughly 30,000 estimate based on John Meares's 1788 listing of the number of warriors by major tribal divisions (1967:229-31). Smallpox and other epidemics had already taken a toll since the first European visit in 1774 by Juan Perez and even earlier as the new diseases preceded European arrival among the Whaling People.

There have been about 30 main tribal and confederacy groupings noted since the mid 19th century; but earlier, when the population was much larger and diversified, there may have been two or three times as many.

The following list names 31 major groups for recent times (based on Drucker 1951:222-41, Edward Sapir's fieldnotes, and information from John Thomas on the Ditidaht and Makah speakers; see also Arima et al. 1991:9-12, and Arima and Dewhirst 1990:391-3). The names of the tribes and confederacies are given first, using their common English spellings. These English names are only approximations, even for the currently "official" names of governmentally recognized bands, but they are easier on the eye for most readers. The actual name of the group, used by the people in the group, follows in parentheses. Official spellings have changed repeatedly over the past century and may be expected to continue to change until a consistent system is established.

Northern Whaling People

Chickliset (*Ch'i·qtłis?ath*). The people of "Ououkinsh" Inlet with territory extending from Cape Cook to the beach opposite Whiteface Island. Their winter village was at ?I·qos and their summer site at ?Apsowis. They have moved to live with the Kyuquot and are no longer a separate governmentally-recognized band.

Kyuquot (*Qay'o·kw'ath*). An old confederacy made up of the Qano·pittakamł (possibly), Shaw'i·sp'ath, Qwixqo·?ath and Tł'a·?a·?ath, who had winter villages at Ma·xk'i·t, Shaw'i·sp'a, Qwixqo· and Ho·psitas, respectively. In turn, these peoples are made up of 14 local groups, each named after its salmon stream in the sound. Overall confederacy territory extends from Whiteface Island to Rugged Point. In the common summer village at ?Aqti·s there used to be 27 houses arranged to conform with the winter settlement. The amalgamated group refer to themselves as the Kyuquot/Chickliset First Nation (*Ha-Shilth-Sa* 2007:34:18:18). Their home community is located at Ho·psitas on the north shore of Kyuquot Sound.

Ehattesaht (*?I·hatis?ath*). This union of three peoples includes the Ehattesaht proper of Zebballos and Espinoza Inlet, possibly the Ha?wihtakamłath of the outside coast and the Chinaxnit?ath of Queen's Cove where they

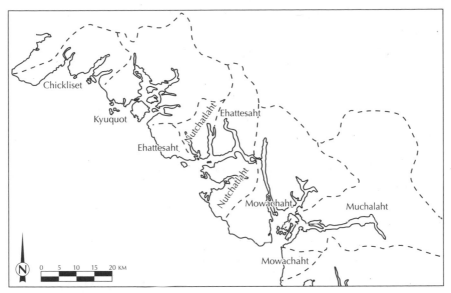

Northern Whaling People.

concentrated at the village of Chenahkint. The former common summer village was at Tatchu Point. The Ehattesaht are now located at the village of Ehattis near the town of Zeballos (*Ha-Shilth-Sa* 1988:15:7:7).

Nutchatlaht (*Noch'a·ł?atḥ*). A confederacy of several groups with a summer village at the north of the mouth of Nutchatlitz Inlet. Winter villages of the constituent tribes were inside that inlet and also at Port Eliza and Espinoza inlet, the lower part of which belongs to the Ehattesaht. In 1988, the Nuchatlaht moved from the village of Nuchatlitz on Nootka Island to Okluge (also spelled "Oclucje") on Espinoza Inlet west of Zeballos (*Ha-Shilth-Sa* 1988:15:2:5.

Mowachaht (*Mowach'atḥ*; previously the "Nootka" Band). A union of two Nootka Sound peoples: the Mowachaht proper, made up of six local groups of Tlupana Inlet, and the Ko·pti·, composed of several groups from Tahsis Inlet and the outer coast of Nootka Island. The confederacy's joint summer village at Yuquot traditionally had 13 houses.

Muchalaht (*Machła·?atḥ*). An amalgamation of perhaps seven local groups who banded together in the 1800s at Muchalaht Inlet and Gold River on the east side of Nootka Sound. They moved to Yuquot in the 1890s and officially merged with the Mowachaht in 1951. These two groups now jointly refer to themselves as the Mowachaht-Muchalaht First Nations. In 1966 they moved to Ahaminaquus at the head of Muchalaht Arm and in 1996 to Tsaxana, inland from the community of Gold River (Mowachaht-Muchalaht First Nations 2000:22).

Central Whaling People

Hesquiaht (*Hishkwi·?ath*). Four or five groups around Hesquiat Harbour merged into one in the 1800s. In the second half of the 20th century, the Hesquiaht dispersed mainly to Port Alberni. Their major community is now Refuge Cove, formerly known as Hot Springs Cove, south of Hesquiat Harbour, about 35 kilometres northwest of Tofino.

Manhousat (*Ma·n'o?is?ath*). A small group on Sydney Inlet that joined the Ahousaht in the 20th century.

Otsosat (*?Ots'o·s?ath*). A once numerous people on Flores Island and the inlets behind it, the Otsosat were practically annihilated by the Ahousaht in the early 1800s (see pages 148–59).

Ahousaht (*?A·ho·s?ath*). A large group originally of Vargas Island and the mainland behind it, who took over Flores Island through war against the Otsosat. The main Ahousaht village is Marktosis on Flores Island.

Kelsemat (*Kiłtsama?ath*). These people of Vargas Island amalgamated with two other local groups and subsequently joined the Ahousaht after most of their men died while fur sealing in the Bering Sea in the late 19th century.

Tla-o-qui-aht (formerly Clayoquot; *Tła?o·kwi?ath*). Originally from Kennedy Lake, these people came to dominate Clayoquot Sound through warfare. Opitsat, on Meares Island, and Esowista, south of Tofino, are their primary villages.

Ucluelet (*Yo·ło?ił?ath*). Shortly before contact with Europeans, these people from Ucluelet Arm and Long Beach took Effingham Inlet from the Hach'a·?ath and Nahmint Bay on Alberni Inlet from the Nam'int?ath. Their major village is Ittatsoo at Ucluelet Inlet.

Toquaht (*T'okw'a·?ath*). These people of Toquart Bay, Mayne Bay and west Barkley Sound suffered extreme losses though warfare by the mid 19th century (Sproat 1868:104). Macoah, their home village, is on Toquart Bay on the north side of Barkley Sound. Abandoned in the 1920s, houses began to be built there again in the 1980s (McMillan 1999:64-5).

Uchucklesaht (*Ho·choqtłis?ath*). This group lives on Uchucklesit Inlet near the mouth of Alberni Inlet. At one time they claimed east Barkley Sound and the outside coast to Tsusiat Falls, dominating the Huu-ay-aht. Their home village is Elhlateese at the head of Uchucklesit Inlet.

Tseshaht (or Sheshaht; *Ts'isha·?ath*). This confederacy unites the Tseshaht proper, Hach'a·?ath, Hiko·ł?ath, Ma·ktł?i·?ath, Nachim'was?ath, Wanin?ath, Nash?as?ath and others of central Barkley Sound. The first three forced their way up Alberni Inlet not long before the coming of the Europeans. The Hach'a·?ath also reduced the *?A?ots?ath* of Effingham Inlet, T'om'aktłi?ath and Ma·ktł?i·?ath. The primary village of the Tseshaht is near the city of Port Alberni on the west bank of the Somass River.

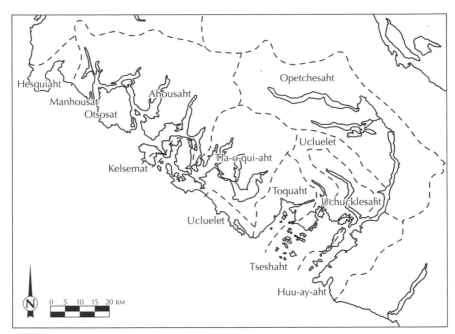

Central Whaling People.

Hupacasath (or Opetchesaht; *Ho·pach'as?ath*). An amalgamation of Tł'ik-o·t'ath, M'o·ho·ł?ath and Ts'o·ma?as?ath, who apparently were Coast Salish peoples on Sproat and Great Central lakes, the Somass River and Alberni Inlet down to Hell's Gate. Displaced by the Tseshaht, they adopted the language and ways of their invaders (Sapir 1912). ?Asw'in?is, their primary village, is near Port Alberni.

Huu-ay-aht (or Ohiaht; *Ho·?i·?ath*). This group occupies the east side of Barkley Sound and was joined, before European arrival, by war-reduced neighbours on the southeast: the Kix?ini?ath, the Ch'imataqso?ath, just around Cape Beale, and the ?An'aqtł'a?ath of Pachena Bay. The Huu-ay-aht took the San Mateo Bay region from the Uchucklesaht and the territory of the ?Aniqshitł?ath along Sarita River. The current home village of the Huu-ay-aht is Anacla at the lead of Pachena Bay.

Southern Whaling People

Tsaqqawisa?tx̱. This independent group in a village just east of Pachena Point on the outer coast faded away in the 19th century, with the last few moving to Nitinat Lake.

Tł'a·di·w?a·?tx̱. This group lived on the outer coast in a village on the Klaniwa River until it died out early in the 20th century.

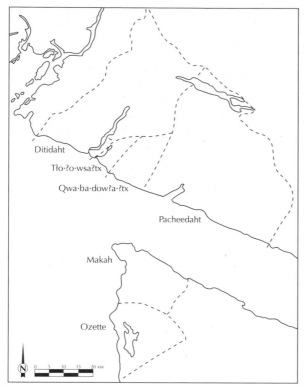

Southern Whaling People.

Tso<u>x</u>wa·d?a·?t<u>x</u>. A coastal group just west of Nitinat Lake that was stronger than the Tsaqqawisa?t<u>x</u> and Tł'a·di·w?a·?t<u>x</u>, but merged with the Ditidaht in the late 1800s.

Ditidaht (*Di·ti·d?a·?t<u>x</u>*) The first Ditidaht people of Nitinat Lake appar-
ently centred the alliance of tribes between Pachena and Bonilla points.
The Da?o·w?a·?t<u>x</u> were later immigrants and have been absorbed. The main
Ditidaht community is at Malachan at the east end of Nitinat Lake.

Tło·?o·wsa?t<u>x</u>. This small group at Clo-oose Beach and on the Cheewat
River, east of Nitinat Lake, stayed separate until it merged with the Ditidaht
in the 1970s.

Wawa·x<u>?</u>adi?sa?t<u>x</u>. An outside group east of the Tło·?o·wsa?t<u>x</u> dispersed
around the late 19th century.

Qwa·ba·dow?a·?t<u>x</u>. The major outside group just east of Carmanah Point
stayed independant into the mid 20th century, then joined the Ditidaht.

Qala·yit'a?t<u>x</u>. A group at Clyde Beach, east of Bonilla Point, apparently
disappeared after warfare with the Tseshaht.

Tł'oqw<u>x</u>wat'a?t<u>x</u>. This autonomous group of Gordon River and West
San Juan Bay vanished early in the 19th century.

Pacheedaht (or Pacheenaht; *P'a·chi·d?a·?tx̲*.) Now the only group east of Bonilla Point, the Pacheedaht claim the coast to Point No Point. This group is an ally of the Ditidaht. The main Pacheedaht village is near Port Renfrew.

Makah (from *Max̲'i·ya*, a Clallam word meaning "alien"; *Q'widishch?a·?tx̲*). This confederacy is composed of several groups around Cape Flattery with villages at Di·ya·, Ts'o·yas, Wa?ach' and Bi?id?da, all of whom gradually concentrated in the post–1855 reservation period at the village of Neah Bay (Riley 1968:58).

Ozette (*?Ose·?ła?tx̲*) The most southerly group of the Whaling People, their village is about 30 kilometres past Cape Flattery just beyond Cape Alava. In the reservation period they, too, gradually moved to Neah Bay and now tend to be regarded as Makah.

The northern and central Whaling People call the Makah and Ozette peoples the *Tł'a·?as?ath̲*, meaning "seaward people", but the Ditidaht and Makah use the same term (*Tł'a·?asa?tx̲* in their languages) to describe the people around Cape Scott at the north end of Vancouver Island. Long ago, according to Pacheedaht Chief Charles Jones Sr, the Cape Scott people moved to Cape Flattery, presumably because the intervening stretch of coast was already occupied. While this explanation may seem a rationalization of the two occurrences of the name, if true it could account for the major linguistic division between the Whaling People of the north and central regions and those in the south. If the coast from Barkley Sound east was Salish at that time, then migrants to Cape Flattery may have been isolated long enough to develop the linguistic separation and then spread across onto Vancouver Island toward Barkley Sound displacing the Salish. But this is speculation only and archaeology in depth is sorely needed along the Whaling People's coast to help establish what happened over the millennia.

Two surviving groups in the above list – the Hupacasath and the Muchalaht – lived away from the open sea and did not hunt whales. Both were originally Salish peoples with adjacent hunting areas in the interior of the island who recently adopted the language and many of the ways of the Nuu-chah-nulth.

Other peoples at either end of the Whaling People's coastal stretch of territory also adopted whaling. To the north, in the Quatsino Sound region, the Kwakwala speaking (Kwakwa̲ka'wakw) nations of the Klaskino (*Tłasqinox̲w*), Koskimo (*Gosgimox̲w*) and Quatsino (*Gwa?tsinox̲w*) used Nuu-chah-nulth-type canoes and gear to hunt whales, though perhaps only since the later 19th century with increased contact past the hazard of Brooks Peninsula. Kwakwala is the other main division of the Wakashan language family, and there are cultural commonalities between the Kwakwa̲ka'wakw and the Nuu-chah-nulth. Two peoples south of Ozette, linguistically and

A Nuu-chah-nulth carver completing the bow of a fine canoe at Mud Bay, Victoria. The streamlined Wolf's-head bow is a masterpiece of canoe-making art. RBCM PN-26009.

culturally unrelated to the Whaling People, also adopted whaling: the Quileute (*Kwo?li·yot'*) of the Quillayute and Hoh rivers (Powell 1990:431), and farther south again on the Queets and Quinault rivers the more numerous Coast Salish-speaking Quinault (*Kwinayɬ*; Hajda 1990:507, Olson 1936:44-48). Both groups used mostly Whaling People's canoes and gear obtained through trade, but also made rougher copies themselves. In his book, *The Quinault People*, Ronald Olson (1936:110) describes an acquisition of whaling equipment through trade with the Makah:

> Chief Peter of Neah Bay (Makah) wished to marry a certain Quinault girl. He came down the coast with a fleet of ocean-going canoes, and they paddled up and down the river in front of *kwi'nail* singing songs. At a signal all the canoes were beached in front of the girl's house. In the chief's canoe were guns, blankets, beads, and so on. His men then carried the canoe, with the chief and goods still in it, toward the house. When close enough he hurled his whaling harpoon at the house with all his might. It pierced through a plank. This was evidently regarded as a good omen, for it was said that he would not have taken the girl otherwise. The father of the girl now came out and was told the whaling outfit, the canoe, all the goods in it, and several other canoes were his if he would yield the girl. It was stated that this form of payment was unknown to the Quinault.

Fine canoes continue to be carved today, albeit not often enough. In the spring of 2009 Tla-o-qui-aht master canoe-maker Joe Martin displays a newly carved, ready to spread *p'inw'ał* (long canoe), five arm spans long on the bottom. Trained from childhood by his father, Robert Martin (1925–2000), Joe has created 42 canoes since 1982. His younger brothers, Carl and Bill, have made a score of their own canoes. Neighbouring peoples also adopted the Nuu-chah-nulth canoe as their big sea-going vessels. The Nuu-chah-nulth canoes have become the predominant style in the Tribal Journeys canoe festival, begun in 1989, which now involves 40 or more big canoes each summer in a two-week-long event of cultural renewal in this region. Eugene Arima photograph.

The Makah obtained many of their canoes in trade from Vancouver Island, home to good Western Redcedar and excellent canoe makers. Today, the Martin brothers of Clayoquot still carve canoes for themselves and others, like the Klallan and Mowachaht. The 11-metre *Hummingbird* that the Makah used to kill a Grey Whale in 1999 is a Martin canoe. In 2006, Ditidaht carver Fred Peters made a huge 15-metre canoe. Unfortunately, he died before completing it with the head pieces of the ends so vital to wave fending and appearance. Peters was likely the last able old-time canoe maker, and the appearance of his last canoe has been ruined by badly shaped heads added by someone inexperienced in the art.

Chapter 1
Making a Living

WHEN THE WORLD TURNS AROUND

To see a little of what it was like to make a living in the world of the Whaling People before the coming of the Europeans, we must try to learn something of how they perceived their world, and how they used their skills and equipment. While, as a whole, the Whaling People occupied several hundred kilometres of coast and knew of many other aboriginal peoples between Alaska and California, most individuals usually concerned themselves only with their tribal area and immediate neighbours. They were not aware of Earth as a planet with all its diversity, or that it circled the sun; some thought the world was a flat disc on a pole (Boas 1890:44).

The Whaling People conceived time as an endless annual cycle. In December, to determine when the winter solstice happened, the wise old men would sit outside the big cedar-plank houses each dawn to watch the sun come up at a slightly different place on the skyline each day as it moved toward a known solstice mark, such as a certain tree on a mountain ridge (Drucker 1951:115, 156; Pacheedaht Chief Charles Jones confirmed this in an interview with Arima in the 1960s). When the sun reached that mark, it would rise in the same spot for four mornings, the "sacred" number of times, then begin moving back again along the horizon. If the sun did not quite reach the solstice mark, it would be "bucking the wind", and a bad stormy winter would follow. If the sun went past the mark, there would be good salmon runs that year.

At the solstice, owls suddenly appeared in the house, and a perfume in the air made everyone fall asleep as if doped. Thereupon, with four thunderclaps, the world turned around – *kwatkwacht* (Dit.) – backing up so that the sun moved back in the sky again, making the days grow longer and repeating the seasons. At the moment of the reversal, the water suddenly rose in a great flood tide, up to the edge of the bed platforms as everyone slept – except for a fortunate few who saw it and gained luck – then quickly went down again without a trace. The Whaling People also noted the summer solstice, which may have marked another backing up of the world, since a Spanish observer in 1792 recorded the months as beginning with July (Mozino 1970:62).

A WORLD FULL OF SPIRITS

The Whaling People's world worked in supernatural ways. To succeed in most undertakings, people had to have power to control the spirits involved. They prayed for power, especially to four great spirits – the four chiefs of the Above, the Horizon, the Land and the Undersea (Curtis 1916:45, Drucker 1951:152). Early European observers at Nootka Sound noted that the Mowachaht recognized a supreme Sky Spirit, whose name was known only to the chiefly as *Ka·ʔo·ts*, meaning "grandchild" (Jewitt 1815:120, 171; Mozino 1970:26). Ka·ʔo·ts's country, up above, was always calm, sunny and warm with plenty of everything – a Whaling People's paradise where chiefs and those slain in battle went after death (Sproat 1868:14). This great Sky Spirit controlled the salmon and other resources, so the chiefs prayed to him on behalf of their followers. There was also the afterworld for commoners and slaves, a poor underground country ruled by *Pin-pu-la*, where there were no salmon, the deer were very small and the houses inferior (Mozino 1970:28-9, Sproat 1868:213). More recently, the Moon, called *Hopał* ("round") or *Ka·ʔo·ts*, was known as the greatest spirit and prayed to by all. The Moon and his wife, the Sun, called *Nʼa·s* (N) or *Dʼa·x* (S), were good protective spirits. Some stars had spirit names too.

Weather phenomena had some interesting explanations that were general among many Northwest Coast First Nations. Thunder (*To·ta·*) was the flapping of the wings of the Thunderbird (*Tʼi·tskʼin*), a huge man on a far off mountain who put on a gigantic raptor suit to hunt whales. Thunderbird had a Lightning Snake (*Hi·ʔitłʼi·k*) for a belt, which would flash down to earth when he dropped it. Thunderbird also caused hail. Snow fell when a big Sky Dog scratched himself letting mange scales fall. Fog came out of the kneecaps of the Crane. The violent storms that came with the southeast wind were the farts of an old man, and since in myth, some animals and birds tried to make him stop, the Whaling People would sing their songs to bring calm weather. Rainbow was once a man. An eclipse happened when the Sun or Moon was swallowed by an immense Sky Codfish (Drucker 1951:155, Jewitt 1815:165).

Under the sea, not far offshore, was a great house with the Salmon People in one half and the Herring People in the other, representing the major food sources. If the Whaling People neglected to perform rites to honour them, the Salmon and Herring people would become angry and dangerous. Also in undersea houses were the Whales and Hair Seals. Killer Whales could come out onto the land and turn into Wolves – both were more likely to be friendly than dangerous. Other fantastic sea beings included giant sharks that could swallow dugout canoes, huge but harmless squids and the sea giantess *Kapcha·*, who slowly floated up with very long hair streaming all about. To pull out one hair for a charm brought riches, but to see her face brought death.

The forest, dark and mysterious, held many supernatural beings (*ch'i·ḥa·*). The *ya·'i·* spirits, who were often in a supernatural canoe, resembled men but had head feathers. They could give power for doctoring, whaling, riches, ceremonial display making and songs. The tall, shaggy, red-skinned *Ch'i·ni·ʔatḥ* chased people with spears. Bristly giants with fangs and claws, the *Matłoḥ* shouted so loudly that people were forced to the ground (Mozino 1970:27-28). To meet such beings brought the right to depict them in dances. Men who nearly drowned and then were lured deep into the woods by flickering fires became the fleet-footed and malevolent *Pokmis*. Doctoring power came from shaman Squirrels, Minks and Ravens who sang and shook tiny rattles over old rotten logs that writhed and groaned on the ground. One might find a person's right hand sticking out of the ground shaking a rattle that gave medicine power, but a left hand meant death. Many more strange beings could be encountered in the forest: headless mallard-like birds, birds with human faces, the shadowy souls of the trees who could kill those who glimpsed them, small snakes that jumped into the openings of a person's body, and dwarfs who enticed people to their homes inside the mountains to dance (the dance resulted in "Earthquake Foot", a sickness that soon led to death).

High on the mountains in caves were the especially strange and powerful supernatural Quartz Crystals (*Hi·n'a*) swaying back and forth while emitting a weird humming sound. They sometimes fell like meteors from the sky, landing like lightning bolts. Most important chiefs had these small crystals as hereditary treasures to be displayed at ceremonies.

SPIRIT POWER IN HUNTING AND FISHING

To be successful in hunting and fishing, a man had to be very careful not to anger the creature he was after by being contaminated with what he believed to be unclean things that they could smell (Sapir 1921:351). The worst of these was a woman who was pregnant or menstruating. Men would carry the canoe to the water rather than drag it over the beach to keep it from touching rotten things or places where a menstruating woman had passed. And to keep the animals from knowing what was going on, hunters talked about their activity indirectly. For example, they spoke of fur-seal hunting as "gathering driftwood" and called the seal "the one that sits yonder under a tree" (ibid.); and inland hunters called deer a *tłochqa* ("tree knot").

More positive ways to succeed in a spirit-filled world included the use of magic amulets or charms worn on clothing or put on equipment, or hidden in houses or the forest. All sorts of things could be used as amulets, but most of them were bits of strange creatures like blind snakes, crabs and spiders. Often obtained during a vision quest when a person sought to meet a spirit, an amulet remained a secret to keep it powerful. People most often met spirits in mysterious, remote places, like the depths of the forest, the open sea, an island or a mountain peak.

The main way to achieve success in undertakings, or health and long life, was to purify oneself in an *?o·simch*, a bathing ritual featuring fasting, abstinence from sexual activity, staying in cold water, scrubbing the body with bundles of twigs and other substances, and praying to the Sky Spirit or Moon. Ritual bathing removed the smell of the warm, sweaty human body that was so disliked by the spirits. It was done while the moon was waxing and days were lengthening, commonly for four nights but often for much longer, even over weeks and months. Many people did *?o·simch* each month as a routine practice for general luck and well-being. For particular goals, such as hunting a certain animal, the ritualist rubbed himself with special secret plants, sang songs and recited prayers; sometimes he used a figure of the animal he sought, made of wood or twigs, and imitated the activity for which the ritual was designed. Each family had its own secluded bathing spot, in a creek pool or in the sea, and its own set of inherited and newly acquired supernatural techniques. Bathing for long periods in the very cold sea was so taxing that the ritualist usually took along a relative in case he needed help. The training toughened the body against exposure and cold, but could be overdone, causing illness or even death.

Power from the spirits had to be properly cared for by observing taboos to keep them satisfied. After a successful harvest or hunt, the fish or game had to be well treated to honour and please their spirits, so that after reincarnation these animals would let themselves be taken again.

MONTHS AND SEASONS

The months differed a little between groups, and of course, the lunar units do not coincide exactly with our own. In the table on the facing page, the "Northern and Central" column roughly correlates to our months (as in Drucker 1951:1, 15-16, but Sapir 1912 has them a month later, relating the first Elder month, for example, to December instead of November). According to Drucker, the Whaling People's month began with the first quarter of the moon, but Sapir noted that it began with a new moon. Month length could vary, apparently, and the correspondences drawn with our calendar months are not absolute. Charles and Ida Jones of Port Renfrew supplied the "Southern" names, some of which appear offset in the table, where the timing overlaps two of our months. The naming could vary between groups within the main language divisions, and the translations given are free and loose. J.M. Mozino (1970:62) recorded the Mowachaht names for months in 1792 and they correspond closely to those in the "Northern and Central" column on the facing page, except September is *?Inkw'achimil* ("burning"), the month for falling trees by burning them through at the base.

Seasons

Compared with the months, the seasons seem looser and easier to describe. If stories mention the time of year, it is more likely the season than the month and usually just summer or winter. Still, finer seasonal categories can be distinguished. Edward Sapir (1912) recorded six seasons as follows, in Central Nuu-chah-nulth:

Tłaqshi ("starts growing") – early spring.

Tło·p'ichh ("warm") – late spring to early summer.

?Ay'i·chhi·ł ("approaching fall") – later summer.

?Ay'i·chh ("leaves fall and rot") – fall.

?I·chhato·?is ("after all the rotten fish float down") – later fall.

Ts'o?ichh ("washed clean by rain and snow") – winter.

RAINY SEASON WORK

The good accounts of economic techniques and gear annual by Drucker (1951), Koppert (1930a), Swan (1870) and others provides a picture of seasonal activities. By November, when the bad weather of late fall and winter set in, the Whaling People had moved to their tribal villages up the inlets, except for a few who only had villages on the open coast. When it was pouring and blowing, it was nicer to stay in the big cedar houses feasting on the stores of autumn salmon and enjoying entertaining ceremonial affairs.

Calendar of Months

English	Northern and Central Whaling People	Southern Whaling People
January	*Wi·yaqhamił* (no food getting for a long time)	*B'abi·qs* (elder)
February	*?Axhamił* (bad weather) *?Ita·mił* (false spawning)	*Pa·kwischis sabał* (canoe drifting up sideways – from storm surge possible even in sheltered inlets)
March	*?A·yaqamił* (herring spawning)	*Pałisabał* (sparkling – from frost in sunshine)
April	*Ho·?oqamił* (flying flocks)	*?Ita·bał* (lying weather) *Ho·?oqwabał* (flying flocks)
May	*T'a·ktła·t'aktłimił* (stringing berries on grass)	
June	*Qawashqamił* ("salmonberry")	*Qawashpł* (salmonberry) *Tł'iḥapaxpł* (red tide)
July	*?Asitsamił* ("wasp")	*Tł'o·p'ichḥats* (warm)
August		*K'ayitsapaxpł* (salal berry)
September	*Hink'o·?asamił* (dog salmon) or *Ch'i·ya·qamił* (cutting fish)	
October	*?Itsosimił* (rough sea)	*Ch'iya·qabał* (cutting fish – for drying) *Qa·łałox* (quarrelling weather)
November	*M'am'i·qso* (elder)	
December	*Qała·tik* (younger)	*Kwatkwacht* (backing up)

Hunter with bow and quiver, wearing a special whaler's hat (*tsiyapoxs*). Woodcut from a John Webber sketch, 1778. RBCM AA-00012.

But when the weather was not too stormy, men still fished, mainly for cod, and women gathered clams and other marine invertebrates. On land, winter huckleberries could be picked until December, and there were deer, elk and bear to hunt or trap, as well as mammals whose fur could be traded (especially after Europeans arrived) or used to trim cedar-bark robes.

Some of the more interior groups – like the Muchalaht of Gold River, Hupacasath around the head of Alberni Inlet and some Pacheedaht frequenting Lake Cowichan – depended much more on terrestrial game and hunted a lot in winter. Deer (*mowach* or *ʔaˑtosh*) and elk (*tɬ'oˑnim*) were the principal game. They were shot from blinds, caught in deadfall traps, or run down in deep snow by hunters wearing snowshoes.

Guns, initially muzzleloader flintlocks, came into use as European and American traders came on the heels of Captain Cook who visited the area in 1778, but the traditional land weapon, also used on water for fowl and Sea Otters, was a bow and arrows made of yew (*moˑstati*). The bow measured about 1.5 metres long and 4 centimetres wide at the grip. It tapered to the tips, with a flat belly (string side) and a rounded back, becoming ridged toward the tips. The sturdy round grip was usually wrapped with cedar bark to enclose the hunting medicine for good aim. Some bows had recurved arms while others were a simple D-shape. The bowstring was made of strong braided whale sinew or seal gut. The arrows (*ts'iˑhati*) could be cedar or yew, with 60-centimetre shafts and feathered with duck, gull or eagle feathers. For land game, as well as for war, triangular points of thin sharpened bone or shell – later iron and copper – were loosely fixed on the shafts so that they would detach after hitting and work into the flesh of the target running away. In shooting, the bow was held horizontally, palm up, and the arrow drawn to the chest while held between the thumb and index finger. Rectangular wooden boxes or cylinders were used as quivers in canoes, but on foot these were too heavy, so arrows were carried in the hand or in the belt. Even bears were killed with the bow and arrow, the intrepid hunter waiting on a high rock or other elevation by the trail to shoot down into the heart at close range. There were also weaker bows of dogwood that were mainly used by boys who, in winter, loved to shoot the little birds that sheltered beside the houses where their overhanging roof planks kept off rain and snow.

Elk were sometimes run down and lanced in deep snow by inland hunters wearing moccasins and simple oval "bearpaw" snowshoes. Framed with vine maple, the snowshoes were strung with elk-hide straps, just two or three lengthwise and two crosswise. After a heavy snowfall, the hunter, often with a younger relative to help, set out with a heavy yew lance about two metres long with a sharpened point that was hardened by fire, oiled and polished to penetrate well. When he found a group of elk or deer he followed it, carefully directing the animals into an area of deep drifts. Then, throwing off his robe, the hunter, naked and free, ran on his snowshoes after his prey, which soon tired in the soft snow. Catching up, the hunter drove his yew lance into the heart of the animal. He would sometimes kill more than one before sitting down to wait for his assistant to bring his robe.

Another way to catch land mammals was to set a deadfall trap (*ṭo·chi·s*) across a game trail. The trap was set with the fall log raised at one end by a loop of line to a support pole above (see Drucker 1951:33). This top support pole or lever was held up near the raised end of the fall log by a pair of posts with a crosspiece on top, while its other end was held down by a line to the trigger pin held by tension under the fork of a stick staked horizontally a little above the ground. From the pin, two trip lines were strung across the trail, diverging to the correct spacing. When a line was struck, it pulled the trigger pin from under the forked stick, releasing the top lever, and the fall log, thus crushing the deer, bear or whatever creature had stumbled into it. The size of the trap varied according to the game. For the Black Bear (*chims*), the fall log was weighted heavily with several logs piled with stones. Often the fall log was set up over a windfall log and guided between two trees. Planted guide posts were left unused for a year to let the ground firm-up around them. Deadfalls for bear were commonly set to the side of a trail with a baited trigger enclosed by a strong fence to force the animal to go under the fall log.

Small deadfalls were used to trap the smaller fur-bearers like Mink (*ch'as·timts*), Martin (*tlitliḫyo·k*), Raccoon (*tlapisim*) and Beaver (*ʔat'o·*); it was the preferred trap for these animals, because the deadfall was less likely to damage the animal's fur or skin. The bait was protected by an enclosure of stakes. A stick, on which a platform of cedar splints rested, held the trigger pin on the inside of the trap. When the animal stepped on this platform,

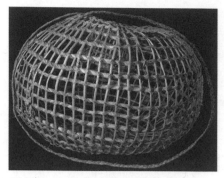

Globular basketry fish trap used to catch kelpfish for bait. RBCM 2219.

the pin was released bringing down the deadfall. Another trap, used for elk by southern tribes on Vancouver Island, at least, was a pitfall armed with sharpened yew stakes set in the bottom.

But aside from the more inland groups, like the Muchalaht and Hupacasath, the Whaling People hunted and ate terrestrial game only occasionally before they acquired guns. Until then, most of their protein and fat came from the sea.

To fish for cod, one first needed to catch some bait, usually kelpfish (*so·ma*) and perch (*kwi·tch'ak*). Kelpfish, about 30 centimetres long, were caught in globular traps (*hopy'ak*, meaning "with a round hole") of woven cedar withes. Before use, these traps were soaked to allow the narrow neck to be pushed inward. Stones and cracked mussels were placed inside for weight and bait. The trap was tied to two metres of line with a float made of an inflated cod's stomach tied to the other end. Several traps were set out to drift with the current across a kelp bed. When a kelpfish was brought into the house, the bearer was supposed to act humorously with it, causing others to laugh. In the 20th century, Whaling People thought of the globular trap as an old-time thing that no family should be without.

Perch were caught in a rectangular enclosure of stakes interwoven with branches. The enclosure was built between the high and low water line at low tide and baited with broken mussels. The perch swam in at high tide and became stranded inside the enclosure when the water receded.

To catch cod, fishermen used a sharp-angled hook with a shank of spruce root to which a barbless point of bone or hardwood was bound with nettle-fibre string. The leader was made of nettle-fibre too while the main line was long kelp stems tied together with pairs of simple hitches – this was the standard fishing line used by the Whaling People. The hook was baited with kelpfish or perch. An oval stone sinker was tied on to the end of the line where the line joined the leader, and a cod-stomach float was tied on to hang the hook at the right depth. Various species of cod were caught, including the common cod (*toshko·h* – probably Pacific Cod), a red cod (*wa·not*) and black cod (*qamah* – probably Lingcod). Often just a kelpfish on the end of a line with no hook was all a fisherman needed, because the cod swallowing it would not easily let go and could be pulled up to be clubbed

Cod spinner lure. RBCM 2225.

A man fishing from a canoe, 1915, perhaps using a cod lure. Edward S. Curtis photograph; RBCM D-08389.

or speared from the canoe. Some men liked to get black cod with an ingenious spinner lure with two vanes. They shoved the lure deep into the water with a pole 9 or 10 metres long, then shook it loose (Swan 1870:42). As it rose, spinning, a cod might follow it up to the surface to be speared with a salmon harpoon or scooped up in an oval dip net (Drucker 1951:25). Cod could sometimes be lured up with just a shiny stone on a line. A live anchovy or herring could also be used (Sproat 1868:230).

In his ethnography of the Nuu-chah-nulth, Philip Drucker (1951:40) reports that pilchard were not harvested until the advent of commercial fishing in the 20th century, but in Drucker's unpublished field notes (n.d.), Muchalaht Peter (1858–1943) described at least one occasion when several canoes came down from the Muchalaht village of A'o·s to drive pilchards into a cove where they caught them with small dip nets.

SHELLFISH GATHERING

Marine invertebrates, mostly shellfish, have traditionally been a secondary but important source of food, especially in winters when bad weather restricts fishing and hunting. With rich shellfish resources, the Whaling People rarely starved, even in times of scarcity. An excellent study of the use of marine invertebrates among the Manhousat, *Teachings of the Tide* by David W. Ellis and Luke Swan (1981), provides much of the information summarized here.

Shellfish can be gathered almost any time of the year. The exceptions, when shellfish should not be harvested, are in March when the herring are spawning and in some summers when there are poison (red) tides. When herring spawn, shellfish suck in the herring milt and become milky and bad tasting. Some kinds of shellfish, like Butter Clams and barnacles, are best in summer; others, like chitons, are good in spring. And some places have more or better quality or kinds of shellfish than others. Traditionally, women have been the main gatherers of shellfish, but men help, especially in winter when the lowest tides are at night.

People gathered clams with a digging stick (*chi·ty'ak*) made of yew or wild crabapple. This stick was about a metre long and three fingers (5 cm) wide with a tongue-shaped blade about one finger (2 cm) thick that was often hardened by boiling in water and oil. A digging stick could also he used for prying seafood from rocks, but the best tool for this was a much shorter, slightly curved prying stick (*kwo·ky'ak*) with a wider, thinner blade. Women carried what they gathered in a strong openwork pack-basket (*qa?o·ts*) made of red-cedar withes bound together with split spruce root winding around their intersections. A load of clams can be very heavy, so the basket was supported by a tumpline (*maqsa·tim*) of tightly woven cedar bark wrapped around the brow. Men preferred to carry their harvest in a woven cedar-bark sack slung over the shoulder. Because shellfish expel water, both men and women wore a back protector (*łiḫtkiyapma*) made of Yellow-cedar-bark matting. They used another mat to kneel on while digging. Clams can be kept alive a few days in a basket immersed in the sea.

Butter Clams (*y'e?isi*) were among the most important shellfish. At a bed, usually in a sheltered beach, a hole was dug and chipped away to the side to uncover the clams. They were most plentiful on the lower levels exposed by the lowest tides. In winter, since low tides occur at night, the men went clam digging by the light of a torch (*hichy'ak*), a cedar splint about a metre long stuck in the sand with a burning lump of cedar bark and spruce pitch held in its split end. Several torches were taken along to be lit in turn.

Butter Clams were almost always cooked by steaming (*n'och?a·*), roasting (*ma·sma·s*) on hot coals beside a fire or briefly boiling (*ni·s*) in a red-cedar

Women with carrying baskets, probably gathering clams. The open work of the baskets allows water to drain and so lighten the burden; it also allows water to re-enter when the basket is immersed in water back home to keep the clams alive. Edward S. Curtis photograph, 1915. RBCM E-00879.

cooking box. The water in the box was kept boiling by dropping red hot rocks into it using wooden tongs (*tl'am'aqly'ak*). For steaming, a pit was dug and lined with rocks. A fire was built in the pit and allowed to burn down. Ashes were removed and a lining of Salmonberry leaves or ferns was laid down. The food was then set in place and the pit covered with more leaves and mats. Water was added to make the steam. When clams were steamed or roasted, each was laid on the side to keep the juice inside, both to cook the clam and to sip later as a broth. The black siphon tip was always cut off. They were dipped in oil to eat, especially when roasted – a process that left them drier.

The smaller Littleneck Clams (ḥichin) were usually eaten raw. The big Horse Clam (ʔami·q), often found buried deeply, was thought difficult to dig because it burrowed down quickly. Horse Clams were usually eaten steamed, and the large shell could be used as a ladle or a cup for fish broth. The Razor Clam (kaka?is) was collected at the lowest spring tides in shallow water where their "eyes" (the siphon tips) could be spotted. The Olympia Oyster (tł'oxtł'ox), Purple-hinged Rock Scallop (tł'i·ḥaw'achi) and Cockle (ho·pisi) were other shellfish gathered. Shellfish harvesters found Cockles by their "eyes" and poked the sand beside them with a stick that had a flat tip that the cockle bit onto. Some thought this fun to do from a canoe. Cockles were usually eaten raw after smashing two together to break one. Sometimes it was fun to hold a Cockle in half a shell and watch the "pointer" (k'opy'ak, the foot) move about and point at someone. Oyster and rock scallops were eaten steamed or boiled.

Mussels could be gathered all year round, except when the herring were spawning and during a summer poison tide. The Blue Mussel (kw'ots'im), usually found in more protected waters, could sometimes be brought up on a branch on which it grew densely. The large California Mussel (tł'och'im) was harvested with a prying stick from certain little islands. Its shell, as much as 20 centimetres long, was used as the cutting blade in chisels, adzes, knives and harpoon heads. Mussels were cooked by roasting, steaming or boiling, though not too long lest they become tough. "Gills and hair" were always taken off before eating.

Goose Barnacles (ts'a?inwa) were pried off rocks at certain places only, being considered, like the California Mussel, to be improved by repeated harvesting. Goose Barnacles are best in winter, cooked before eating. Other barnacles (tł'a·noł) were only occasionally eaten. They were best in summer when the bigger ones (tł'imḥin) were eaten steamed. To pick a barnacle, the prying stick was pressed to its base and given a sharp blow with the palm.

Other creatures taken off rocks with the prying stick are limpets and chitons. Limpets (ḥoḥo?a) are occasionally eaten raw or steamed. Black Chitons (ḥay'isto·p) are also eaten either raw or cooked, after the back plates and insides are removed. They are tough in winter but tender in spring. In May and June, the women used to feast on them. The Giant Red Chiton (p'a?im, a name that brought a smile) is very tough. Only young people with good teeth could eat it raw. Everyone else cooked it in water, brought almost to a boil, or pit-steamed it for about an hour. The Manhousat believed that chitons had to have eight back plates to be edible. Abalone (ʔapsy'in) can be harvested with a prying stick and eaten raw (usually) or cooked.

Sea urchins (also called "eggs") are collected in a number of ways. The green or brown ones (no·schi·) can be picked by hand during a very low tide, but more often were taken using a canoe and a long-handled nettle-fibre dip net (*ts'imi·htama*) with a hoop of cedar withe about 45 centimetres wide and a straight front edge. Giant Red Sea Urchins (*t'ots'op*) were skewered from a canoe with the sea-urchin spear (*t'otshta*), a red-cedar pole three to five metres long with two to four sharp prongs of yew lashed on. In winter when low tides were at night, the Giant Red Sea Urchin could be speared by feel where they were abundant and the man knew the ocean bottom. Purple Sea Urchins (*hi·ix*) are extracted with a prying stick from their small holes in tide pools in the rock. Sea urchins are cracked open at the mouth, cleaned of weeds and guts, and the five gonads scooped out and eaten.

Sea anemones (*k'inlimts*) are gathered usually in spring with the prying stick. They are steamed and, if offered one, you had to eat it all or be a widower. Sea cucumbers (*te·?inwa*) could be picked by hand on flat beaches at low tide. On steeper shores, a long pole was used with a cross stick to drape the animals over. The head was usually bitten off and eaten raw. The body was scraped clean of its slime and eaten raw or boiled. Dungeness Crabs (*hasa·mats*) were skewered with a sea-urchin spear or single-pointed spear. This was easiest during the low spring tides. The crab hunter in his canoe often wore a visor of red-cedar bark to see into the water better, but still needed good eyes to spot his quarry four to six metres down. Sea stars (*qasqi·p*) were not eaten.

THE DEER AND THE WOLVES

To the Whaling People, living creatures were much more than they appeared to be. As characters in myths, they talked and acted like people, each with a certain personality. As an example, and to remind us that such creatures were more than food to the Whaling People, here is a well-known story in which Deer foolishly insults the Wolves (Sapir and Swadesh 1939:19–26).

The Deer and the Wolves

Deer was out fishing with hook and line one day when the weather was fine. While he was there at Deer-standing-on-the-point [a place], the Wolf people were moving. They passed by Deer and he said, "It's a fine day that you're all moving in your canoe, you big-nosed bone-eaters," saying this last part in a lower voice.

This is what Deer said. And another canoe-party would pass by where he stood fishing, and still another would move by, and "Is that you, young Deer?" said they who were moving in their canoe. "What are you doing, young fellow?"

"I am standing fishing with my hooks," said Deer.

And then another canoe-party moved by.

Deer insulting the Wolves. Tim Paul drawing, 1983.

"You people in the canoe are having fine weather," said the Deer again.

"What is it that you are saying, young fellow?" said they.

"'You people are having fine weather as you move in your canoe,' is what I was saying."

"Oh, that is not what you were saying."

"It's what I said," said Deer once more, and added again in a lower voice, "Oh, the bone-eaters, big-nosed ones, the eaters of dead bodies!"

"What did you say, Deer?"

"I said, 'You people are having fine weather as you move in your canoe.'"

"That is not what you said. 'Big-nosed ones' is what you were saying."

Now truly it was the chief of the Wolves who was moving with his people in a canoe, bound for M'a?qo·?a. And then they took Deer along with them and he journeyed in the same canoe as the chief of the Wolves. They arrived at M'a?qo·?a. Deer had not his wife with him, and the chief owned him, but Deer retained the little canoe that belonged to him.

Now they settled down in the house when it began to get dark. It

had not been dark long when the chief became sleepy, so he said to Deer,
"Come, now, and put me to sleep first of all, come and sit here at my side
while you keep on filing so as to lull me to sleep."

And Deer took his file and started in filing [his mussel-shell knife], and
as he did so, he sang:

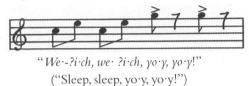

"*We·-ʔi·ch, we· ʔi·ch, yo·y, yo·y!*"
("Sleep, sleep, yo·y, yo·y!")

"Sing a little louder, my friend," said the chief. "I am falling asleep, my
friend."

"Lie comfortably," said Deer. "Just let your head tilt back a little more."
And Deer started in to sing again, "Sleep, sleep, yo·y, yo·y!" and, as he sang,
he kept on filing his mussel-shell knife.

The chief of the Wolves fell asleep. The chief was asleep with his head
tilted back. Then Deer took his knife and cut off the head of the Wolf
chief. He jumped out of the house, carrying the head with him. And then
he seized his little canoe that had been left on the roof of the house. He
started off in the canoe with the head placed at the very end of the bow,
and away he went. Deer sang:

"*Ho·-pa·tɬ- ya·-ni ho·-pa·tɬ- ya·-ni·*

t'oḫ-tɬi·-ta·k -mo·t Qwa-ya·- tɬ'i·k-mo·t, tɬ' i·k —mo·t!"
("Round thing in the bow, round thing in the bow,
The former head of the former Wolf!")

And then she who had been the wife of the dead chief of the Wolves
awoke, having becoming aware of something wet under her. She thought
that her husband was wetting himself.

"Wake up! Here you are wetting yourself!"

He did not speak. She felt for his face but she discovered that to her
fingers there was merely the feel of a hole on top.

"Wake up, all of you! Here you are with a chief whose head is cut off."

They knew that it was Deer who had killed him. The Wolf people were
in an uproar and they had a council to decide on what they should do.
"Well, let us cause him to be lost in a fog. You people go and borrow the
fog-bag of Crane."

So they borrowed it from Crane and made a fog. Deer was lost in the fog and turned around. He started back, and, as he pursued his course, he sang, "Round thing in the bow, round thing in the bow, / the former head of the former Wolf!"

These were his words as he sang on his way. The Wolf people heard that it was Deer. They got ready on the beach. Truly, Deer returned to his starting point. He arrived on the beach and got out of his canoe. And then he took up some of the sand.

"Goodness, but you look like the sand of M'a?aqo·?a." But he called out to his wife, "I have a chamber for you here in the canoe!"

But just as he said this, the Wolf people jumped on him and chewed him up.

"Aha! Go ahead, all of you, and leave but my intestines," said Deer before he was torn to pieces.

And this is why the Wolf people are in the habit of leaving only the intestines when they devour their kill.

Storytelling was a well developed art. In the original Whaling People speech, characters often talk in their own special ways and sing songs at times. Actions are motivated as in real human life. Insults are serious attacks on prestige, which was all important. Deer is made a slave for insulting the Wolf chief. Taking his head is typical fighting action. As for the fog, everyone knew that it was kept in a bag by Crane.

THE HERRING SEASON

About the beginning of February, just when food stores from the previous year were running low, the weather grew less stormy and the herring (*tlosmit*) began appearing near the coast. People moved from the winter villages up the inlets to spring camps nearer to the coast. They rafted their large canoes together in pairs with poles lashed across their bows and sterns, then loaded on house planks removed from the framework of the big house. The planks were generally layered lengthwise in the canoes, leaving the ends open for the paddlers. People could live on the canoe raft, moving in easy stages from place to place. Cooking could be done on the planks with fires built on a bed of split green alder or bark covered with sand or gravel. At the major camps there were house frames on which the planks were attached for the roof and walls. Possessions were well adapted to a life of annual movement according to the seasons.

When the herring came, the Chinook (Spring) Salmon of the sea (*so·ḥa·*) also appeared in large numbers, feeding on them. These salmon were trolled

Halibut and herring spawn drying at a village near Ucluelet. The racks in front of the houses support boughs covered with eggs; those at the left, against the house, include strips of halibut. RBCM AA-00048.

for with sharp-angled hooks baited, of course, with herring. As he paddled, the troller held the line in his hand, moving the hook along jerkily. When a Chinook bit on the hook, it had to be pulled in carefully because the hook was barbless. Only enough for immediate eating was caught, since it was forbidden to keep springs overnight.

For the herring the fishermen set out to sea or an outer inlet, two or three to a small canoe, watching for the gulls that hover over schools of little fish when they are near the surface. The sternman paddled violently to excite the fish and get them closer together. At the right moment the bowman lowered his dip net of fine-meshed, nettle-fibre string into the circling school. This dip net (*ts'ichitl*) was a long, tapered bag with a one-metre square mouth, hung on two cross sticks attached to a pole, four to five metres long. Also used was the simple but efficient herring rake (possibly *ch'itxwi·y'ak*), a long cedar pole an inch and a half thick set with a row of sharp bone pegs for almost a metre at the end. The herring raking (*chocha·*) was done by the sternman wielding the pole like a paddle, impaling fish on each stroke and shaking them off into the canoe. Great quantities of herring were taken. They were eaten raw, broiled on sticks near the fire, or boiled in rectangular wooden vessels using hot stones to heat the water. Many herring were also cleaned, split and dried, either indoors over the fire or outside in the sun. After about a week they were stored in boxes.

Around March, the herring roe (*k'oms*) could be seen loosening inside the fish, signalling that spawning was about to begin. Unless it was an early, light "false spawning", which lasted only about a day, the herring continued spawning for several days. Spawning fences of large hemlock and spruce boughs were set out underwater where it was about four metres deep at low tide. The boughs were weighted with stones and fastened by lines to floats of cedar logs. After the spawning, the branches with their thick coating of eggs were taken out, cut into smaller pieces and hung on poles to dry in the sun. It took several days to dry the eggs. They were then stored in boxes where they would keep for eight months or more. To prepare dried herring eggs for eating, they were soaked overnight, boiled, and sprinkled with whale oil for a sauce (Koppert 1930a: 70-71). When possible, people gathered seaweeds and sea grasses with the herring spawn attached by cutting them with a knife tied to a pole.

About the end of the herring season, a seaweed (possibly *hashqwits*) was gathered for its roots, to be eaten raw, using a long pole with two cross sticks to twist among the plants and pull them up (Drucker 1951:42).

Since herring spawn at different times in different coves, the season lasted a few weeks. Chiefs owned the coves, so commoners needed their permission to set fences in them. For this, they paid a part of the harvest as tribute. The great quantities of herring taken, their prized eggs, and the fact that both could be preserved by drying, made these fish a major food resource, second only to salmon, at least among the more northern groups. In mythical terms the Herring People and Salmon People lived under the sea in the same house. Like the salmon, the first herring of the season were honoured with a respectful welcoming ceremony.

Chapter 2
Seasons of Plenty

SPRING

In the Flying Flocks moon (April), waterfowl travel north along the coast. In stormy weather they come into deep coves and inlets for shelter. When they did, the hunters went out at night, two to a canoe. They took with them a two-metre-square net of nettle-fibre string stretched between two crosspieces on a pole about four metres long. They lit a fire on a sand-covered board across the stern behind the steersman who paddled holding a rod in his mouth from which hung a mat. The waterfowl were bothered by the light when the canoe came up in the dark, so they would swim to the shadow cast by the mat. When they had gathered, the bowman cast the net over them. With the right conditions, a canoe could soon be filled with ducks, geese or swans (Drucker 1951:34, 42-3). Firelight hunting was also done with bird spears, about three metres long, with three or four barbed prongs (Swan 1870:48).

Where ducks wintered, they could be hunted any stormy night. If the weather was not stormy enough to drive them in, canoes went out with the hunters in them hidden by fir boughs. These canoes circled well out to sea and drifted in on the ducks that usually swim just outside the breakers. The hunters then shot the birds with arrows, often requiring several shots before making a hit (Swan 1870:48). Chiefs observed rituals for stormy weather and dark nights when they owned the coves and inlets suited for netting or spearing by firelight (Drucker 1951:174). The ducks they hunted included Mallards (*na·ht'ach*), mergansers (*tsa·pin*), Buffleheads (*ts'ik'ints*) and Harlequins (*wa·ts?ish*).

Halibut fishing also began in April for men whose chiefs owned the grounds. Bait, usually octopus (*ti·ło·p*) had to be obtained first. Octopus was found at low tide in cracks and caves, stabbed with a barbed pole to mark

Muchalaht people in the summer of 1896, gathered in front of a large duck net and, at the far right, a section of lattice work that was probably part of a large fish trap. "The duck net, for use with the firelight night hunting, was a rectangle of fair-sized mesh of nettle fibre on the same type of frame as that of the herring dip net..." – a pole about 3.5 metres long with two 2-metre-long cross sticks tied to it at their centres, one near the end of the pole and the other 1.5 to 2 metres back. "The frame was made as heavy as it could be and still be thrown a short distance, for its weight was what prevented the ducks from escaping." (Drucker 1951:34.) Edgar Fleming photograph; RBCM PN-11440-A.

its movements and poked with another sharp pole until it came out or was killed. Tentacles, skinned and split, were tied over the lower arm of the special, curved, halibut hook (*chimo·n*). Being made of the dense heartwood of hemlock, fir or balsam, the hook sank in water. This type of hook was also used to catch Lingcod (black cod), red cod, red snapper, dogfish, bullhead, skate and even octopus. The fishing line (*sanap'at̓*) was made of long kelp stems tied together, thick end toward the hook, with paired single hitches. For Pacific Halibut (*p'o·ʔi*), the line was made about 50 metres long because the halibut banks are 30 to 40 metres deep. Banks were located by using landmarks as reference points. Fishermen set out early to be on the banks at dawn before the wind came up.

The Whaling People caught halibut in three main ways. Where the fish were abundant and bit quickly, they used hand lines, in the past with a single hook on the line, but recently, to catch more for commercial sale, with a pair of hooks held apart by a spreader pole a couple of metres long. On the Swiftsure Bank, four men in a big canoe could get more than 100 halibut in a morning by hand lining.

The second method was to anchor over a bank and put lines out from a pair of poles angled out over the sides in the front of the canoe, plus, perhaps, a third pole over the stern. This could be done by one man in a small canoe.

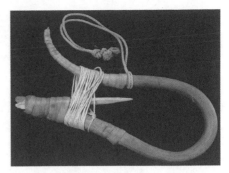

Halibut hook with a bone barb. RBCM 2210.

The third and most complex method was drift-line fishing in which the lines were attached to a float made of a seal bladder with a bigger marker bladder several metres up the length. Allowing for wind and current, the fisherman set out his drift lines one by one, perhaps a dozen or more if he had an assistant, so that they drifted over the halibut bank. When a hook was taken, the smaller first float moved or was pulled under, while the larger marker-float remained in sight. The halibut could then be pulled up, clubbed with a heavy yew club with a ball-shaped end, and slid into the canoe. If the fish was a big one, the canoe would be tipped to the water-line to slip it in.

Halibut fishermen returning to Neah Bay, Washington, about 1914. Edward S. Curtis photograph; RBCM D-08340.

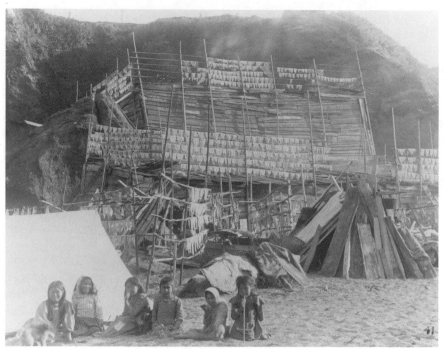

Halibut drying on Tatoosh Island off Cape Flattery.
Burke Museum of Natural History and Culture Ethnology Archives L4123.

There is a good story about halibut fishing by Raven (*qo'ishinm'it*), that clever rascal, and the slow-witted Black Bear (*chims*). As in the previous story, the plot hinges around a concern for prestige when Bear is afraid to go home without catching any halibut because he would be laughed at. With Raven involved, a lot of fun follows in this version of the myth collected by George Hunt (Boas 1916:900-03).

Raven and Black Bear

Raven was one of the chiefs of the Mowachaht tribe. One day he met his friend Black Bear. When they met, he said to Black Bear, "Will you go out to fish for halibut, for we have no food to eat?"

Then Bear said, "Yes, I will go with you if you will promise to take good care of me."

Raven said, "Why, what harm can I do to you? You are four times larger than I am. It is your place to take care of me, for you have greater strength than I have."

Bear replied, "That is so. Let us be going now!"

Raven told him to get his halibut fishing line; and Bear went into his house, got his halibut fishing line, and took it down to the beach. He also had a piece of octopus for bait, and he put it into Raven's canoe. Then he told his friend Raven that he was ready, "For," said he, "my paddle and my halibut fishing-line are in your canoe."

Raven took his halibut fishing line and his paddle from the corner of his house and went down to the beach, where his canoe was.

Then Bear went to the bow, and Raven sat in the stern. They paddled out to the mouth of Muchalaht Inlet. Here Raven said to Bear, "We are far enough out. I will let go the anchor. We will stay here anchored while we are fishing." And he put the anchor overboard.

After he had done this, he turned his face toward the stern of the canoe, away from the bow, for he did not want Bear to see him putting the bait on his hook. Bear took his halibut hook, put a piece of octopus on it and fastened the hook to his line. Then he put the two hooks on the spruce-pole crosspiece, tied the stone sinker to the middle of the cross-piece, and threw it over the side of the bow. Raven did the same to his line, only Bear did not see what he put on his hook for bait.

As soon as Raven's hook reached bottom, he got a bite, and hauled up his line. There was a large halibut on it. He took his hook out of the fish, and then threw the hook overboard again. Soon he had another bite, and he hauled up his line with another large halibut on it. He kept on doing this until the canoe was half full of fish.

All this time poor Bear did not catch a single fish. Then Black Bear said to Raven, "Friend, tell me how it is that I do not get a bite, and you have nearly filled the canoe with halibut? Will you not give me some of your bait to put on my hooks?"

Raven laughed, saying, "O friend, the bait that I put on my halibut hook I can not give away, for after I have finished using it for bait, I shall have to take it from my hooks and put it where it belongs. You have the same thing on you. Why don't you take yours off and put it on your hook for bait?"

Bear replied, "What have you put on your hook for bait, that the halibut bite it so much?"

And Raven said to him, "If I were to tell you what I have done to myself, you would not do as I did."

But Bear said, "O friend! I would do anything to myself rather than go home without getting one fish, and be laughed at by our friends."

Then Raven laughed, and said, "I will tell, I have used my privates for bait. Therefore I am getting all the halibut to bite at my hook."

Then Bear asked him how he could take off his privates, and Raven said, "I cut them off."

Bear replied, "Does it not hurt you when you cut them off?"

"What have you put on your hook for bait…?" Tim Paul drawing, 1983.

But Raven said, "I think it would hurt me more if my people should come to the beach and laugh at me because I came without any halibut. I think it best to stand the little pain of cutting off my privates rather than be laughed at by our people, for it would hurt my feelings enough to kill me."

While they were talking, a man came paddling out to them in a canoe. It was Cormorant. He anchored close to where Raven was fishing, and he could hear every word they were saying. After he had let down his anchor, he put some octopus bait on his hooks, and dropped the line overboard. While he was waiting for a bite, he heard Bear say, "Come and cut my privates off, for I believe I could stand the pain for a short time better than being laughed at by our friends."

Raven said, "Why can't you cut them off yourself as well as I can?"

Bear inquired, "After I have cut them off, how shall I put them on again?"

Then Raven laughed while he was chewing gum, saying, "Why, of course, I can put them on; for you see that I always chew this gum, and after I finish using my privates for bait, I gum them on. And when I want to use them again, I pull them off without any pain."

"Well," said Bear, "come and cut them off, for you know how to do it."

Raven said, "I will give you a chance to get some halibut, for I don't want our people to laugh at you until they kill you. It is better to stand a little pain now than to be killed slowly by shame." And he took his large mussel-shell knife from the stern of his canoe to where Bear was sitting. When he came up to him, he said, "Now, my friend, lie on your back, with your two legs as wide apart as you can get them, so that I can make a clean cut."

Then Bear lay on his back, as he was told; and just as Raven was taking hold of his friend's privates to cut them off, Bear asked if it wouldn't hurt when the cutting began.

"Well," said Raven, "you must be foolish if you think that a cut from a knife doesn't hurt for a short time. When I cut my privates off, it hurt me, I know, but it is better to stand pain for a short time than to be laughed at by our people until dead."

"Well," said Bear, "cut away, then!"

Then Raven took hold of his friend's privates and cut them off as quick as he could. After he had cut them off, he said to Bear, "Now go to sleep for a short time; then, when you wake up, you will feel well again." And he went back to the stern of his canoe.

He had not been sitting there long, when he saw Bear give two kicks, and stretch out his body. Then Raven went to look at him and found his friend dead.

Then he said to himself, "Now I have my wish, for he was a fat man. I will go ashore and cook him and eat him before I go home."

Then he looked round, and saw Cormorant close to where he had been. He had heard everything he was saying to Bear before he killed him. So he hauled up his anchor. After he got it up, he paddled to where Cormorant was, and said to him, "What are you doing here?"

Cormorant said, "I am halibut fishing, but I can not get a bite of any kind of fish."

All the time they were speaking to each other, Raven was wishing in his own mind for Cormorant to ask him for some of his gum, and they had not been speaking long, when Cormorant asked Raven what he was chewing.

Cormorant said, "Will you give me some of your gum, for I have been here so long that I want to drink some water, and where we are I can not get any water to drink. Your gum will moisten my mouth."

Raven said to him, "I can not give you any gum unless you will let me take it from my mouth and put it on your tongue, for I am not allowed to put it in your hands," said he.

Then Cormorant said, "Put some of it on my tongue!" and he put out his tongue as far as he could.

Then Raven took some of the gum from his own mouth and put it on Cormorant's tongue. As soon as he had done so, however, he took hold of Cormorant's tongue, pulled it out, and threw it into the sea.

Then Raven said, "Now, friend Cormorant, speak!"

Cormorant tried to speak, but he could not say a word.

Then Raven said, "Now I have punished you for trying to come to spy on me. Go home; but now you can not tell our people what I have done to my friend, Bear." And he went toward the shore of a small bay.

Then he went ashore and made a fire. He put stones on it. And while the stones were getting red-hot, he went down to his canoe and took out his dead friend, carried him up the beach, and laid him alongside the fire. After he had done this, he saw that the stones were red hot. He then took the fire away, went for grass and moss, and carried them to the heap of red-hot stones, then put Bear on top of it. Then he took the moss and covered him up to keep the steam in.

After this he went to his fisherman's box and took all his spare halibut hooks out. When it was empty, he filled it from a little stream of water, and poured the water on the moss that covered the dead Bear. It had not been cooking long, when he uncovered it and saw that it was done. Then he began to eat, and continued until he had eaten his friend up. After he had finished eating, he picked up all the bones that were left and hid them in the woods. Then he went home in his canoe.

When he drew near to the point of Yuquot, he turned the heads of six halibut toward the bow of his canoe, as though they had been caught by Bear – these were the largest six he had in the canoe – for all Indians, whenever they catch halibut, always put them in their canoes with the tails away from them and the heads toward them. After he had done this, he paddled until he came round the point, where the people of the village could see him. Then he began to cry as loud as he could to make the people of the village hear him, and this is what he said while crying:

"I lost my beloved friend Bear while I was fishing halibut with him. He had caught six large halibut, and was hauling up the seventh one, when his leg became entangled in the line. While he was trying to club the fish, he missed his blow, and the large halibut went down and carried him down also, and I never saw him again."

This he said as he was paddling. The Mowachaht went down to the beach to meet him. At first they did not believe him. Some said, "Oh, Raven killed our friend Bear, and has eaten him up!" and some said, "He has left him on some island to die."

But as soon as they saw the six large halibut headed toward the bow of the canoe, they said to one another, "It must be true that he was pulled over by a large halibut, for we can see these six large halibut our poor friend Bear caught; and it is true that sometimes the line will get tangled round either our arms or legs and nearly pull us overboard."

While they were talking, Cormorant was trying to tell his friends the Mowachaht that Raven had killed Bear, but they could not understand him, for his tongue had been taken out by Raven so that he might not tell his friends of what he saw. And Raven told some of his friends to take their large halibut and give them to Bear's friends. So some were given to his wife, and Raven kept the rest.

And that is why there are ravens on Yuquot Island, but no bears.

CANOES

The canoes of the coast have fine lines. We briefly describe them here because they are so central to making a living from the sea. Canoe makers use the trunk of a Western Redcedar to construct their canoes. They use just a few tools – before contact with Europeans these were made of stone, bone, mussel shell and hard wood.

Traditionally, a single canoe maker would rough out a canoe in winter and finish in the spring with perhaps an apprentice, often a son or nephew. As usual, he first engaged in ritual fasting and praying for success, before going out to find the right cedar tree, usually straight-grained and clear, close to the water, or in a place where it would be easy to move out of the forest on rollers. Before the availability of metal, the tree was felled by burning it at the base; wet clay was put on the trunk above the fire to keep it from spreading. Felling by fire was apparently done mainly in September (Mozino 1970:44, 62) when the tree would be dry. When metal became accessible, trees were cut down with big chisels (*qay'axwas*) up to a metre long. A stone hammer (*pinaxpinax*) pecked into a shape to fit the hand was used

Nuu-chah-nulth style canoes at Victoria's Inner Harbour.
Richard Maynard photograph; RBCM PN-2571.

to drive in the chisels and wedges of yew (*tlanat*). The canoe maker needed only half the thickness of the tree, so he used wedges to split the trunk after it was felled. Sometimes, just half the thickness might be split out of a tree to the desired length by notching it deeply at the right height and starting a split in which a cross stick was placed to work down, aided by wind action (Drucker 1951:79-80).

The bottom of the hull was usually shaped first, then the inside hollowed. In the past, it seems, this was done by controlled burning and then, at intervals, adzing out the charred wood (see Olson 1936:69). Alternatively, notches were cut crosswise to allow the wood between to be split out. For gauging hull thickness, small holes were made at intervals, formerly with a simple hand drill (*so·ta·*) made from the bone of a deer, bear or eagle. For finer work, the small chisel (*kowo*) and D-shaped adze (*ch'ahay'ak*) were used. When the hull was roughed out, it was brought from the woods to the village by water. The Ditidaht, outstanding canoemakers along with the Tla-o-qui-aht, sometimes crowded onto the canoe at this first launching, until the rough canoe sank, to wish it luck for seaworthiness (Touchie 1977:24).

It is the addition of the high end pieces, the heads, that make the canoe look right. The heads, and any patches on the sides, are fitted exactly by painting the joint surface of either the head or the hull with charcoal paste, then holding the piece in place and striking it to mark the high spots in black that have to be taken down. Pegging and lashing with twisted cedar withes fasten the pieces permanently. There are several ways to patch splits and holes (Arima 1975:71). The surfaces are finished smoothly, especially the exterior to lessen drag. Formerly it was sanded with sandstone blocks and dogfish skin, then rubbed with rushes. The hull is usually spread, raised a little on blocks and partly filled with water. Red hot stones are added repeatedly over the several hours of "steaming" needed to make the wood pliable. To keep the heat in the top is sealed with a covering, now usually a plastic tarp but formerly bark or rush mats whose stiffness kept their edges off the sides and allowed fires to be built along the hull outside for more heating. When pliable the hull is spread with gentle pressure using sticks until the thwart poles of hemlock or fir of the desired lengths can be inserted and lashed in with twisted cedar withe. Seat thwarts of boards are now added, but formerly there was just a seat in the stern for the steersman and the rest sat on their heels on the bottom on canoe mats. The low centre of gravity allowed the hull to be made narrower and faster, if so desired. The inside could be treated with a reddish hemlock- or alder-bark infusion for appearance and perhaps as an anti-insect preservative. Red ochre could also be used for the interior. The outside is usually left plain except for white collar stripes at the ends. Formerly it was dark brown from scorching and perhaps dogfish oil, both preservative finishes. The past century has seen the

A giant canoe built by ?Oˑdayo that proved unmanageable in winds and tides.
RBCM AA-04626.

use of commercial paints, especially black, at least for larger canoes. Atop the bow is a long notch for a harpoon shaft without which the animal head-like end will not look right.

Paddles (*?oxwa·p*) are made from yew, maple or Yellow-cedar, about the length of an arm with a crosswise "crutch" handle at the top. The blade is about a hand-span wide with an elongated sharp point that enabled the paddler to use it as a fighting weapon when needed. To paddle silently, the long tip allowed the paddler to keep the paddle in the water to prevent dripping. The bailer (*hay'im*) was shaped like a pyramid for quick and easy scooping of water inside the hull. Poles were used to push the canoe up rivers. After seeing European sailing ships, the Whaling People used sails of different kinds, most often spritsails. Some observers have said that the flat-bottomed canoe could only sail before the wind (Drucker 1951:86, Waterman 1920:26), but it could tack moderately because of the skeg-like cutwaters (*sipo·s*) at the ends of the bottom and the hull configuration (Arima 1975:86). Its apparent ancestor, the rounder-bottomed type of the neighbouring Coast Salish, has a bottom-end skeg at the bow, recently accentuated, but not at its well-raked stern.

With its long, rakish "Clipper-ship bow" and high upright stern, the west-coast canoe looks like a lithe animal. The prow, with its snout-like tip and ear-like harpoon notch, looks like the head of a deer or wolf (*qwayats'i·k*). On the throat-like part below the tip of the prow was a little lump called the heart where magic medicine might be placed. In the past, war and ceremonial canoes could have animals or birds painted on the sides (see Meares 1967:263); otherwise decoration was spare and tasteful. Inside, under the gunwales, is a pretty fluting of two to four little grooves running the length of the hull. The grooves provide grip for handling the canoe. The top of the prow might be lightly grooved crosswise for better foothold. Special canoes, like a prized sealer or whaler, sometimes had several rows of opercula, the oval door-like discs of sea snails, embedded inside under the gunwales. Some big canoes have a white face up front.

Kinds or classes of canoes are not distinguished consistently, but we offer a tentative list. Although Whaling People recognize canoe size by the bottom length in arm spans, the following class sizes are given by the overall length in metric to avoid confusion. Measuring by the bottom leaves out the overhanging ends, mostly the prow projection of 50 to 120 centimetres or so, depending on the size and design of canoe. For instance, typical whaling canoe size of five arm spans long on the bottom (about 9 metres) would be about 10 metres with the bow projection included.

In addition, there were children's play canoes, about two metres long, sometimes without heads. In the 19th century, the surviving utility and trolling canoes came to be built without head pieces and were either fitted

Classes of Canoes

Class	Name	Size
Moving Canoe	*shitł'ats*	12–14 m long, ~2 m beam
War Canoe	*wi·taqsats*	12–14 m long, <2 m beam (for speed)
"White-face"	*tl'itso·ł*	usually 15–17 m long, but reported up to 18 m

A huge old-time war canoe with painted ends and a high, wide prow to shield against arrows.

Class	Name	Size
Whaling Canoe	*ʔoʔo·taxsats* or *p'inw'ał*	8–11 m long, ~1.5 m beam, 0.5 m deep
"Three persons" Utility Canoe	*hashmaqats* (N, C) *ʔatłakwodiyak* (S) *qaqatsi·sti<u>x</u>* (S)	~7 m long, 1.2 m wide, but size varied considerably
Sealing Canoe	*yashmaqats* (N, C) *yasha·ba<u>x</u>sts* (S)	6.5–7.5 m long, 1.2 m wide, 0.4 m deep

A speedier model was about a metre wide tapering to half a metre on the bottom, but it could not carry as many seals.

Class	Name	Size
Sea Otter Canoe	*kw'akw'atłasats*	5 m long, narrow (for two people)
Trolling Canoe	*chi·tssats*	4–5 m long

This two-man fishing canoe was enlarged in the late 1800s to become the commercial fur-sealing canoe made to fit between the masts of the sealing schooner: 5.8 m long, 1.2 m wide, 0.4 m deep.

Class	Name	Size
One-man "Sit in the Middle" Canoe	*takaʔodiyak* (S) *hopinwash* (C) *xashin* (N)	3–3.5 m long

---

"<" = less than; "~" = approximately.

The Whaling People made skilful use of sails introduced by Europeans.
Edward S. Curtis photograph, about 1915. RBCM AA-00877.

with cabins and inboard motors ("put-put" trollers) or with outboard motors. Oars came into general use late in the 19th century. Less commonly
adopted was the rudder.

The Whaling People were expert canoeists, able to travel in heavy seas
and to surf through breakers in to land. From childhood, they raced in play
and practised recovering from a capsize. Even in the narrow, cranky models
they kept an easy balance.

WHALING

The whaling season – the great hunt for the mightiest of living creatures –
began each spring, in the Flying Flocks month of April. Killing a whale was
the highest glory of the Whaling People, reserved for their chiefs, who were
anxious to claim the fame that accompanied such a deed.

Of the several kinds of whales hunted by the Whaling People, perhaps
the most important was the Grey Whale (*ma·ʔak* (N,C), *ch'it'ap* (S)). These
whales are about 12 to 14 metres long and each spring migrate north to
Alaskan waters, slowly since there are some new calves born in Baja California. Since Greys travel near the shore, feeding on the bottom, they are fairly
accessible though still not the easiest prey. The spring Grey Whale hunting
season is roughly April to June. On the return migration south in November and December the whales travel fast and farther from shore while the
weather is bad, but some Whaling People still pursued them.

Whaling Ritual. Calvin Hunt (Mowachaht Chief Ts'awna) silk-screen print. If a whaler prepared himself well, the whale would be attracted to his canoe.

Another important species was the Humpback (*ʔiˑhtoˑp*), which spends more time in this region, even year round in places like Barkley Sound. The Northern Right Whale (*ʔiˑchqi, sixwaʔox* (Dit.)) was hunted, but has been a bit forgotten following commercial overhunting. These huge species are slow swimming, especially the Right, and good eating. Whaling People have also hunted the Sperm Whale (*kotsqiˑ*, meaning "mussels-on-head"). They did not hunt the Blue Whale (*yayach'im, yachoˑbad* (Dit.)), because it was too big to handle, and an unknown species that they called *chichichwan* (Drucker 1951:49). The difficult-to-catch Killer Whale (*qaqawin, qaqawad* (Dit.)) was pursued only as a test by young whalers.

For the grand pursuit of whales, ritual preparation was especially elaborate, long and hard. It varied with the individual whaler, but an example from the Mowachaht (Drucker 1951: 169-70) will give an idea of the proceedings. The chief bathed nightly, during the waxing of four moons, in fresh running water, rubbing his body with bundles of nettles and secret plants. (Some whalers went to extremes, dragging their bodies over rocks covered with sharp barnacles instead of scrubbing themselves with twigs and plants.) He prayed long for help to the Four Chiefs to have the whales allow him alongside to harpoon. Wearing his whaler's bear-skin robe, a Western Redcedar-bark headband and secret marks on his face, he walked slowly to and from his ritual place so that the whales, too, would move slowly. Then for another four waxings of the moon the chief bathed in the sea, swimming slowly counter-clockwise, diving, surfacing and blowing, then floating quietly to get the whales to do the same. Every four circuits he came out to rub himself with plants and to pray. All the while he refrained from sexual activity, but his principal wife was often with him during his ritual. She might hold a rope fastened to him, as if he were harpooned, while he sang the song he would sing to a weakened harpooned whale. He might walk around her slowly while she repeated, "This is the way the whale will act!" (Curtis 1916:38; see also Sapir et al 2004). His canoe crew also had to

Part of the whaling ritual. Edward S. Curtis, 1916; RBCM D-08444.

perform rituals before the hunt, though not for so long. Hunters of other kinds of sea mammals also tortured themselves in the same way before going out.

The most successful whalers possessed charms of odd creatures like a double-headed worm or a certain crab (Curtis 1916:16). Whales and other sea mammals are all like ordinary people in their houses under the sea. It is when they go fishing that they get into canoes that are their animal bodies (Sapir 1912 6:8).

A large amount of equipment was used in whaling. A heavy harpoon shaft (*hi·na·n'oḥsom* (N, C), *dopi·y'ax̱* (S)) four to five metres long, sometimes even longer, was made of two lengths of yew securely scarfed together. The big harpoon head (*takaml* (N, C), *xwishiml* (C), *qwi·qabł* (S)) had a sharp blade of a large mussel shell, held with spruce gum between a pair of antler or bone barbs, around which the end strands of a thick sinew lanyard were tightly wound, then wrapped with nettle-fibre string, Yellow-cedar bark and cherry bark before a smooth coating of gum was applied (Waterman 1920:31-32). Seven metres of sinew leader was attached to the lanyard with a loop at the end, for the main line, a strong three-stranded cedar-withe or split-spruce-root rope. There were two kinds of main line – one heavy and 70 metres long, the other light and 110 metres long. The floats were made of the whole skins of Harbour Seals (ko·ko<u>h</u>w'isa), scraped, smoked, fitted at a front flipper with a mouthpiece for inflation, and lashed at the ends to a line that could be tied to the harpoon line. Four floats were commonly carried in a canoe, with uninflated spares. Other gear included a spare harpoon shaft, extra heads in kit boxes, a wide bladed "spade" lance for crippling the whale, a killing lance, more harpoon line, and a wooden bucket of fresh water because the canoe might be out on the sea for several days.

Besides all this gear, the canoe had to carry 6 to 12 crew, ideally a harpooner, a steersman and six paddlers. No wonder the canoe had to be long and beamy. The following description of a whale hunt is mainly from an account recorded from ʔAtlyu, one of the last Ahousaht whalers (Drucker 1951:49–56).

When all the equipment and ritual preparations were complete, the whaler set out with his crew, often after a sighting of a whale or sometimes after dreaming of one. The special canoe was carried down to the water on lifting poles. Other whaling canoes would accompany the main one, frequently with younger kinsmen of rank in command, as well as a swift sealing canoe to carry the news to the village when a whale was harpooned. The fleet set out before sunset for the whaling grounds, not far out for Grey Whales but farther for Humpbacks. The whalers spent the night at sea, at the proper distance from shore – there they checked their gear and inflated their floats. At dawn, they spread out in their canoes to look for whales. A sighting was signalled by waving a paddle overhead to get the other canoes to approach, paddling hard but noiselessly. The chief stood in the bow, harpoon ready.

It could take a long time to get close to a whale while it was on the surface. Eventually, the crew brought the canoe alongside approaching on the left side and from the rear where the whale could not see them. According to Chief Charles Jones, the right time to harpoon was when the whale was just submerging, with its flukes well under and swung towards the canoe so that the animal would swing away in reaction and not smash the canoe. The steersman watched to see when the flukes were in the right position, then gave the signal to the harpooner, who immediately drove the harpoon in behind the fore flipper. At once the canoe swung sharply to the left away from the whale, and the first float was thrown out by the first right-hand paddler behind the harpooner who quickly crouched in the bow to avoid the line paying out. The second right-hand paddler held his paddle under the line to have it run out smoothly from the space before him. The dangerous moments lasted until all the line and floats were all out because someone could get caught in a loop or the canoe could be capsized or smashed

INDIAN WHALE HUNTERS- NEAH BAY

56519 ASAHEL CURTIS

56519

A Makah whaler about to plunge a second harpoon into a Grey Whale, about 1908. Ida Jones remembered his name as Do·kmi·s (Arima 1975:92). A crewman is holding the line from the first harpoon head that is already in the whale's flesh. The line goes back to several large floats. The second harpoon has a small float attached to it. Apparently, this float was designed to "turn" the whale toward the shore and so avoid a long tow if the whale died far out to sea.
James Phillip or Shobid Hunter photograph (Asahel Curtis wrote his name on a copy he made of the original, but he did not take this image.); Washington State Historical Society 56519.

in the first violent struggles of the whale before it sounded. Any disaster that happened was thought due to the incorrect observation of taboos or performance of rituals.

The harpoon shaft, which had detached, was then picked up and usually sent to the village in the fast messenger canoe. All the while the whaler's wife was lying still under new mats at home to make the whale act quiet and not run far when harpooned.

The whalers prepared a second line with floats to harpoon the whale again when it surfaced. The other canoes came to plant their harpoons too. If any of them happened to get near the whale first, they waited for the chief to harpoon first, if he could. As the whale was repeatedly harpooned, it grew weak. Sometimes it ran out to sea (to the whalers this happened because of lapses in ritual preparation), which necessitated a long tow back, perhaps taking days. With songs and prayers the hunters would try to head the whale back toward shore. To kill the weakened whale, the first paddler cut the tendons to the flukes to "hamstring" it, then lanced under the flipper to the heart. As soon as the whale died, one of the crew dove in, cut a hole through the upper lip and another in the jaw, then tied the mouth shut to keep the great carcass from filling with water and sinking. The crew attached more floats to the whale to make it ride higher. With a line tied

Saddle of Whale's Blubber. James G. Swan drawing; Beinecke Rare Book and Manuscript Library 1013444.
Swan did not explain why he did not include the dorsal fin, but this might be a Grey Whale's saddle.

to the loop closing the mouth, the canoes began the hard work of towing. The whalers sang songs to the whale, which, like a high-born lady (*ḥakom*), was attracted both to the whaler's wife and a drink of fresh water,.

At high tide the whaler beached his prize, at his own village if possible, to get the bones of all his whales in one spot. The carcass was staked down for butchering. First to be cut off was the whaler's special and large piece, the saddle of skin and blubber of the dorsal fin at the back of the head, which was taken to his house in a procession led by his wife. It was hung over a pole held up on two posts with a trough below to catch the dripping oil. Eagle feathers were stuck in a row on top and white down was sprinkled on in honour of the whale. At the ends of the pole were hung the harpoon lines. Bunches of feathers were stuck on the posts and, alongside the saddle, the whale's eyes were hung, at least by the people living around Cape Flattery (Swan 1870:21-22). The next pieces of blubber went to the crews of the canoes and any others who may have joined in the towing. Then pieces were given to the rest of the tribe in order of rank, a procedure that was always carefully observed.

The whale was appeased, for being taken, by ceremonies performed around its saddle (*chakwa·si*). For four nights the whaler, his wife, and whaling crew gathered to sing special songs in honour of the whale, represented by the saddle. During this period, the whaler and his wife drank water from a special spring brought in a special bucket. Both spring and bucket were marked with feathers, no doubt on behalf of the whale who as a sea mammal was thought to thirst for sweet, fresh water. Then all the men came on invitation to a feast where the saddle, having been taken down, was cut into

Blubber being stripped from a beached whale.
Asahel Curtis photograph; Washington State Historical Society 19253.

thin strips and boiled. Dress was festive and, at every step in the proceedings, people sang and danced. The oil from the saddle was saved in sea-lion bladders marked with feathers as a special food for winter feasts.

A successful whaler enjoyed great prestige. But most of all whaling was economically important (Arima 1988).

DRIFT WHALING

Even if many of the whaler's harpoon strikes did not hold, the wounded animal could die from infection and became a drift whale that might be recovered later. Whales that died tended to float about, buoyed up by gases that had formed inside them. The Whaling People believed that whalers did not come upon a drift whale by chance, but because of a special magic ritual performed by a chief to persuade the whale spirit to give up its body (see Jonaitis and Inglis 1999). A drift whale (*ho·n'i·*) might be found at any time, either floating on the sea, in which case canoes hurried out to tow it in, or beached on a shore. Drift whales happened more in the stormy winter season (Drucker 1951:37-8).

The carcass belonged to the chief who owned the sea or beach area where the whale was found, or to him who owned the rights to drift whales, which could be held separate from ownership of territory. The Whaling People were particular about the ownership of all kinds of property and disputes of ownership often arose. Such a valuable prize floating on the ocean, where boundaries were poorly defined, could provoke rival claims. If the whale had died from a hunting wound, any harpoon head found could be claimed back by the hunter as payment for the blubber.

After ownership was established, the chief took his special piece first, the saddle of the back near the fin. Then other chiefs of the village took their pieces of the blubber that was highly valued and usually good even if the meat was rotten. Followers of the chiefs took their pieces for them. Other choice parts owned as chief's rights were the tongue, lower jaw, flippers and flukes. Men swarmed over the carcass to butcher it. The smell was very strong. A piece of blubber was taken by attaching a line through a hole cut in it so, while one man pulled, another cut the fat from the meat. At times there were loud arguments over pieces and accidents when knives slipped. Afterwards came feasting and festivity.

The tale of "Always Lifts Up and Sorehead Hunter" (Sapir et al 2004:189-203) is about drift whaling by the whalers of Cape Beal (*Chi·mataqsaɬ*, so named for a canoe-swallowing undersea monster there). The first whaler's name means he is always lifting up his harpoon to strike a whale. The second whaler is a hunter of the Sorehead whale, likely the once numerous Northern Right Whale, which has big calluses on its head that appear white against the dark skin of the whale. This engrossing tale has a typical theme of rivalry and revenge, the plot hinged around the nature of the drift whale. Again we are provided with a lively inside view of the intense world of the Whaling People. A little-known canoeing practice described in the account is the use of a look-out ladder in the canoe to help spot the whale drifting among the waves.

Always Lifts Up and Sorehead Hunter

Their name was *Ch'imataqso?a?atḥ*, a large tribe. They were a tribe that always got many whales, for whaling was their only occupation. They were wealthy on this account, which is why they were always doing only that.

"Say!" said Always Lifts Up (*?I·ch'a·?apshi·l*). "Come here you people. Let's go out and sit and chat on the rocks."

He asked them to do this, so then the young men started out to the rocky place out to sea at Ch'imataqsol. They went to their lookout place where they were in the habit of looking out in the morning. There were many young men out on the rocks on the fine cloudless day.

Always Lifts Up caught sight of something.

"Say! Come and look! Do you see the drift whale (*ho·n'i·*)?" said he to those who were with him.

One of the young men, another youthful chief spoke up: "Stop telling lies! There is no drift whale at all."

The many young men started to talk about it all together, sitting and chatting on the rocks.

"Hey!" said Always Lifts Up again. "There it is, surely. It's clearly visible on the surface of the water."

"Hey!" said that young man again, and they started to laugh among themselves for Always Lifts Up has to be lying, there being no drifting whale carcass to be seen. He was the only one who could see so far out on the water; he was one of whom you could say, "Good for you!" But he really was the one who could see for this reason: he was gifted with piercing sight, having obtained supernatural power from an eagle.

"You are lying more than ever," they said to him.

He still wasn't believed as there was no one among the other young men who could see so well though they were all trying to get sight of the whale.

"Say!" said Always Lifts Up again, "Have you all eyes like that? There it is on the surface of the water. There is nothing in the way."

The young men jeered in mockery, laughing because they for their part could not see the whale carcass that was supposed to be drifting on the sea. Always Lifts Up spoke again:

Now, the Chief named Sorehead Hunter (_ʔIˑchqiqmiˑk_) was staying home.

"All right!" one of the young men was told. "Go and get Sorehead Hunter so that he may come and see, being the only other one gifted with piercing sight."

The young man stood up and said within his heart that he would go and call him. He went down and ran to the house, that young man who had been sent to call the chief.

"You are called for, Sorehead Hunter, by Always Lifts Up. He says that you are to come and see a drifting dead whale that he speaks of. Always Lifts Up is the only one who can see it," said the young man.

Sorehead Hunter went with the one who had come to fetch him. He got to where they were all together on the rocks.

"All right!" said Always Lifts Up. "Come and see the whale drifting, for there it is on the surface of the water with nothing to keep it from sight. I do not understand why these people cannot see it."

Sorehead Hunter started to look for it.

"Oh!" he said as he, too, caught sight of it for he had the gift of piercing sight, he who had obtained his supernatural power from an osprey.

"It is only a little ways out at sea," said Sorehead Hunter.

"What do you think about our going after the drift-whale carcass?" he was asked.

Sorehead Hunter did not answer.

He was asked again: "Say! Perhaps we had better go to get the drift whale. Let's go and get it. We should not be long away for it is not far out

Sorehead Hunter on his lookout ladder searches for the drift whale.
Tim Paul drawing, 2008.

at sea. We should be early in returning."

Said the chief: "Oh! It is well."

Sorehead Hunter arose, willing to do what he had been asked. All the kinsfolk of Always Lifts Up, as many as there were of them, got ready and carried their whaling canoe down to the water's edge. Then they called out to Sorehead Hunter: "Come on! We are tired of waiting on the beach."

Into the canoe went the whole whaling outfit, the line of twisted cedar branches, the floats. Everything went in that they were in the habit of using whenever they went out sea-hunting, for the family of Always Lifts Up got many whales. They set off, moving out from the rocky bay of Ch'imataqsol. They were moving out from the rocks by way of a small channel in the middle.

Chief Sorehead Hunter was alone. There was no one of his own people who went along with him to go out whaling on the sea though he was a chief. He was the only one in the canoe that was of another family. And he was with his enemy Always Lifts Up, who was trying to get him killed on the sly.

"All right!" said he to those that were with him in the canoe. "Let's go straight to it. There's what we're after."

He had with him a ladder [a wide board about two metres long, used in the house to reach the roof]. When travelling he had a ladder that he was in the habit of having stood up in his canoe.

They set out, started off from the beach. All day long they paddled. The day was sunshiny and fair. It was fine out on the water.

"All right!" he said. "Stand this ladder of ours up in the canoe."

They stood it up, two of them holding it. He climbed up to see where they might be. He saw that, sure enough, they were heading straight for where it was. He stepped down, took down his ladder, and stowed it lengthwise in the canoe. This ladder had holes cut in it, chiselled through with a bone chisel [half-moon-shaped step holes with the straight side down].

They paddled off. As it was warm and windless they started sweating.

Then Always Lifts Up spoke, saying, "There it is now. Looks like we weren't far off the mark. You people must be able to see it now."

Again they stood the ladder up in the canoe. It was now past the middle of the day.

"All right! You be the one to go up and see," said he to Sorehead Hunter.

So he went up as he was told and saw.

"Let's go straight ahead," he said.

He stepped down and seated himself in the canoe. Again they paddled off. Yonder appeared in full view a drifting whale carcass. Sure enough, the whale carcass had one of its side fins up.

"Let's paddle a little harder," said Always Lifts Up.

They began to paddle with more rapid strokes as they wanted to get there quickly. They were getting nearer and nearer, reassuring themselves that yonder really was a drifting whale. They reached it when the sun was halfway down toward the horizon – that was the time of day they got there. They reached it just before they were beginning to feel faint from paddling, for they had been a long time paddling, since the morning.

They came alongside the Humpback and recognized that it really was such. Always Lifts Up then spoke, addressing the one who was along with him in his canoe, the one called Sorehead Hunter: "All right! Climb up! You be the first to cut, cutting off the *chakwa·si* as your share." [The dorsal fin with its supporting saddle where the whale spirit dwells is the prize part taken by the one who gets the whale and is proudly displayed with much ceremony.]

Sorehead Hunter unclad himself and climbed up.

"Get on the other side! Start cutting the whale from that side," he was told.

So then he began, having been told to go ahead and start cutting on the other side. As soon as he got on the other side of the dorsal fin he lost sight of those who had accompanied him in the canoe. Just then they shoved off with their paddles. He was just left up there, thrown away, the doomed chief. But he still didn't know about it, didn't know how they were treating him. Unmindful he cut and cut away.

Then suspicion came, for of those who were with him none had climbed up. He was alone. He stopped cutting, looked up and saw them off yonder paddling hard. He has just been left behind up there. Sorehead Hunter called out: "Why are you doing this? Come back here! Let me go with you in the canoe! Do not treat me so!"

The canoe party did not stop. They paddled and paddled away, saying to themselves that they were hitting him and putting him to death, for they had been unable to kill him secretly. The reason they were doing so was that the family of Always Lifts Up were the ones who wanted to be head chiefs.

Paddling on and on the canoe party disappeared. Sorehead Hunter lost sight of those who had come with him. He burst into tears, cried because he would die there as there was no way he might live being far out at sea. The islands barely showed above the surface of the water. Sure to die in this way he wept. He wept, just cried until nightfall. Then all night long he wept. Daylight came, and he was weeping the length of the day. Again the sun descended into the water and he was crying for himself that he was going to die.

Now back ashore the ones who had gone in search of the drifting whale came out from behind the point.

"It's them," said people on shore.

They landed at Ch'imataqsol, and people came down to the beach. One of those who had come to see the landing spoke: "Why is it that one of you is missing?"

"We were spearing and he got entangled, caught up by the harpoon line as it left the canoe," said Always Lifts Up.

They had been breaking up the gum on the faces of their harpoon heads to bits. They made them all like that, and the harpoons in the canoe had no mussel-shell blades on them. [Harpoon blades are held in place by spruce gum.] They treated them like that so they might falsely claim that they speared but the whale got away. That's why they broke up the gum stuck around the harpoons. But as soon as the gum dropped they put it in their mouths and were chewing it. [A habit and a relief from parched mouth and throat.] All the men were doing this when they landed.

Now, there was one who wondered why the canoe party was doing this, why they were all chewing gum. The man spoke of it to himself because he did not believe them, mistrusting their words in his heart. He suspected at once that the chief had been slain.

Yonder he was indeed, as if truly struck with a club. He had now been two days crying. Another day came, and he cried and cried away knowing he was to die. When it turned into the late afternoon, it began to storm. Clouds darkened and a squall came up quickly. When it was about to turn into night he stopped crying for a while and considered what he might

Sorehead Hunter in the drift whale. Tim Paul drawing, 2008.

possibly do, for he was naked. He was completely naked, for all his clothes were in that canoe with those who had been with him. As soon as the evening came on, the fog began to turn into fine spray and the east wind – the storm wind – rose. At once he cut into a spot on the whale on the side of its dorsal fin. The young man cut out only as much as the size of his waist. Then he cut out the fat inside and threw it away. He left only the skin of the whale and a small piece of blubber. When night fell it rained and stormed. Straightaway he sat down in the hole and put the whaleskin back in place covering himself with it. Only his hand was sticking out on the surface of the whale holding down his cover. Thus set up he was comfortable.

Then he began crying again, more bitterly than ever. A big storm came on. All night long he wept. He was bent on doing so for four days and then to cease doing so, because he knew that he was to die. Daylight came and he fell asleep. The storm changed to a south wind. He heard something. Sure enough, now he was about to hear what the nature was of that on which he was resting.

They spoke to him: "Hey! Stop your crying! It's you that makes the canoe so slow."

So they said to him. He woke up. The chief knew he'd been spoken to. He stopped resting in the spot where he was and got out. At once he began to pray and asked that he might be made to move on to dry land. He stopped crying. The chief knew it wasn't dead where he was placed. He heard that it was a party travelling, canoemen and canoe. He went back to the same spot he had occupied. His throat had got dry, sore because of the saltwater he was breathing in. He sucked the blubber, began sucking it now and then, and his throat got better. Then he fell asleep again. He listened again to try to hear as clearly as possible. He listened, and this time he succeeded in hearing clearly.

"Stop your crying! It's you who is making it impossible for us to reach the rocky shore."

This is what they told him. At once he sat up and prayed again. Now he knew that it was people travelling in their canoe. He began talking, asking that he might be brought home, that he might be able to reach the rocky shore. Such words he spoke, pleading piteously. Again he went to the same spot and began to suck on the blubber. This is what he had for food, drinking the oil of it, and why he stayed alive. He fell asleep. When evening came again the weather was fine and he fell asleep.

Once more the same words were said to him: "Stop your crying! You shall be brought to land. We shall take you home, taking you to a rocky shore."

The he saw – it flashed within his heart. There they were, a canoe party, and he was in a canoe. He looked and saw that he was sitting on front of the steersman's place in a whaling canoe and that this canoe had thwarts. He had gone into the middle of it. They had made him stop being where he had been on top. And he heard. There they were, a canoe party, with many. Now they began to talk to one another.

"At what place shall we land?"

"Let's go straight to the rocky shore of ʔOmoˑs [Seaweeds Drifting on the Beach]."

This is what he heard, the one who had been a man, for now he was another being. He had gone into the heart of the drifting whale. It turned dark.

"All right! Wake up, all of you so we can start paddling. We've been too long drifting about on the water. We'll be on shore before the day comes."

They set off.

"Ho̱···!" cried the canoe party in a prolonged call, and then shorter, "Ho̱! Ho̱!"

Sure enough, this is what they were doing right along. Sorehead Hunter heard what it was all like when he found himself in the canoe. It was daylight. They of the canoe fell asleep and set to drifting about on the water. Then it turned dark once more, and he spoke again, the one who was in the habit of speaking. Indeed, he was the one who attended to waking those who were with him in the canoe.

"Hey! Wake up, all of you who have blood running over you in the canoe!"

The ones who were addressed in this way were whatever was inside the whale, the parts that weren't firmly attached in the canoe. Indeed, they were the ones who paddled vigorously. It turned dark, and again they made the same kind of call as was sounded before:

"*Ho̲*⋯! *Ho̲*! *Ho̲*!"

They set off and paddled all night.

Then came a fog. The canoemen stopped for fear they might not see the place to which they were going – that's why they stopped. Then they fell asleep again. This, in truth, was their way: they paddled only at night, they did not paddle by day. They had fallen asleep again. And there in the canoe was Sorehead Hunter. He saw everything and knew that he would keep living. When daylight came they were close to shore. There was Ch'imataqsol!

Then they spoke to Sorehead Hunter: "Now listen! You will take revenge on him by whom you were murdered. Listen! We shall tell you what you are to do to him for revenge, for we know by whom it is that you have been injured."

This is what they said to him. He listened. Sure enough, he was about to land on the rocky shore with the coming of night. They said to him, "Look and see."

There it was, a little whetstone.

"This is what we are in the habit of putting on for one who is wicked when hunting. We always make him spear at that. We always put it on for him, flat under our skin, at whatever part the spear comes flying to."

This they said and gave him the whetstone.

"You shall use it for rubbing. You shall have it under the palm of the hand. Because of it you will get stronger and stronger, biding your vengeance, for you will pay him back."

Thus he was told. And another thing was given him. It had the appearance of a smooth stone, flat and rounded.

"You shall use this for the rubbing of your body, passing it over the soft inner parts of your limbs in order that you may gain strength."

So he was told, and that number of things was given to him. Then one of the canoe party spoke again: "Wake up all of you! We have been drifting about on the water for a long long time. We shall be ashore before day comes."

And they were in the cliff-lined bay before the coming of the day. Now his heart rejoiced. Now he knew he would live.

His father had not been far from dying, sore at heart for he had but one grown child though there was also a little boy who as yet had come to only slight intelligence. There he was, on the rocks at the other end of the beach, with only a half beamed house left to him for they had burnt down his former home. [When in mourning half the house is burnt down, the other half being taken away to rebuild in another place.]

The drift whale began to paddle off.

"*Ho̲*⋯!" they called out, "*Ho̲*! *Ho̲*! *Ho̲*! *Ho̲*!"

Then the lookout man spoke up: "We might hit a rock! Our canoe might break! Let's go straight in the channel so we won't run aground."

They entered the narrow channel in among the rocks.

They came to the rocky bay of ?Omo·s, a calm place sheltered from the breakers. The whale turned around, flattening down along the rocks. Sorehead Hunter jumped out of the canoe, naked, but he did not really feel the cold for he had been rubbed down by them. He jumped out onto the rocks.

Standing there on the rocks he saw two men. As it turned out that dead whale had been towed along. Indeed, it was Ya𝑧i· spirits who had been towing. The men walked off. Sorehead Hunter followed behind in the same direction, started going after them and found out for certain where they disappeared into the rocks. Then he gave up the pursuit.

Day came and off he went to where the many houses were, he, Sorehead Hunter, of whom it was not known that he had come from far away. Nor was it yet known that a dead whale had drifted to shore. Out of the woods he came, there he was, his house gone, burnt down. He saw and knew that off yonder on the rocks it was the house of his father who had but a half beamed roof over his head. Then his heart was grieved from seeing that his old house was no longer standing there.

Sorehead Hunter started off and went to where they got drinking water, his heart telling him that his little brother would be coming for water. He sat down on the ground and clothed himself with ferns. These he wore and under them next to his skin he had moss on account of which it was warm. He had the ferns stitched together. He was not made to wait long. There appeared the younger brother coming for water without hair on his little head for it had all been cut off [in mourning]. Then spoke Sorehead Hunter, very gently lest his brother be startled out of his mind. The little boy looked to see who it was and laughed.

"Come here, my dear boy. Don't be afraid of me. It is I, Sorehead Hunter. Here on the rocks is that ho·n'i· on which I was as it came to shore."

This is what he said. Then he took him and sat him on his knee.

"I am alive, my dear boy. I was just left behind on it," said Sorehead Hunter.

And the little boy spoke, too: "They pretended that you got entangled with the line and fell out of the canoe."

Sorehead Hunter took his little pail and put water in it for him.

"All right! Listen to me. You shall tell your father, but do so secretly. Say to him, 'Father, I have seen Sorehead Hunter.' And you shall make a hole for me there in the corner of the house, and I'll go and get me a blanket as soon as it turns dark. Now be off!"

So he said, and the little boy went away.

Darkness fell. The village still had no news of him, the chief, that he had come back. Only the family of Always Lifts Up was rejoicing. The boy went off and found his father lying in bed. He came close to his father and put his mouth to his ear.

"Father," he said, "I have seen Sorehead Hunter. I have seen where he is. He is over there by the water. 'Come here, my dear boy,' said he to me, 'Do not be afraid of me. I am alive. Here is the drift whale on which I was,' said he to me."

"Damn! Have you not rather been visited by a spirit?"

"Not so. Keep quiet. He says you are to make a hole for him here in the corner of the house."

It was growing dark. The old chief asked in his heart if it was really him. He put out his fire. When darkness came the fire was out. The old man did not go to sleep but remained awake in the house. He was sure he heard a creaking sound coming from the corner. Someone appeared. It was really him there, Sorehead Hunter. He sat down. At once the mother burst out crying.

"Don't," said Sorehead Hunter. "Be silent. Just leave that sort of thing," said he to his mother. "Father," he said, "There is a drift whale on which I was as it came to shore. I have it there on the rocks of ʔOmo·s. You shall go for the drift whale. Do so early, before it dawns. All of you shall go out in the whaling canoe. Then I'll go out of the house."

And with that he went away. The father got out of bed, went off, and approached his younger brother.

"My boy has come back. He says that we are to go and get the drift whale."

They got ready, prepared themselves in silence, and went down to the beach carrying the canoe on their shoulders. Then they set off and got to where the drift whale was. They cut it up in a hurry and were quick to fill the whaling canoe. They wanted to get back before anyone else stirred, to come out at the point while it was still early in the morning. And this they really did, for it was early when they rounded the point. As soon as they came close to the beach they called out:

"There is a drift whale yonder on the rocks at ʔOmo·s!"

All were seized with excitement and made ready. The family of Always Lifts Up went down to the beach. Sorehead Hunter was there on the rocks, lying in wait for him when he should come down to the beach. Now Always Lifts Up got hold of his canoe and started to lift it up. Sorehead Hunter rose and walked, coming out from among the rocks. He walked on and approached the one who was about to lift his canoe, Always Lifts Up. He took hold of the bow of the canoe, bringing him to a halt. Then he gave a slap at the whaling canoe. It broke to pieces, crumbled to bits. He went up to him and took hold of him with his left hand. He got hold of him under the chin and by his collarbone. He died. He got hold of the other one as well and did the same to him. Him, too, he killed. And it was known that it was he, Sorehead Hunter. They died, they who had gone to seek the drift whale. There they were on the beach, dead. Thus Sorehead Hunter took his revenge and the people began to weep. Now the Ch'imataqso?a?at<u>h</u> tribe set off in their canoes to get the drift whale.

Commercial whaling's great slaughter of the Grey, Humpback and Northern Right whales to near extinction by the early 1900s also meant the virtual death of traditional whaling by the Whaling People (Bowechop 2004:404-09). According to information provided by the late Pacheedaht Chief Charles Jones Sr, the Makah carried out the last whaling on the south coast in 1907. The Pacheedaht and Ditidaht had stopped whaling earlier. Henry St Clair towed his canoe out to Swiftsure Bank and took several whales that last year. By this time many men had been engaged in the relatively short-lived fur-seal industry that provided successful hunters with a significant income. Whaling was still "the symbolic heart of the culture, but practically speaking it brought little in the way of cash income" (Marr 1987:25). This activity may have been the Makah whaling revival referred to by Curtis (1916:40; see also Waterman 1920:48). The famous photograph of the Makah whaler, Do·kmi·s, about to throw a second harpoon (page 62) was taken just a few years before Henry St Clair's last hunt. The Ahousaht in 1906 or 1908 took their last whale in the traditional manner. The whaler was either ?At̲yo or a man named Ahousat Amos. ?At̲yo was Philip Drucker's primary informant on whaling. Drucker's fieldnotes of interviews with ?At̲yo indicate a significant hiatus in whaling among the Ahousaht. ?At̲yo and his cousin, Ahousat Amos, were able to go whaling because their families had kept the technical and ritual knowledge alive. Whaling was also carried out in the Barkley Sound area by the Huu-ay-aht whaler John Moses. In 1963 Edwin Frank became the last of the Whaling People in British Columbia to kill a whale; he used non-traditional equipment from a fish boat.

Grey Whales had been decimated in the 19th century after the discovery of the whales' breeding grounds in Baja California (Scammon 1968:20-33). Commercial whaling only stopped when the low population no longer supported a viable commercial harvest. After 1900 and the establishment of the factory ships that allowed processing of captured whales at sea, the Grey Whale hunt was again resumed and the population plummeted to about 2,000 animals. In 1946 an international agreement banned the killing of

Grey Whales. In 1994 Greys were removed from the United States' list of threatened and endangered species.

In 1998 the International Whaling Commission recognized the Makah's right to whale under an 1855 treaty with the United States, allowing them to take 20 whales through the year 2004 (Marine Mammal Centre n.d.). Apparently the United States delegation won this approval by linking the Makah application to a separate Russian proposal to allow aboriginal Chukotka whalers in the Bering Strait area to kill 145 Grey Whales (LaBudde 1998). In the summer of 1999 a Makah whaling crew from Neah Bay, Washington, killed a Grey Whale off the northwest side of the Olympic Peninsula (Sullivan 2000, Peterson and MCRC 2002, Bowechop 2004). This hunt was sanctioned by both the Makah Whaling Commission and the United States Marine Mammal Protection Act. In September 2007, five men, "weary of waiting for US court approval to hunt whales", were arrested after killing a Grey Whale in Juan de Fuca Strait. They did not have a permit or waiver to do so and were denounced by the Makah Tribal Council for whaling without the permission of the Tribal Council and the Makah Whaling Commission (*Ha-Shilth-Sa* 2007:34:18:6).

It can be argued that the Grey Whale population would not be threatened by limited hunting by Whaling People. Apparently the International Whaling Commission agreed as they allocated the Makah a harvest of five whales per year through 2002 (Shukovsky and Barber 2001).

HUNTING OTHER SEA MAMMALS

The Whaling People hunted other sea mammals from narrow, fast two- or three-man canoes with sharp low cutwaters for silence. They used a two-pronged harpoon to spear most animals but a bow and arrows for Sea Otters. Sea mammals could be hunted at almost any time of year, but the prime season began in late spring when, with good weather, many groups moved out to the open coast. To ensure success, hunters performed arduous rituals for weeks before the hunting season began. They also performed short rituals each time, before they set out. Sea mammals were believed to carry a little stick to deflect the harpoon of a hunter who had not done his ritual properly (Sapir 1912 6:18 n5).

The double-headed harpoon (*m'achy'ak* (Dit.)) had a slender shaft about four metres long. According to Chief Charles Jones Sr, the harpoon was usually made of fir, with two unequal diverging foreshafts, the longer being about 60 centimetres. A finger rest with two notches was cut in the butt end to aid throwing. The socketed harpoon heads, about 15 centimetres long overall, were armed with a blade of mussel shell held between a pair

Using a sealing harpoon to catch seals from shore.
Edward S. Curtis photograph; RBCM D-08366.

of antler or bone barbs. A braided sinew lanyard, about 30 centimetres long, was tied around a notched section of the barbs and neatly wrapped. The main line was made of sinew or a rope of twisted cedar withe. Metal blades and trade ropes came into general use soon after contact with Europeans. A good hunter could accurately throw the harpoon about twelve metres.

The Hair (Harbour) Seal (*kokoẖwisa* or *k'a·sch'at̓*) was the most commonly hunted sea mammal. Setting out before dawn and arriving at the sealing grounds early, the hunter and his steersman looked for only those seals that appeared easy to catch. They got as close as possible to the seal, moving silently while it was feeding underwater. When ready, the hunter stood in his canoe and threw the harpoon on a slightly downward angle. When one of the blades struck, the shaft came away, because it was held to the line by a slip knot. After some playing to tire it, the seal could be brought alongside, clubbed, and rolled into the canoe.

It was believed that if the seal disliked the hunter for having done something wrong in his ritual preparation and observation of taboos, it could put a whetstone about 15 centimetres square on the point of aim to shatter the harpoon blade when it struck (Sapir 1912 6:18 n6). A hunter's best harpoon, which was a prized family heirloom, was used only in fine weather with the hunter sure of getting his game (Sapir 1912 6:20).

Hair Seals could be harpooned from shore in a few places, such as from a rock in the narrows of a stream where they passed. They could also be netted in special locations, such as where a stream went over a rock ledge where a bag net could be set below. The more common method of catching seals on land was clubbing the ones that had come ashore in caves. Especially productive were caves with submerged entrances that opened behind in the woods. Such lucky finds were made by men who were scrupulously clean from proper ritual bathing. The cliffs at Cape Flattery have caves at the bottom into which men could swim at low tide with pitch torches tied to their heads to light the seals on ledges inside. The Whaling People valued seals not only for their meat and blubber, but also for their whole skins that could be used as whaling floats.

A sea-lion (*toko·k*) puts his head up to the surface every few minutes to breathe. When it is at the surface but with its head still down in the water, the hunter and his steersman paddled up quickly to harpoon it (Sapir 1912 6:18). The line was usually tied to a thwart, though a seal-skin float was sometimes attached to the line. Also, some men held the line in their hands to play the sea-lions. The Whaling People did not value sea-lions as highly as seals for food (Drucker 1951:46).

They prized the Northern Fur Seal (*k'it·ano·s*) for its fine fur, its meat and its blubber. A Fur Seal stays on its back at the surface, whether sleeping or looking for fish, with its head turned back into the water, so it could be harpooned in the belly. To catch a female, the harpoon could be cast low to bounce on the surface, but the much bigger and more powerful bull had to be hit hard, directly, to kill it outright; a wounded male fur seal was strong enough to break the line. According to Chief Charles Jones Sr, if the harpoon was slightly overthrown, the head of the shorter lower prong would get him.

Southern groups hunted two kinds of porpoises for food in Juan de Fuca Strait (Sproat 1868:30): the Dall's Porpoise (130–200 kg) and the Harbour Porpoise (*ts'itk'oh*, 50–90 kg). The central Nuu-chah-nulth hunted only the Harbour Porpoise and "only in passing" (Koppert 1930a:67). After harpooning a porpoise, the hunter released the line with a marker float (an inflated cod's stomach) attached. Since the skin of a porpoise is weak, too much tension on the line could tear the harpoon free before the animal could be subdued. On occasion, hunters went out at night to attract porpoises by throwing sand or fine gravel over the water to mimic the sound of schools of small fish (Drucker 1951:46).

Traditionally, Sea Otter (*kw'akw'atł*) was prized for its meat and for its fine fur, worn by high-ranking people. In hunting Sea Otters, the hunter went by canoe with his steersman to the kelp beds before dawn, trying to catch one asleep at the surface. If he found a sleeping otter, the hunter would steal up soundlessly and shoot it with bow and arrow. A wounded otter could not swim far underwater, so it was easy to follow and shoot with another arrow or harpoon for retrieval. Another hunting method was to go at night along the reefs listening for a crying pup. On finding such a pup, the

A hunter ready to release his arrow at a Sea Otter.
Edward S. Curtis photograph; RBCM D-08364.

hunter tied a rope around it and made it swim about whimpering to attract the mother within harpoon range.

When European traders came in search of the Sea Otter's precious pelt, from 1785 onward, chiefs of the Whaling People organized mass hunts so efficient that they virtually wiped out these animals from the region. On a clear, calm, summer morning many canoes would line up, from just beyond the breakers out to sea, then follow the shoreline in formation, spaced well apart (Drucker 1951:47-48). In such a way, the Mowachaht used to put out over 20 canoes in a line a kilometre or two long, sweeping that breadth of water along the shore. When someone saw an otter, he waved his paddle overhead, bringing the canoes in to form a big circle around the spot. When the otter surfaced, they shot arrows at it but the target was hard to hit from the canoes rolling on the swell. The one to put in the first arrow owned the pelt and paid off with pairs of trade blankets those who put in other arrows and harpooned it. The skin was hung outside with heavy stone weights attached to stretch it several inches since the traders priced it by length. The tail was cut off and sold separately. The meat was often served in a feast for the steersmen who were usually older kinsmen of the hunters.

Following the end of the maritime fur-trade period, about 1820, Sea Otters disappeared from the west coast of Vancouver Island. They were re-introduced in northern Nuu-chah-nulth territory in the late 20th century, without consultation with Nuu-chah-nulth people, and are now flourishing. In the 100-year absence of the Sea Otter, sea urchins flourished and the great kelp forests were diminished, resulting in significant coastal erosion.

The increased predation of sea urchins by Sea Otters has resulted in an increase in the kelp forests and a concomitant increase in biodiversity. But some people have raised concerns about the decimation by Sea Otters of sea urchins, abalone, crabs and intertidal clams, traditional sources of food for many Nuu-chah-nulth communities (Okerlund 2007a, 2007b). The Nuu-chah-nulth are now considering harvesting Sea Otters to provide their hereditary chiefs with tradional otter cloaks (*Ha-Shilth-Sa* 2007:34:16:20 and 34:17:20).

The foregoing provides only a rather abstract outline of complex activities that occupied great sectors of the life of the Whaling People. To strike a balance we can do no better but to turn again to one of their many oral traditions, a graphic account that features hunting seals in caves and includes an endearing picture of the seals at home. The intriguing human interactions described are also quite revealing again of the Whaling Peoples' psyche, as it were. This story (after Sapir et al. 2004:181-8) is thought to originally belong to a particular family, but it is now a general story enjoyed by all. As in many folktales, it has a grim aspect.

Hair Seal Hunter and Porpoise Hunter

These two were both good hunters, but one was not so lucky. Porpoise Hunter (*Hi·tsswatqmi·k*) was behind, and Hair Seal Hunter (*Ko·h w'isaqmi·k*) was lucky. They would go out in the evening, the two good hunters, hunting at night. In the morning they would come in. One of them would come in with lots in the canoe, Hair Seal Hunter would; but Porpoise Hunter would come in with nothing. That is how it was that he was behind his rival. Right away Porpoise Hunter thought about what to do. He called on an old man, and they deliberated.

"Ask Hair Seal Hunter for some seal to eat and watch for what is between its teeth," he said.

"All right! All right!" said the old man.

They went out again, Hair Seal Hunter and Porpoise Hunter, the latter hunting porpoise at night. He would have just one when they came in in the morning while Hair Seal Hunter had many in his canoe. Hair Seal Hunter would come in with lots of seals.

Because his rival was besting him, Porpoise Hunter got ashamed and angry at the same time. Then the old man spoke: "O great Seal Hunter, I want to eat a seal that you catch."

"You shall eat seal," he was told, the old man, and was being cooked for.

After the invitation he went to dine. The seal was all cooked up. The old man began to eat and was eating the head of the seal as he had been told to do by Porpoise Hunter. Then he saw that what he was eating had dirt between its teeth. He finished eating and took some leftovers home

"Hair Seal Hunter and Porpoise Hunter." Tim Paul drawing, 2008.

from the seal head. He went home and told Porpoise Hunter that he found out why Hair Seal Hunter was getting lots of seals

"He must have a cave. I saw from what I was eating that the seal he gave me had dirt between its teeth."

"That's the evidence I needed. That's why I suggested that you ask to eat seal. Now I'll get some."

That night he went out again, Hair Seal Hunter, going out with his sister. The other followed, his brother with him. They arrived at the secret cave. The two brothers watched where the seal hunter went. They went closer to where Hair Seal Hunter went. There against the edge of the rocks was the sister, looking after the canoe. They went alongside.

"What is Hair Seal Hunter doing?" they asked the girl.

"He's gone to get young cedar branches," she said.

He took his sealing harpoon, Porpoise Hunter did, and said, "Ha! You will die!"

He grabbed her by the hair and wrapped it around the end of his harpoon. Thrust underwater with the pole, the girl drowned. They sank her down with a stone. Her canoe was capsized and all broken up. Then Porpoise Hunter went looking for Hair Seal Hunter. He went up on the rocks and pulled on the bushes. He found that the bushes were only stuck there in the ground, not rooted to it. He went up farther, pulled on the bushes, and the same thing happened: the little bushes just pulled up. Then he noticed that it was disturbed, evidence that this was his trail. He went up farther still and saw that there were seals down below.

"All right! I've got you now!" he said.

Then he walked some more and saw a harpoon resting on the ground. He knew it belonged to Hair Seal Hunter. Right away he began moving along stealthily and as he drew near he saw that it was a cave down there. And he saw Hair Seal Hunter walking about on the cave floor, holding a seal by its hind flippers to club it. There was a rope ladder hanging over the edge. Porpoise Hunter suddenly jerked it away and said, "Hey!"

He tried to jump for his ladder but barely touched it.

"You will live," said Porpoise Hunter and ran back down the rocks to his canoe.

"I got him!" he told his younger brother.

They went home that night with no porpoise in the canoe. Hair Seal Hunter started to cry for he knew that they must have killed his sister. For four days he cried, crying for himself too.

The seals used to go out in the morning. In the evening they would begin to come back in and talk about being in faraway places. Some of them would say, "I was just close by."

Hair Seal Hunter began to understand what the seals were saying, for he had now wept there for four days. The biggest seal would be left behind when the rest went out, left behind with the young ones who would be crying. He would try to stop them from crying.

"Don't cry, don't cry! Or the humans might roast you on their fires," the big seal would say.

That was the one who told him, "Stop crying over there inside! You are becoming a nuisance! Come right in the house. Now we'll see what we can do for you."

"All right!" said the chief of the seals. "Let's assemble." They assembled.

"You will take him back," said the chief. "All right, which one of you is long-winded?"

One spoke and said, "I'm not very long-winded; I only stay under for four breakers on the rocks."

Another spoke up: "I stay under for six waves on the rocks, then I come up."

And another spoke: "I stay under for eight waves on the rocks, then I come up too."

Another spoke: "I stay under for ten waves on the rocks."

Said again another: "I go right across the sound without coming up."

Another spoke: "I go right across two sounds without coming up, and I'm short-winded too."

Hair Seal Hunter was listening to what the seals were saying for he now could understand their speech.

Another spoke: "I can stay under across three sounds without coming up. That's how long my wind is."

Also: "I can stay under across four sounds without coming up."

Also: "I can stay under across five sounds without coming up. That's how long-winded I am."

Also: "I can cross six sounds without coming up. That's how long my wind is."

Also: "I can cross seven sounds without coming up. That's how long my wind is."

Also: "I can cross eight sounds before coming up. That's how long my wind is."

Also: "Nine sounds I can cross before coming up. That's how long my wind is."

Then a cute little one spoke up, a little seal with big bulging eyes: "I myself can cross ten sounds. That's how long my wind is."

"Alright, alright, alright, alright!" said the chief, "You will be the one to take along this human. You and he will be in one canoe to take revenge on the other human who pulled up his ladder."

They started teaching and training him for what he was expected to do. He put on the swimming-skin, and they tried him out.

"Float on the water!" they told him.

He learned how by practice.

"All right," said the chief, "here is something to poke away the spear and make him miss. Go out now. Time it so you arrive there in the morning."

He set out, went underwater and arrived where Porpoise Hunter lived. He came up to the top of the water, floated there, and was seen by those sitting outside.

"Go and wake Porpoise Hunter. Let him spear. It looks like an easy kill."

Porpoise Hunter woke up, got ready and went out. The seal came up. Porpoise Hunter strung up his double-headed sealing harpoon. He was out with his brother again. They began chasing. The seal came up again.

"My! It looks like an easy kill," said those sitting in front of the house.

Paddling hard, Porpoise Hunter went closer. The seal went down. Porpoise Hunter watched for it to come up. It came up again, the seal. He moved in closer. Porpoise Hunter speared, and missed. It had poked the harpoon away, making him miss. The seal came up once more.

"Catch his harpoon this time," said those who had accompanied Hair Seal Hunter.

Porpoise Hunter speared.

"His harpoon found its mark," said those who were sitting outside.

The seal started running as it submerged. It dragged the two brothers in the canoe straight out of the sound to sea. The seal did not come up. It was running very fast and impossible to stop. The younger brother in the stern spoke: "It's becoming difficult it seems," said he to his older brother.

"There seems to be no stopping this," said the older brother.

They were now far offshore.

"Say! You watch out!" said the younger to the older. "We are now far off shore. Cut the line!"

"Say! I prize it too much! I'm too proud. I have a fine harpoon."

The seal had rubbed his harpoon head with medicine that would cause

the owner to prize it more. He was really running now a way offshore.
The mountains became low in the distance, just the snowy peaks now
showing above the water. The younger brother got scared, for he knew
that they were going to die. When only the snow capped mountains
showed, the seal came up.

"Hey!" said the seal. "I am Hair Seal Hunter. You'll become like I am
now. You'll become supernatural."

Porpoise Hunter just bowed his head. Seals were coming up again,
three of them. They shook their heads, the seals: "*Toch'e···, Toch'e···,
hitakwise?i!*" ("East Wind, East Wind, come out!")

A storm arose, and the canoe of the two brothers capsized. Hair Seal
Hunter went back to where they had left from.

"We got them," he said. "We left them with their canoe capsized far
out at sea."

Hair Seal Hunter took off the swimming-skin.

"All right!" said the chief. "You will send him home. I guess his old
folks are in poor state back where he left shore. All right, listen! You stop
killing us, okay? I guess you saw these children on the floor here. They
don't have fathers or mothers on account of you."

Hair Seal Hunter spoke too, to the chief: "You stop being at the small
bays because you are easy prey when you are there. Be at the points, at the
tips of the points so that you can see both ways whether a canoe is coming. That way you'll be hard to get."

The chief spoke again: "You give us something when we are swimming
behind you, okay?"

"Yes, I will do that," said Hair Seal Hunter.

"All right! Take him home," said the chief.

Back home Hair Seal Hunter was still absent. They considered him
dead, and his old folks began to mourn for him. Realizing that their son
was dead, they were crying all the time.

Hair Seal Hunter went home, arriving at night. He knocked on the
side of his parents' house.

"What are you, teasing us?" they said. "We are in a poor state. The way
we are here, we never stop crying. We're always crying."

"It's me, Hair Seal Hunter, your son!"

"Ha! What did that voice say?" They were surprised that it mentioned
the name of the one for whom they were constantly crying.

"It really is me. I've become supernatural," he said.

The mother got up, looked, and saw that it really was her son.

He asked his father, "Where is Porpoise Hunter?"

"He's not around," his father said. "He's still gone. He harpooned a seal
and it dragged him along."

"I took revenge on him. He won't come back. He pulled up my ladder."

"They are crying for him where he left shore."

"Don't tell anyone that I came home. I will go and see those who are crying."

He got to Porpoise Hunter's house, sat right beside the wall, and listened to those who were crying. Then he took his beating stick, beat on the wall and started singing a song he made up: "You, too, now, / You, the one who pulled the ladder up on me, / You, too, turn into a supernatural, / You, Porpoise Hunter."

"Aha," they said, "Who is that singing? He is not very polite to us at a time when we are in such a poor state."

Then they found out it was Hair Seal Hunter come back from the dead. Everyone found out that he had had a supernatural experience and had come back out of the woods after the necessary days of isolation. They saw that he was very much alive but that Porpoise Hunter was gone. Both brothers were dead, never to come back.

MORE GATHERING OF PLANT AND SEA FOOD

With the sunnier days of spring the luxuriant plant life of the west coast revives. Around May the gathering season on the land began. At the same time, hunting and fishing on the sea were giving good returns too, so that from spring to fall the people enjoyed a long season of abundance. It was a time generally free from want and of drying and storing for the leaner winter season certain foods obtained in surplus amounts. The plant foods described below were gathered mainly by women at different locations in a group's territory as the people moved about. Only the common ones are discussed, based mainly on information from the unpublished notes of Denis E. St Claire (1977). Many have not had their native names clarified yet, and not all were used by every group.

Tender new shoots were the major spring plant food, especially the shoots of Salmonberry (m'a·yi) and Thimbleberry (ch'ashxiw'a). Refreshing raw, after peeling, these shoots could also be steamed. Also eaten raw were the young stalks and leaf stems of the Cow Parsnip. Fiddlehead shoots of the Bracken Fern were steamed or boiled. But the Sword Fern was sought for its large rhizome, dug up before the leaves sprouted and roasted or pit steamed. Also dug before sprouting was the bulb of an unidentified, white-flowered plant collected in winter. A spring plant food unusual to us perhaps but widespread among native peoples was the cambium layer of Western Hemlock (qwitł'aqmapt).

As spring turns into summer, many berries ripen. The most important early berry was the Salmonberry (*qawi·*), patches of which were owned by chiefs who directed their harvest. Another exceptionally abundant and important berry was Salal (*y'am'a*). Salal berries were eaten both fresh and dried for winter by parboiling, preliminary drying in frames over fire, then sun-drying in cakes (Drucker 1951:65-66). Also picked was Trailing Blackberry (*qa·łqawi*), Coastal Strawberry (*kałkintapih*), Saskatoon, Red Huckleberry and Black Gooseberry. Later in summer came the Thimbleberry (*tłachłał*), Bog Blueberry (*xwi·lasim*), Red Elderberry (*ts'ini·pi*), Oval-leaved Blueberry, Alaska Blueberry, the haws of Black Hawthorne and Common Bearberry. Blueberries and Thimbleberries were often dried, the latter, at times, together with clams.

Several roots and bulbs that developed in summer were dug by the women with their digging sticks (*ti·qwa·yak*). These included the roots of Springbank Clover (*ʔaʔi·ts'o*), Silverweed (cinquefoil, *tłichsy'op*), and the bulbs of Northern Rice Root, Tiger Lily, wild onions (only around Port Alberni), and Common (Blue) Camas (*kwan'is*). These were eaten steamed or roasted. In the fall, rhizomes of Bracken Fern, Licorice Fern and Lady Fern (*shitła*), and roots of Skunk Cabbage (*tima·t*) were dug up.

In the fall a few berries are still ripening, such as those of the Evergreen Huckleberry (*sinmoxsy'ats*), Low-bush Cranberry and Bog Cranberry (*p'ap'iʔis*), which were gathered green, then steamed until red and soft. Wild Crabapple, most plentiful around Alberni, was also picked green in late summer and stored to ripen before being eaten either raw or cooked. Other plant foods particular to the interior location of Alberni are currants (*ʔołʔo*), rose hips (*patʔo*), and perhaps Western Dock (wild rhubarb, *hom'a·q*).

Among gathered plants, seaweeds must be included as significant foods. Eelgrass has sweet roots and stems that were enjoyed raw. Surf grass and sea grass were formed into square cakes and dried for winter. This considerable variety of plant foods eaten by the Whaling People was supplementary to the main diet of fish, shellfish, mammals and birds, but important for nutritional balance.

These plant foods could also help get people through occasional periods of scarcity. Shellfish gathering, described earlier for the winter, continued through spring and summer. The very low tides of spring, which were not in the dark of night as in winter, were used to exploit the rich subtidal zone. Also many kinds of shellfish, like the Black Chiton, are at their best just after winter. The Black Turban Shell (*tł'achkwin*) was eaten raw only in spring, by the Manhousat at least, because of an interesting belief that the creature grew legs each summer (Ellis and Swan 1981:29). Barnacles are best in summer, as noted before. Butter Clams are eaten in August and September when most were dug, then pit-steamed, sun-dried or smoked

A berry-picker at Clayoquot.
Edward S. Curtis photograph; RBCM AA-00158.

on cedar skewers, and stored in baskets for winter. Dried clams (*saḥaw'a·sht*) were soaked overnight to soften them, and dipped in oil for eating.

Another plant product, while not a food, often occupied the mouths of Whaling People – spruce gum (*ʔishts'i·p*). Gum had other uses, like patching canoes or a smooth coating for harpoon heads. It could be collected in quantity, according to Chief Charles Jones Sr, by building a fire under a good tree, then catching the dripping pitch in big clam shells. For chewing, the gum could simply be picked off a tree any time. Whaling People were avid gum chewers, and this characteristic is even featured in myth. Prohibition of gum chewing for ritual reasons likely was a trying self-denial.

Gum is prominent in the first part of the major creation myth of Andaokot (also called ?Inthtin, Mucus-made or Snot Boy). This is a Mowachaht
version of the myth (Boas 1916:903-07).

How Andaokot First Came to this World

Once there was a village of Indians at Mowin'is. The name of the tribe
was Deer tribe (Mowachaht). One day all the little boys of that tribe
wanted to go up the river Mowin'is; and among these little boys were
three noted ones. The first was Dogfish (*Yachakas*), the second was Spirit
of the Dogfish (*Kw'its'kas*) and the third was Small Clam Boy (*Hichin?qas*).

These little boys went up the river, and they had not gone far, when
they met a great woman chewing gum. She had a great basket on her
back. She came to the little boys and blew at them with something that
took all their strength away, so that they could not run away from her. The
first one she got hold of was Dogfish, then Spirit of the Dogfish, and last
Small Clam Boy.

Now, as soon as she got hold of them, she took some of the gum from
her mouth and put it into their eyes, and then threw them into her basket.
All the other little boys were treated in the same way. The first three, however, went through the netting of the basket as soon as they were thrown
in, for Dogfish, as soon as he found out that he had been thrown into the
basket, stretched his body and went through, and the other two did the
same. All the other little children were carried away by the great Woman
of the Woods (*Małahas*). Dogfish, Spirit of the Dogfish and Small Clam
Boy helped one another take the gum out of their eyes; and as soon as
their eyes were clean, they went to their people and told the news.

But Woman of the Woods went into her house, took a long round pole
and a rope, and tied the children's legs to this pole; and, after she had tied
them on, she hung them over the fire alive, and smoked them to death.

Now, one woman in the village of the Mowachaht, as soon as she
found out that her little boy was among those carried away by the great
Woman of the Woods, went back to her house and cried, and she kept on
crying for four days. On the fourth day she blew her nose and threw the
mucus on the ground. Two days later she saw the mucus begin to have a
little head on it, and arms and legs. Then she began to shut her eyes, and
she cried again. On the third morning she looked at it, and found that it
was as long as her longest finger; and on the fourth day she heard the little
boy begin to cry. Then she took a piece of her Yellow-cedar-bark blanket
and wrapped it round the little baby boy, and she hid it under a tree.

She thought then that she had better go and tell her husband about it;
so she went and called her husband, and showed the little boy to him, and
he told her to take him home. After that the boy began to grow very fast,

How Andaokot First Came to this World. Tim Paul drawing, 1983.

and in a short time he began to talk. Then he asked his mother to make
a bow and two arrows for him, and they began to make a bow and two
arrows; and after they were finished, he asked his mother what made her
cry so much.

She told him about losing the only little boy she had. The child
wanted to know where he was lost. Then she said, "Don't go up the little
stream Mowin'is, for there is a great woman there who killed all the little
children that went there to play; and one of them was my child, who was
killed with all the rest."

After he heard this, he told his mother that he wanted to go and see
the woman. His mother told him not to go, but he insisted. One day his
mother put abalone shells on his ears, and one on his nose, and made her
little son Andaokot look very pretty with paint on his face. That same day
Andaokot disappeared, and his poor mother and father began to think that
he had gone up the river Mowin'is to see the Woman of the Woods. Now,
they were right in guessing that he had gone up that river.

He had not gone far, when he came to a well or spring near a large
house, and alongside of the spring stood a tree. He said to himself, "This
is the well where the great Woman of the Woods comes to get water to
drink, so I will climb up this tree and sit on the top of it, and wait until
she comes for water."

He climbed the tree to a fork on top of the tree, and he had not stayed there long, when he saw the great Woman of the Woods come out of her house, carrying a large box to fetch water in. When she came under the tree, she saw the reflection of Andaokot in the spring. Then she stopped and looked at the pretty shadow in the water, with abalone shells on its ears and nose; and she said, "Oh! I did not know that I was so pretty as that, and I did not know, either, that I had abalone shells in my ears and nose."

She was saying this while she was feeling her ears and nose for the shells. After a long while Andaokot took some moss and threw it down on the great Woman of the Woods. Then she looked up, but Andaokot hid himself; and again the great Woman of the Woods said, "Oh! It's my own reflection, only I never had a chance to see how pretty I look."

Again, Andaokot took some moss and threw it down at her, and again she looked up. But Andaokot did the same thing as before, and she did not see him, for he hid himself in the fork of the tree. Once more the great woman looked upward to see who threw down the moss. But, as before, she did not see him, and she said to herself, "It is my own reflection that I see."

A third time Andaokot took some moss and threw it down on her, and before she looked up he hid himself, and she did not see him this time, and again she said the same thing as before. The fourth time he threw down the moss he did not hide, but he let her see him. When she saw him, she said, "Ah, come down and be my husband!"

Then Andaokot came down the tree; and the first thing the great woman said to him was, "How pretty you are! What did your mother do to your face to make it look so pretty?"

Then he said, "It's no good for me to tell you, for you could not stand being killed first so as to make your face the shape of mine."

Then the great woman said, "Now, tell me about it, for I can stand any pain to become as pretty as you are!"

Then Andaokot said, "My mother took a large flat stone to lay my head on, and she took another one and hammered my head with it, and kept on hammering until my skull was all pounded to pieces. After that she began to squeeze my head until I was made as pretty as I look now. Then I was made to come to life again. So here I am now!"

Then she said, "Shall I get a flat stone to lay my head on, and will you hammer my head as flat as your mother did yours?"

Then Andaokot said, "Well, if you want me to do it. Don't blame me, for I don't want to do this to you, but if you want me to make you pretty, get a good flat stone, and a stone big enough to hammer your head flat with."

Then she went to find the two stones. It was not long before she brought two stones, and she showed them to Andaokot. When he saw the two stones, he said, "These two stones are too small; the bigger the stones are, the prettier you will look."

Then she said, "I will look for larger stones, for I want to be very pretty, as you are, for I mean to have you for my husband." And she ran to find two larger stones.

She had not stayed away long, when she came back with a stone just as large as she could carry. Then she put it down close to where the young man was standing. She put it flat on the ground, and then she went after the other one for a hammer. She brought this also and put it down. Then she said to Andaokot, "Come along and hammer my head flat, and make me look as pretty as you are!"

So Andaokot told her to lay her head on the flat stone. Then she did as she was told, and Andaokot took the stone to hammer her head with. But she jumped up, saying, "I don't think you can bring me to life again after you kill me!"

Andaokot said, "I thought you would do that. Now you had better remain ugly. But I will not marry you," said he, as he threw away the hammer.

Then the great woman said, "Come and hammer my head flat, for I want to marry you!"

This she said as she went and laid her head on the flat stone and before she could move, he hammered her head flat and killed her.

Then he went into her house; and as soon as he was inside the door, he heard someone calling out loud, "Come, my master, for here is a man that has come into your house!"

Andaokot looked for the man who was calling out, and then he found that it was the chamber-pot of the great woman that was calling. Then he took a stone and threw it at it, and broke it to pieces; but this caused only more noise, for all the broken pieces began to cry out louder. Then he picked them up and threw them into the fire, but they cried still louder.

Then Andaokot saw the great woman at the door dancing, and she said, "Ah, Andaokot! You thought you had killed me; but you are mistaken, for I shall never die. Even if you cut me to pieces, I shall come to life again unless you shoot at my heart – that object you see hanging up there," said she, pointing to a black object hanging up in the corner of her house.

And Andaokot saw the great woman turn her head from him. Then he took a good aim with his bow and arrow, and shot at her heart; and as soon as his arrow struck it, the great woman fell down dead on the floor.

Now she was really dead. Then Andaokot saw all the dried children hanging up over the fire, and he took them all down and laid them in a row on the floor.

After he had finished laying them down, he urinated on their bodies, and they all came to life again. Then he took them home to their parents, who were made happy again.

The story of Andaokot continues on page 227, where he takes the role of Q'anixi·nax̱ the Transformer.

SALMON

Traditionally, fall was the main season for salmon, when most groups caught great numbers of them, particularly Dog (Chum) Salmon (*hink'o·ʔas* (N), *ʔak* (C)). But the early salmon runs begin in spring, starting with Sockeye (*miʔa·t*, or *hisit* when in the sea), then Spring (Chinook; *so·ḥa*) and the early light runs of Coho (*tsow'it*). Whaling People also fished for Pink Salmon (*ch'a·pis*) and Steelhead (*qiw'a·th̲*). All these species were caught mainly in traps set in weirs (fish fences). Trolling began at the end of winter, around February when the Spring Salmon followed the herring closer to shore. It continued into the early summer as the salmon came into the inlets and bays before running upstream to spawn. The Dog Salmon of the fall were especially welcome, because they ran last and in great numbers, and because they had less fat than the other salmon, so they dried better for preservation with less spoiling. From the "Winter Springs" of February to the Dog Salmon of the fall, the people could catch their staple salmon over three quarters of the year with dried stores to tide them over the winter.

Salmon traps of several kinds and sets were used (Drucker 1951:16-18, Koppert 1930a:73-75). The tidewater trap (*po·ʔis*) was set on tidal flats at river mouths where salmon hung about before going upstream to spawn. Between low and high tides, stakes of fir were driven into the bottom with a heavy, flat stone to make a large rectangular enclosure parallel to the shore, four metres (or more) long by two metres wide and two high. Branches were fastened horizontally to the stakes to make a lattice work that kept the fish in while allowing the water to flow through. On the shore side of the trap were two entrances, narrowing on the inside to a V-shape to encourage entry but not exit. From the sides of the entrances, a pair of guide fences – one from each entrance – diverged toward the shore, stopping short of the high-tide line. Sometimes a third fence was put between the two entrances. At high tide the trap and its fences would be under a couple of feet of water. The salmon swam over the fences or around their ends, and as the tide went down those inside were stranded in the trap.

People also built traps in the streams and rivers. These river traps (*mo·s*), made of rod latticework, were set with guiding weirs to capture the salmon

A tide-water fish trap near Friendly Cove, 1912. Edward S. Curtis photograph; RBCM AA-00540.

either as they swan upstream or were turned back downstream. In a fast current, a cylindrical trap with its wide mouth facing upstream might be used. Such traps were set fastened to stakes with the mouth submerged while the smaller closed end was raised just out of the water. To turn the salmon into them, weirs were built by driving pairs of crossed posts into the stream bed two to four metres apart, joining them at the top with horizontal poles on the upstream side, and putting sections of lattice work, weighted with rocks, against them. The layout of the weir across the stream varied, but it basically slanted from either midstream or the banks toward the traps to turn the salmon back to them. The force of the current swept the fish into the wide mouth and up into the narrow end where, high and dry, unable to back down or turn around, they died.

A similar type of upstream-facing conical trap had a pair of weirs diverging right from its mouth. The salmon were driven into the trap by beaters splashing upstream, while other men at the trap took them out of a door in the closed end. These cylindrical traps were usually built flat with rods three to five metres long tied about two to four finger widths (4–8 cm) apart, to several hemlock cross-branches with a winding line. The branches were then bent around into hoops with the lengthwise rods inside to make the trap. A trap door could be built into the narrower, closed end.

When such traps were set facing downstream, they needed a funnel-like entrance turned inward and narrowing down to a small opening through which the salmon could just pass but find it difficult to get back through. There were also box-shaped traps about two metres long with inturned,

A wooden weir on the Somass River, 1896.
Edgar Fleming photograph; RBCM AA-00547.

funnel-shaped mouths. The weir was commonly angled to lead the salmon into the mouths facing downstream. They could be raised to remove the salmon.

Salmon were also taken by harpooning, which was more productive when the run was not heavy, either before or after the main runs. The salmon harpoon had up to three double-barbed heads in various arrangements on the shaft. The basic type was like a small harpoon for hunting sea mammals, having a pair of foreshafts of unequal length. Such a harpoon could be thrown from a canoe at salmon at the surface in the wide mouths of rivers but, more often, it was thrust at the fish from the bank or a rock in the stream. One variant for harpooning downward had two foreshafts angled out to the sides while the centre shaft projected beyond them to save the heads from hitting the bottom if the harpoon missed the salmon.

Drying salmon, and also herring, halibut and cod, for later consumption enabled the Whaling People to stretch their seasonal superabundance of fish over the winter so that they rarely went without food. They smoked fish in the traditional big communal houses with their open fires. Above these, and farther up in the rafters, the fish filets were hung. With salmon, the typical procedure was first to wipe them clean of the protective slime with ferns or moss, then to cut around the body behind the gills and in front of the tail, leaving the backbone intact. Large mussel shells were the traditional knives used by the women preparing the fish for drying. The salmon was then split from either the back or the belly, removing most of the flesh as

Salmon drying on racks at Clo-ose, about 1930.
Dorothy Bayne photograph; Alberni Valley Museum PN02804.

one piece, and leaving the head, backbone, and tail in another piece. Later, the backbones, still with much flesh on them, could be separated, stuck on a split stick, broiled or smoked. When the salmon was split from the back, the sides were smoked overnight to dry the flesh. Filets were cut out of them, leaving about half an inch of meat still on the skin. Cedar splints were inserted in the skin to spread it out, and both skin and filets were thoroughly smoked, then stored in bundles. When the salmon was split from the belly, the filets were cut but left attached to the skin along the back. Hung on the drying racks, these bulkier pieces had to be turned every day or so. The especially fat strips of the throat and of the belly behind the ventral fin were preserved separately. Fat parts, though prized, underwent special care to be dried without spoiling. Because the Dog Salmon had less fat than other species, it could be dried easily – this abundant salmon was the main winter food supply.

Salmon roe was a rich food that was packed in boxes or seal bladders and hung in the smoky rafters where the contents changed into a compact cheese-like delicacy. The first salmon taken, especially Sockeye and Dog, were treated with respectful rituals, in what amounted to welcoming ceremonies like those done for people received as honoured visitors. Among the northern groups, the first catch of Dog Salmon was laid on new mats in the chief's house. He sprinkled eagle down – the symbol of peace and goodwill – on the salmon and said to them (Drucker 1951:175): "We are glad you have come to visit us. We have been saving these [feathers] for you for a long time. We have been waiting a long time for you, and hope you will return to visit us soon."

Then the salmon were dressed and cooked for a feast. All bones and guts were put back in the water. During the Dog Salmon season many prohibitions were observed, such as not chewing gum, not carrying fire along the beach, not making loud noises there or shredding cedar bark by pounding with the bark shredder – basically, not causing any disturbance that would displease the salmon and stop them from running.

This is explained in the myth of Chief Ya·ł'o·ʔa, who marries the Dog Salmon princess (Boas 1916:928-30):

> All that the salmon come to the rivers for is to get the eagle's down that
> drifts on the waters.... [And before the chief returns to the human world
> from the salmon people he is visiting, a wise old salmon man says,] "We
> had better tell Ya·ło·ʔa what we want his people to do for us, and what we
> should like them to put on the water for us to get. Now, the first things
> we always liked to get from them are eagle's down, and mussel-shells,
> the large ones, and the *hap'a·chim'ł* – these three things we always like to
> have. We also do not want them to use blunt-pointed spears on us, for it
> hurts. And whenever they make salmon traps to catch us with, let them
> shave the sticks well and put a good sharp point on them [at the funnel
> entrances]. Also, whenever they cook salmon in any way, and whenever
> they finish eating it, let them pick up all the bones and pieces of skin and
> throw them into the salt water. Then we can come home again. If they do
> not do that, we can not come to life again."

Chapter 3
Living Together

VILLAGES AND HOUSES

To see how the Whaling People lived together, we will first look at the physical settings they created for themselves – their villages and houses. For ages, certain places have been the best spots to live. There has to be a landing place for canoes, ideally a smooth sheltered beach of sand or gravel. If the shore was rocky, landing and launching skids could be built with poles and, where a narrow spot made it necessary, the canoes could be handled sideways in and out of the water. Sometimes rocks were cleared in shallow waters into neat rows leaving channels for the canoes to go in or out. A short steep bank near the water was handy to get the canoes above the high-water line. There on the bank, the rectangular cedar houses were built, usually broadside to the shore.

The winter villages were located up the inlets, sheltered from the storms that rage on the open coast. Acquiring fresh water was no problem in winter when the plentiful rain made freshets. It could also be caught directly in containers. But the spring and summer villages on the lower parts of the inlets and outside coast needed a nearby stream or spring that ran even in the months of dry weather. In general, the Whaling People established villages and camps near the food resources they exploited. In times of war they moved to special, easily defended sites, like a hill with slopes dug away to steepen them, or a small island. They sometimes built palisades of posts or heavy split planks for protection during wars.

The houses of the Whaling People were similar to those of neighbouring peoples, such as the Kwakwaka'wakw (Macnair 1986:501), in that their main framework was permanently set in the ground while the roof and walls were detachable shells of cedar planks. As the people moved about during their seasonal round of economic activities, they took their house

House covered with cedar planks, Neah Bay, about 1915.
Edward S. Curtis photograph; RBCM G-01010.

planks along on their canoes and put them up on the permanent frameworks that stood at the major seasonal villages. Houses were largest in the
winter villages and about half this size in the other camps used when people
were more dispersed and social units smaller. The framework was made two
plank-lengths wide, 9 to 12 metres (house planks were 4.5 to 6 metres long).
The length of the house could be from about 12 to 30 metres, while the
height was about 4 metres (Drucker 1951:69). Running the length of the
house were three thick, strong roof beams, the centre one about half a metre
higher than the outer pair.

This gave the roof enough pitch to run the rain off. The strength of the
house beams had practical value, particularly when snow fell deep, wet and
heavy. But their great size mattered just as much as a display of the wealth
and might of the chief who could command the resources needed to put
them up. The three roof beams were mounted on stout posts, one at each
end. Longer frameworks often had another set of posts in the middle.

The chiefs built the houses with much ceremony, using a great deal of
manpower to get the heavy posts and beams into place. Big cedars were
felled and transported by water to the village. There, they were rolled up the
bank, on inclines of well-supported planks, by many men hauling on strong
ropes of many strands of twisted cedar bark. The ropes were anchored to
stakes above and passed around the log. Chocks were used to stop the log
from rolling back. To plant a housepost in its deep hole in the ground, it was
raised by a combination of hauling on a rope tied to its top and lifting on

House-frames and temporary shelters at Friendly Cove, September 1874.
Richard Maynard photograph; RBCM PN-4652.

poles passed under it. A pair of poles, crossed like scissors, held it up while
the operation was under way. A plank was placed in the hole to make the
end of the post slide down along it instead of digging into the earthen side.
About 80 men were needed to raise house posts (Koppert 1930a: 14). The
side posts were ordinarily about 3.5 metres tall while the centre ones were 4
metres. Centre posts could also be doubled and capped by a short crosspiece
on which the ridge pole or centre beam sat. The roof beams were also rolled
up plank inclines. The houseposts were notched on top to receive them,
and the beams held in place by their own great weight. The huge ridge
pole could be a metre or so thick, smoothed with an adze, and decoratively
fluted like a Greek temple column with neat grooves, also made with an
adze. Or it might be painted with simple designs like red or black bands, or
white spots, always representing some storied, chiefly right. Sometimes the
chief had the right to have the ridge pole project over the front of the house
with the projection carved into a stylized animal head, like that of a sea-lion.
At times, centre posts were also carved into simplified human figures, for
example, again according to hereditary privilege.

The interior of a house at Yuquot, Friendly Cove, 1778.
A carved wooden whale saddle stands in front of the left house post.
John Webber drawing; RBCM PN-16344.

For the plank shell of the house, pairs of light poles were driven into the ground around the sides at the right spacing. These held the wall planks between them. The planks were laid horizontally, overlapped like clapboard, and held up on slings of twisted cedar-withe rope tied between the pairs of poles. The top planks were fastened to the framework. The roof was constructed by bridging the beams with rafter poles over which other poles were tied lengthwise. The best and longest planks were used for the roofing, laid crosswise to the length of the house. They were loose and could be pushed aside from the inside to let out smoke or increase light. To keep the roof from leaking, more boards covered the places where the main planks met (Drucker 1951:70), or the planks could have grooves at their edges to fit into each other to be weathertight (Koppert 1930a:16). Rocks and logs kept the roof planks in place when strong winds blew. The entrance, in the end or side, was usually covered in olden days with only a mat, but in historic times with a plank door. Informal back entrances were simply spaces left between plank ends. The house had no windows, but light came in through the smokehole and the spaces between the wall planks.

Inside, a low plank platform extended around the sides. Each family had its place along the platform, according to rank, the highest chiefly ones at the rear wall and the lowest commoners and slaves at the front by the entrance. The family spaces were partly partitioned by piles of storage boxes (*p'at̓aḥy'ak*), baskets, tubs, cooking boxes, trays, mats, and all the assorted gear for fishing, hunting and gathering. Bedding consisted only of mats of cedar bark or rushes, together with clothing robes. Each family had its fireplace on the earth floor. Tall, pyramidal racks of four poles tied together at the top with horizontal poles below were erected for drying fish. More drying and storage racks were hung high up near the roof. Early European observers did not find the Whaling People's houses the neatest places inside because of their different concept of order. From the outside, too, the houses looked a bit ragged, with planks projecting here and there at the ends. But they were big, solid, spacious structures, well suited for the climate and to the seasonal movements and social order of the people.

Firewood was mainly driftwood. Before commercial logging on the coast, driftwood did not cover the beaches in huge quantities (Drucker 1951:107). Women gathered small pieces in burden baskets, while men went in canoes to get the bigger pieces. Windfall logs near the water were levered down the beach and towed home. The thick bark of Douglas-fir made a hot, smokeless fire, while partly rotted Western Hemlock made a smoky fire for drying fish. Before contact with Europeans, the Whaling People started a fire with a fire drill of red cedar spun between the palms, a method so arduous that fires were kept going as long as possible, being banked up at night to keep coals live to the morning. When travelling, people carried a slow-burning length of twisted cedar bark as a match.

DRESS

Apparel, including ornaments, is a vital dimension of human life, not just for practical purposes but also for social reasons. Among the Whaling People personal appearance was an important marker of rank in a class-conscious society. Despite the often raw weather of the west coast, the Whaling People wore relatively light clothing. People went barefoot except when a few hunters put on simple moccasins to go after deer or wore snowshoes to hunt elk. On the occasional hot days of summer the men wore only their ornaments (Drucker 1951:99). Women, however, always kept well covered. Shredded Yellow-cedar bark was the main clothing material. The basic clothing item was a robe (*lichayahom*), commonly woven of shredded cedar bark and edged with fur. Men frequently wrapped the robe around the body under the left arm and pinned the top corners over the right shoulder, leaving both arms free. A belt was optional. Women wore longer robes, almost ankle length, covering the shoulders and with short loose sleeves down to the elbows (Jewitt 1815:74). Beneath the robe, men wore nothing, but women had an apron-like skirt of shredded cedar bark. With the arrival of Europeans, woollen trade blankets were soon adopted as the basic piece of clothing, but European-style clothing did not come into general use among the Whaling People until about the last quarter of the 19th century. When the weather was wet and cold, a short, poncho-like, conical

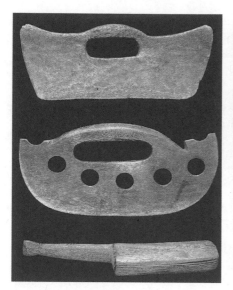

Two bark shredders and a bark beater, all made of whale bone. RBCM 459, 9611 and 10226.

A Tla-o-qui-aht woman wearing a woven cedar-bark rain hat (*mitloxsim*). Edward S. Curtis photograph; RBCM D-08447.

cape (*mil?in*) was worn over the robe. There was also a rain cape of double matting to cover the back. The Whaling People's rain hat was woven of red-cedar bark or split spruce root – it was smaller than the hats of coastal peoples to the north, and shaped like a blunt cone.

Chiefs and high-ranking women dressed better than the commoners, especially on ceremonial occasions. Chiefs had designs painted on their rain hats. If they were whalers, they had special hats with a pointed knob on the top and designs of whales and whaling canoes woven in. Their robes had wool woven into the cedar bark. Northern groups obtained Mountain Goat wool from Kwakwaka'wakw peoples on the mainland coast and southern groups had special woolly dogs, likely adopting them long ago from the neighbouring Coast Salish peoples. For formal occasions the chiefs wore particularly fine robes, including those made from the pelts of Sea Otters, or sometimes Mink or Martens. Whaling chiefs wore bear-skin robes when they went out whaling or while doing their preparatory bathing ritual. High-ranking men sometimes also wore bear-skin vests. In recent times, the more northern chiefs bought pearl-button and Chilkat blankets from their Kwakwaka'wakw neighbours. In the old days, war chiefs sometimes donned a special display robe of thick white elk hide with painted designs – they wore this as armour (Jewitt 1815:67).

A woman in shredded cedar-bark clothing, about 1914. She carries bundles of cedar bark and holds a D-adze in her left hand.
Edward S. Curtis photograph; RBCM D–08330.

A woman weaving a blanket of Yellow-cedar bark.
Charles S. Sely photograph; RBCM PN-1139.

Hair was worn shoulder length by the men and longer by the women, without braiding, until well into the 19th century. On ceremonial occasions men tied the hair, well oiled, on top of the head, with a hemlock branch, and chiefs added a sprinkling of white eagle down. Headbands of shredded cedar bark, dyed red, were common for ceremonies. Dancers stuck feathers from eagles, hawks and swans in these bands. Men, more often than women, painted their face and body, using red ochre, charcoal and hemlock sap that turns black. Chiefs put on shiny, powdered mica over a base of deer or bear grease. For ceremonials the painting was done in assorted geometrical patterns (Jewitt 1815:76-7), probably symbolizing rights. Plainer face painting was also done, particularly by the young people who were concerned with protecting their complexions from sun-burn.

Jewellery worn by both men and women included ear and nose pendants of abalone shells, dentalium shells, copper and trade beads. Women wore bracelets and anklets made of Sea Otter fur for those of high rank, or of elk hide or woven cedar bark for commoners. Young girls wore tight bands around the ankles to make them appear slim and the calves above full. Wives of chiefs might also wear necklaces and bracelets of valuable and beautiful dentalium shells.

SOCIAL RANK AND CLASS

The Whaling People lived in a society in which all members of each social group, whether large or small, were ranked in order from top to bottom. The highest ranking individuals were the leading chiefs of the several confederacies of tribes that are recorded for the northern division of the Nuuchah-nulth, at least in historic times. They headed the highest ranking tribes. Where the tribe was the largest social grouping, rather than the confederacy, its highest ranking chief was the top person. He was first in rank because the local group he headed was first among the number of such groups making up the tribe. In each local group all other members were ranked in order of closeness of kin relationship to the chief. Slaves belonged to a separate class at the very bottom. They were not even considered to be on the scale of rank, because as war captives they had become property, to be used like any other personal possession.

If any level of social grouping can be considered basic as a unit, it was probably the local group – a number of people living together through much of the year at locations centred on a natural resource like a salmon stream and being related in some way to the group's chief. The local group had a name usually taken from the name of their original main location with the suffix *?ath* added that meant "people of ...". The chief, the first or highest in rank in the group, held his position through hereditary right, ideally being the first-born son of the preceding chief. He owned the territory and resources of the group as inherited rights, as well as numerous other privileges, including things that may seem immaterial to Europeans, like ceremonies and songs, but were regarded as valuable properties by the people. Next in rank were the chief's younger brothers who might head subgroups of which they would be chiefs, or if there were no subdivisions they might serve in their older brother's group as war chiefs, orators or "talking chiefs", and the related messengers who were like ambassadors to other external groups. Sisters of the chief held high rank as well, but they would generally marry out of the group and live with the husband's group most of the time. Wives for high-ranking men were chosen from roughly equivalent ranking positions in their family groups and, so, brought assorted inherited rights, material and spiritual, as their marriage dowry from their fathers and mothers.

More distant kin of the chief were also ranked after him, their relationship traced through either male or female ties – the closer the relationship the higher the rank. According to Ida Jones, lines of descent from high-ranking individuals were in the forefront of social consciousness, so that a person looking at his ancestry might see it like a branching plant with a number of descent lines coming down to him. Through these lines the person inherited names that marked position and everything else of value as rights or privileges (*topa·ti*), regarded as property. The inheritance or transfer of such property rights was made public and legalized or accepted as proper through the potlatch, which was the formal public announcement of the social transaction whereby individuals took on new rights and positions. Potlatches included ceremonies, feasting (usually) and a distribution of goods that were like payments to all who witnessed the act. These witnesses made the announced transfer of rights valid by accepting it as proper. This was why the potlatch was such an important institution. In a potlatch, everything was done in order of rank, from the seating of individuals to the serving of food and giving of gifts, with everyone announced in turn by name and item given by the host, so that the rank of everyone in relationship to each other was clearly and formally shown in public. The potlatch was a primary mechanism of the social order of the Whaling People, organizing the way they lived together.

In this continuous grading of ranked positions, with individuals placed in terms of their distance from the chief, those who were ranked higher than a certain loosely distinguished point in the system were generally regarded as chiefs (*ḥaw'iḷ*), while those below that point were considered commoners (*maschim*). This demarcation came, typically, at the rank of the descendants of the chief's younger brothers, who were the lesser ranked chiefs. A chief sometimes gave minor rights to especially able commoners who were valuable supporters, so elevating them above the undistinguished run-of-the-mill. When this happened the ranks of chiefs and commoners overlapped, and individuals could marry up or down a step, raising or lowering the positions of their children.

But this did not disturb the upper layer of chiefs, the highly privileged ones with titles to major resources and the limited number of named positions or seats at potlatches, as well as to a body of supporting followers who were generally, though not always, immediate relatives. Chiefs had wealth and power; indeed, the Whaling People's word for chief means "wealthy". Rank and wealth coincided, and the Whaling People were much concerned with both. Thus, a ranked social system could be regarded as a way of organizing the exploitation and distribution of the wealth of natural resources.

Each local group usually had one or more big communal houses in the main villages. Again, spaces inside were occupied according to rank. An ideal pattern was to have four chiefs occupying the four corners of a house, the first-ranked and real owner of the house taking up the back right-hand corner (when facing the entrance), the next the back left, the third the front left and the fourth the front right corner. There were various other arrangements by rank, though, with the head chief owning the house and other chiefs, likely brothers or close paternal kinsmen, owning the right to their places within the house. Between these "owned" places lived the lesser ranked chiefs and the commoners, who were like tenants and often moved about between houses depending on which group they were related to and chose to be with. Generally, the higher the rank the more stable the location of residence. Commoners closely related to a chief tended to stay near him, enjoying economic and social advantages as his loyal supporters, while commoners who were less clearly linked with the chiefs of a house moved on more frequently for one reason or another. People sometimes moved just for a change, even the chiefs, although they did so less frequently than commoners. Slaves (qo·ł), being property, stayed in the least desirable part of their owner's house, near the entrance, and did not move unless their chiefly owner did or they were sold.

Chiefs were the focal points of Whaling People's society. They inherited their position, unless unfit for it, and they owned practically everything of value and importance, from village sites and houses to salmon streams, fishing banks in the sea, herring-spawning grounds, shellfish beds, hunting territories, berry-picking and root-digging patches, and the beaches with anything that washed up on them, including drift whales (Drucker 1951:247-8). They also inherited the knowledge and rituals for managing the supernatural realm. Chiefs and their families wore richer clothing, especially on formal occasions when they were the ceremonial leaders. Ideally, chiefs directed their groups' activities and did not work, except at pursuits of glorious prestige like whaling or hunting Sea Otters. A council of knowledgeable elders advised chiefs on serious matters affecting the group, such as war or a high-ranking marriage with another group – but final decision rested with the chiefs. Ownership of resources meant that, each season, the chief opened each resource to exploitation. He might, for example, order his men to get the first catch from a fishing ground for him or he might lead the first expedition. Anyone else using his resources would pay a tribute of no set amount. This tribute was willingly given, because the chief would use it to host a feast for the group (Drucker 1951:251-52). Large sea or land mammals, however, belonged to the hunter, who gave a feast from his catch.

The chief of a group was like a father looking after his children, dominant but kindly (Wike 1958:219-20). He and his family actually formed the core of the local group. He provided feasts, potlatch distributions and security, or his following would diminish. If disliked, he could be killed and replaced by a rival relative preferred by the group. When threatened by a revolt, a chief could have his slaves protect him or use his supernatural powers against his enemies. But when a chief and his followers were good to each other, the group prospered. Despite the seemingly total dominance of the chiefs, there was a balance of power. The chiefs needed a strong following to be successful, and tried to live up to their ancestors' reputations in giving feasts and potlatches. Any exploitation of commoners had to be measured against the possibility of losing his following. But there were good chiefs and bad chiefs in this regard.

Being a slave was a disgrace. Relatives tried to pay ransom for those captured in war and made slaves. Although the lot of a slave was not physically much worse than that of the commoners, to serve others was unpleasant, especially for the high-born who had been captured, so slaves often tried to escape. Whether they escaped or were ransomed, on return to their group, ex-slaves were given a potlatch to announce their restoration to freedom and assumption of new names. Male and female slaves often lived together as if married, especially if they belonged to the same master. Rarely a master might buy a woman slave for a good male slave. A young slave was commonly made an attendant to a chief's child of similar age and the same sex, the two often becoming companions. Such companion slaves were as well treated as their chiefly partners in daily life, but if their young masters died, they were often killed to accompany them. Slaves were property and could be bought, sold, mistreated or even killed – their lot was not a happy one.

In summary, Whaling People's society was made up of three main classes: chiefs, commoners and slaves, although the first two classes sometimes overlapped. The rank of chiefs and commoners was determined by the distance of kin relationship to the top position. Ideally, a chief's position passed to his eldest son, or if he had no son, then to his next oldest brother (Drucker 1951:245, Jewitt 1815:170, Mozino 1970:31, Sproat 1868:116). Specific rights, depending on their nature, could be inherited by the eldest son, shared between more than one child, held by an eldest daughter until her marriage when it might be transferred to a brother if she did not take it along with her, or given to a new son-in-law (Drucker 1951:267). Portable privileges, like songs, dances and names, might be taken out of a group by marriage, but there was a sense of patrimony of rights to be kept as intact as possible over the generations (Sapir 1915:363-64).

FEASTING

Feasting was one of life's great pleasures for the Whaling People, and enjoyed as frequently as possible. They had the resources to provide an abundance of good food most of the time, but they also experienced times of scarcity, so feasts must have always been appreciated. Feasts also gave the Whaling People an opportunity to be formal and ceremonial, a situation they loved. In a way, a feast was always a ceremony, and only the most minor ceremony did not include a feast. As a social event, feasting may be associated with many social purposes, but its essense is the sheer pleasure of eating a lot of delicious foods, wearing festive clothing and being entertained with oratory, songs, dances and skits.

Chiefs gave most of the feasts. The most common occasion for a feast was when a chief obtained a lot of food. This usually happened at the opening of a seasonal resource, either collected by his own people or paid as a tribute from another group for the use of one of his resource properties, or as a gift from another group (perhaps the leftovers brought back from another feast). Feasts were part of many public events, such as potlatches and group rituals (like the Wolf Ritual). They also served to publicize and legalize changes in social status for commoners and, sometimes, chiefs, without the costly distribution of goods of a potlatch. A common feast was one given by a father, uncle or grandfather for a child passing from one stage of life to another. A chief could be asked to give a feast of a kind of food his followers were hungry for, like salmon or herring. The request was usually made by the war chiefs, speakers or the clowns who did funny things to make people laugh during serious public occasions.

A feast could be held for a few persons or for several tribes or for a special group, such as the four chiefs of a house or the warriors or the old men of the tribe. For any feast, the seating order of the guests was important, because it signified their rank in the social order. Therefore, the arrangement had to be correct so that no one would be insulted.

The usual order had the chiefs at the rear of the house, with the first ranked in the middle and the succeeding positions on alternating sides of him, or perhaps in a single row beginning from the right as seen by the speaker facing the entrance. War chiefs would be seated in a double row down the middle of the house. The rest, including retired chiefs, sat along the sides, men on the right and women on the left. At a feast, long mats (*lits'a·sim*) running the length of the house were unrolled before the guests. The host first sang a feast song then his speaker announced what the particular occasion was and where the food that was being served came from. There were many courses. Between each course, young men would serve fresh water for drinking and washing hands. Extra food was often on hand so the guests could be given leftovers to take home. The guests, in appreciation, gave small presents to the hosts. Entertainment was provided by singers and dancers while the speaker or a special jester clowned for laughs, performing funny imitations and feats of excessive eating or drinking. The war chiefs also ate enormous amounts. Finally the host thanked the guests for coming and asked them to remember the reason for the feast.

Feasts could serve to distribute food. Between groups, the special food resources of one could be enjoyed by another as in the following case described by Drucker (1951:372-73).

It is related that once the Kyuquot war chiefs began to remark that they wanted to be invited to a Sockeye feast by the owner of the first Sockeye rights at Queen's Cove, the Ehattesaht-Mowachaht Chief M'okwina. (The Queen's Cove group was independent, not belonging to either the Ehattesaht or Mowachaht confederacy; Chief M'okwina held rights there for a time following a marriage to the daughter of a Queen's Cove chief). Chief M'okwina heard the news.... He announced that he intended to bathe ritually to bring a good Sockeye run, and delegated four men to make 200 bundles of nettles to rub his body with. He began his ritual bathing, and as a result the Sockeye were soon jumping all over Queen's Cove. His next step was to set his 4 traps, and to have some women cut and dry 400 of the Sockeye for him. He sent a party to Qaˑ'yoˑkw to invite the war chiefs. Meanwhile he readied his feast dishes, *Wi'ta?a?ik* and *Wotwotwoha?i.*

In a few days the Kyuquot arrived in three large canoes. The combined Ehattesaht and Queen's Cove people assembled on the beach to meet them. The war chiefs with faces painted black, danced, flourishing guns and knives. Chief M'okwina gave his guests a small feast of Sockeye and dried herring eggs announcing that the real Sockeye feast would be on the following day.

In the morning the war chiefs assembled in the house of the Tɬichyaˑ?atḥ chief to break their fast, and to practice their songs. Then they were called to Chief M'okwina's feast. The two great dishes were brought in, one filled with rice and molasses, the other with herring eggs and whale oil. The 400 dried Sockeye were piled in a great heap nearby. All the Ehattesaht had assembled, in the role of hosts; they sang as the Kyuquot entered. Then an Ehattesaht chief stood up to speak for the host:

"Chief M'okwina was very glad to hear you people wanted to eat dried Sockeye from Queen's Cove, because the Kyuquot and Ehattesaht tribes are just like one family, and you can ask for anything you want. All Chief M'okwina's tribe, the Ehattesaht have helped him prepare these Sockeye for you."

Then the Ehattesaht sang a shanty. The Kyuquot replied with a song. Then the chief who acted as the hosts' speaker called on one man for each of the two dishes, and the two named, with half the party to assist each of them, sat at the dishes. They arranged themselves so there were 20 men at each dish (10 on either side). After they had eaten, the two war chiefs to whom the dishes were assigned gave gifts to M'okwina, one giving him a gun, the other a good woollen blanket.

They moved back away from the dishes, sitting on long mats. Each man was given 20 dried Sockeye, only 2 of which were cooked. They ate the cooked fish, then made ready to leave. M'okwina gave a sealing canoe and an iron kettle to the men who had given him the gifts. In addition to the 18 uncooked Sockeye, which each man was to take home, they were given other leftovers, including baskets of herring eggs. Now they were ready to go home, but it was stormy and raining so they stayed over a couple of days. Other chiefs feasted them. Finally they set out for Qaʼyoʼkw and that was the end of the affair, except for the gleefully told sequel that the war chiefs were storm-bound for 6 days on the way home, and ate up all the Sockeye, reaching Qaʼyoʼkw at last with nothing but the herring eggs, which they had been unable to clean of the fir needles.

The Whaling People were fun-loving, a quality easy to lose sight of when trying to describe their social institutions with all their serious complications. You may be curious about their kind of humour. The following is an example of a skit by two Kyuquot clowns satirizing a ceremony, taken again from Drucker's detailed work on the northern and central tribes (1951:270-71).

Yoʼmotq and Wowoʔih were the two speakers of the Tʼashiʼsʔatḥ chief at Qaʼyoʼkw and were clowns as well. (Yoʼmotq was of fairly high rank; he owned the third corner of the house and held many privileges. Wowoʔih was a commoner.) They liked to clown whenever a feast or potlatch was being given. They kept their paraphernalia in a battered old box that they called their treasure chest. On one side they had painted a frog and on the other a fish. They always dragged it out to the centre of the house, with a great fuss, when they were performing. (The Tʼashiʼsʔatḥ chief owned a very large elaborately painted treasure chest of Kwakwaka'wakw provenience.)

Once they found some kind of a cast-iron "face" washed up on the beach (apparently a piece of ornamental ironwork) that they painted and put in their treasure box. At a dance they brought it out covered with cedar bark. They announced they had encountered a new supernatural being; it was alive, but they didn't know what it was. Women were called out singly to unwrap and identify it for them. As each woman was about to touch the bundle, one of the clowns would jiggle it to make it seem to move. The women were all afraid (or pretended to be); none of them would open it.

The clowns made long speeches thanking each for trying, and very ostentatiously gave her a payment — a five-cent piece. It was very funny the way they talked about the "money" they were giving (as though it were a great sum), then give those little coins you could hardly see. (Calling a person out to perform a ritual act, and "paying" him for his performance was a common ceremonial device.) Then they unwrapped the "face" themselves, singing that it was a White man's supernatural being.

POTLATCH

Potlatch (*paƚaꞏch*) is a word from the Chinook Jargon, a simplified trade language, that came from the Nuu-chah-nulth *pach'iƚ*, meaning "to give". Potlatch giving of goods was done mainly by chiefs, primarily to transfer chiefly rights and position to their successors at social occasions, like times of major change in a person's life, or the great Wolf Ritual ceremony. Chiefship was commonly transferred while the heir was still a youth, establishing the succession firmly so that rival claims hardly ever arose and to discourage the competitive potlatching by rivals for the position. Except in rare cases, the Whaling People did not emphasize competition, the shaming of rivals, the destruction of property or cheating in their potlatching. Good feeling prevailed, and the aim of the performance was to do as well as the great ancestors did (Drucker 1951:383-84).

To stage a potlatch, a chief began with a feast for his group to announce his intentions and to plan the event. For a major potlatch, like the one at the puberty of a chief's daughter, a new house might be built. Supporters volunteered contributions. If other groups were to be invited, another feast was held to form an inviting party. This party, often including the chief and sometimes the child to be honoured, went by canoe to the other groups, singing as they arrived. A speaker loudly announced the purpose of the mission and then called out the names of the village's chiefs in order of rank. This automatically invited the followers of these chiefs as well. To remember them, the speaker, as he called out the names, threw down cedar splints in two lots, one for the chiefs with potlatch seats and the second for the rest. The canoe, occupants and all, was then often carried up to, and sometimes even inside, the house of the top chief of the invited village. The inviting party was feasted, entertained, and given gifts by the village chiefs. When the party returned home, the host chief held a feast again to tell what each of the invited chiefs had given and to finalize plans for the ceremonies surrounding the potlatch.

When the guests arrived for the potlatch, both they in their canoes and the hosts on the shore before their houses, all dressed in ceremonial clothing, began singing and dancing. Each guest was invited to stay with friends or relatives. If the potlatch was one associated with the Wolf Ritual (see page 202), the principal novice to be initiated into the Wolf Ritual society would be kidnapped dramatically as the guests were arriving. Before the main event, the different chiefs of the host village held feasts for the visitors and gave them gifts. Then the ceremonies began with the names of the guests being shouted out loudly from the top of the host chief's house, all in proper order of rank. Chiefly guests were escorted, one by one, to their seats inside. There was a set number of named potlatch seats for each group

Guests arriving for a potlatch at Opitsat and being carried ashore in their canoe to the accompaniment of two drums and a welcoming song. RBCM PN-2727.

whose holders engaged in the giving and receiving between groups. Generally, people were seated the same as for feasts, with the hosts at the entrance end when they were not serving food, dancing, performing ceremonial displays or distributing gifts.

The feasting usually came first. When the potlatch goods were brought out by the young men, the chief stood and, through his speaker, announced in whose honour and on what occasion the potlatch was being given, what was to be given away, and where the wealth came from – whether from his property, followers who helped, potlatch gifts he had received in his potlatch seat from other groups, gifts received by the inviting party or any other source. Ceremonial privileges were also announced, and the songs, dances and special features associated with the privileges were displayed. The guests were thanked for looking at these inherited "supernatural treasures", for ceremonial privileges were originally obtained from the spirit world. The goods were then given away while the host chief sang his wealth song, the speaker calling out each guest's name and the gift given. The giving might be done in stages following different displays of ceremonial rights – first those in return for gifts received by the inviting party, then the potlatch gifts and finally the presents to contributing followers of the host.

The amount given depended on what the potlatch donor had managed to accumulate. The size of the individual gifts varied according to the rank of the recipients, but there was no fixed rate or strict proportioning related to rank. The potlatch donor amassed much of the necessary wealth of goods through his own efforts, although substantial contributions were provided by kinsmen of high rank in junior lines of descent to the chief's and also by some of his commoners who had means. Although the chief reciprocated with gifts for such supporting contributions, they were not regarded as loans to be repaid. A consistent major supporter might be given a right, like a minor fish trap site or a war chief name, that bound him closer to the chief.

Potlatches were returned but not necessarily with greater or even equal wealth. Even a chief who rarely potlatched, continued to receive according to his ranked position (Drucker 1951:381). There was, however, a second-ary form of potlatch in which the amounts given back and forth escalated. This was an elaboration of the invitation visit with a chief going to another tribe to display his ceremonial privileges and give blankets or money to the chiefs there, who then gave back more than they received. The chief and his party returned home to hold another potlatch giving still more to the invited tribe, which then ended up ahead; but sometimes this third potlatch was omitted. Generally, the giving of gifts evened out in Whaling People's potlatching. Wealth circulated and was consumed, while hereditary rights were validated by their active representation in ceremony, rights and their associated social positions were transferred, and the lines of social de-scent through male or female ancestral links were publicly recited (Drucker 1951:385, Rosman and Rubel 1971:104).

A couple of accounts of particular potlatches may give an idea of their flavour and perceived significances. The first one describes a 19th-century oil potlatch given by a great chief of the Pacheedaht, the southeasternmost tribe on Vancouver Island, to his neighbours of Cape Flattery. It is a transla-tion of a text dictated by a great Tseshaht trader, Tom Sa·ya·ch'apis (Sapir and Swadesh 1955:299-300).

Kwi·sto̱x's Big Potlatch

The people of the inside region (around Victoria) heard that Kwi·sto̱x was going to invite many tribes. He set out and went across. He had only his wives and his slaves with him. He went to the place called ʔOsi·ł, seaward of Neah Bay, where there are many whale hunters. The ʔOsi·ł are a tribe of whalers. He landed. He said he was after oil, that he was going about looking for oil. The Seaward Tribe plotted to set their price up. My! They valued it high, a measure was really expensive. The women alone were buying. They had all kinds of beads and things to buy with and their sea-lion bladder was filled up. They were there another night. They began filling another bladder.

My! Kwi·sto̱x got angry at the way he was treated. At night as soon as the tribe went to sleep, he went to bathe and to do ritual for buying. He would make their spirit weaken. All night long he blew spray from his mouth and prayed. At dawn he returned to his vessel. The morning came as he sat in his canoe without having slept that night.

Kwi·stox's Big Potlatch. Tim Paul drawing, 1983.

As soon as the people came out in the morning, he told his slaves, "Bring the goods down to the beach, so we can set out. It is good that the tribe here wants to keep their oil, because none of the tribes will come to buy. They will be afraid because the news will travel quickly that the price has gone up. I will tell them of my bad luck."

They brought the goods down to the beach. My! Two Seaward People came to help him pull his vessel out.

"I will take your blankets. I have oil in the house. My price is the same as always. My price hasn't gone up," they told Kwi·sto<u>x</u>.

They dragged his vessel. They did not pull it right into the sea, but only brought it to the edge. He unpacked his bag of blankets. There were two who came to sell oil. They shouldered the blankets and carried them up the beach. Well! They bought and it was measured out. The large measure sold for a double blanket. They put it into a large cooking vessel. It had a notch where it came to two measures. My! Down the beach came two full sea-lion bladders, each worth five blankets. Again those first two who came to sell oil carried blankets up the beach.

"Only I have good oil, only I have good oil," said the Seaward People.

He did not take notice of the people talking to him. He only bought of the first ones to come to him. They each received 15 blankets. Then he bought from two others. He used up 40 blankets and got 10 bladders of oil.

Then he stopped and loaded in the goods. He returned home and landed at *Kana·yit* [*Qala·yit* (Dit.), Clyde Beach]. They carried the oil up the beach. Then they had someone go in a canoe to invite the tribes of the inside region. They invited the ?I·?iɫxwa, the Clallam, the Victoria Tribe [Victoria: *Mito·?i* (N,C), from *Bito·li* (Dit.)] the Chiya·nox, the Sooke, the Neah Bay Tribe. They invited 20 of the Seaward Tribe.

The tribes came to the feast. They all entered. For lunch they had wild onion root, though the Salish tribes were eating dried halibut. At night came the Salish tribes, along with the Seaward People they had invited. He had a long house with a middle door. Since he had his younger brothers living at both ends, the house was very long. Now Kwi·stox poured oil on his fires.

"O Tribes, this firewood was obtained at ?Ose·ɫ [Ozette]," he said. "I went there to fetch wood that you might have fire while in my house. The ?Osi·ɫ Tribe plotted against me. But I did not seek oil in order to become rich. The whalers of different tribes do not want their oil to drip away. That is what I am now burning while I have you by the fire."

Thus he used nothing but oil as fuel as long as they were in the house. He was pouring oil of the Seaward People on the fire as he spoke in that manner. That is why he invited them to be among his guests. My! He distributed many gifts to the invited tribes.

There were two famous chiefs when I was a boy, Becomes-Ten of Nootka Sound and Kwi·stox. That was what Kwi·stox did to make the Seaward Tribe miserable, the ones who did not give him oil. His fuel consisted entirely of good whale oil that he had just recently bought with many blankets. Well, I have come to the end.

Personal accounts like this provide many significant details about the Whaling People's society. They also give some insight into the thoughts and feelings of the storyteller. "Kwi·stox's Big Potlatch" reveals the contending interests that could come into play in a trade exchange when the ?Ose·ɫ, a tribe of whalers just south of Cape Flattery, raise the price of their whale oil. Chief Kwi·stox retaliates by doing a bathing ritual to weaken their spirits. He breaks off his trade visit by having his slaves bring his goods back to his canoe and stating that no tribes would come to buy ?Ose·ɫ oil after he spreads the news of the raised price. He effectively forces the ?Ose·ɫ to return to the usual rate of a double blanket for a large measure. Whaling People were accomplished traders.

The story shows the Whaling People's talent for hard bargaining and a chief's ultimate aim of prestige rather than material profit. Kwi·stox puts down the ?Osi·ɫ before several other tribes "of the inside region", as people from Juan de Fuca Strait were considered, by burning the oil he had bought from the ?Osi·ł at his potlatch. This action also displays his wealth and power. The potlatch was the reason for his trading – he says that he did not seek the oil to become rich and he gives out many gifts. Certainly his burning of the oil was a wastefully conspicuous display, but Kwi·sto<u>x</u>.'s fame as a great chief rests partly on memories of this occasion among the Whaling People.

The next example of a potlatch (also from Sapir and Swadesh 1955:301–306) describes an exceptionally grand one given by the other famous chief of Tom Sa·ya·ch'apis's boyhood – Becomes-Ten of Nootka Sound. The occasion was the building of a house with an extra high roof, a claim to extra greatness that Becomes-Ten bolsters by giving away blankets in an overwhelming fashion. Many interesting details about getting Sea Otters, Hair (Harbour) Seals and oil from drift whales (ten in a season!) to buy trade blankets, occur in the description of preparations. There is also a reference to the making of the old-style Yellow-cedar bark blankets, highly valued by the older Kwakw<u>a</u>ka'wakw guests at the potlatch. The description of the blanket potlatch will give an idea of what one was like. It amply demonstrated the greatness of Chief Becomes-Ten.

Becomes-Ten Gives a Potlatch

We heard that Becomes-Ten, the Nootka Sound chief, was building a house. It had four thick beams. We heard he was starting to put the beams up. They were square. We also got word they were four boards long and four thicknesses wide. Two beams were ... in the middle of the house, three fathoms [5.5 metres] apart, and on that were placed cross-beams, two handspans wide. It had a ridge roof. We heard that the roof was on and that it was very high. One did not hear the rain, the house was so high. We heard that Becomes-Ten's house was very high.

The Kyuquot chief spoke about it. "Wonder why he wants the house so high. Wonder what he will put on the rafters to dry."

Becomes-Ten heard that he said it. He gave a feast for his neighbours, the whole tribe, including the women.

"I want you because of what I heard the Kyuquot chief says of me, O Nootka Sound people," he said. "You will indeed go hunting on the water. Now go hunting, so I may put things up to dry in my house. Sea Otter hunters, you will now hunt Sea Otter. Bark pickers, women of Nootka Sound, you will gather bark, find things with which you can acquire a small blanket. You will sell your Sea Otters, you hunters of otter, and turn it into blankets."

He said this in the winter time to get ready for when the heat came through.

"You who are good blanket makers will work."

He ordered a hundred women weavers of Nootka Sound to make blankets. They began. They trimmed all they made with Sea Otter. The bark gatherers collected cedar bark. They used it as trade goods for blankets and went peddling among the Ahousaht and the Tla-o-qui-aht. The Hair Seal hunters hunted seals as trade goods among those tribes. The Sea Otter hunters hunted Sea Otters. There were two leading Sea Otter getters in the tribe, one called *Tsahso·ta* and another called *Kwa·tipi·ya*. The Nootka Sound Tribe worked one summer and finished as winter came.

Another summer approached and they went to Yuquot, their summer village site. Becomes-Ten also caused ten whales to drift on the rocks and thereby got many additional blankets. Now he gave a feast and all the men and women of the tribe came.

"Now, give me all the wealth you have obtained, neighbours," spoke Becomes-Ten.

First the women who had been weaving brought out to view one hundred good Yellow-cedar blankets, which the old time people used for robes. Women who gathered bark showed four or five or as much as six blankets they had bought with cedar bark. The Hair Seal hunters had six or eight or ten to show. Sea Otter hunters had one hundred or two hundred. The two outstanding hunters each had four hundred. All the people in the tribe, two hundred of them, gave their two, six, ten or twenty. The blankets amounted to many, because all contributed.

Then he asked people to be in his crew when he set out. They went to the 'Namgis and Kwagu'ł, Ahousaht, Tla-o-qui-aht, Kiłtsma?ath, Kyuquot. There were many inviters. Then the inviters arrived. They said they carried them along on the sea. The Nootka Sound people now got wood. Becomes-Ten's firewood was two and a half fathoms [4.5 metres] long, green raw wood, alder, spruce; they got thick logs a man could hardly reach around. He had collected food: dried herring, herring spawn, dried halibut. The tribes began to arrive. The Tla-o-qui-aht came in early. Becomes-Ten was half Tla-o-qui-aht.

All the tribes entered in the evening. They lit a fire in the house. They started putting wood on the fire. It got to where the men putting on the wood could no longer reach it. Underneath in the fire was very dry split wood. Then they put on lengths of pitchwood. The fire was set in the middle of the room. Still the heat was felt all the way to where the people were along the walls. The smoke hole in the roof was opened. Becomes-Ten's house was lit up.

When the guests had been there ten days, they got ready to distribute the gifts. They would light the fire and pile on wood just once for all day, because they were burning raw wood. All the tribes entered in the morning. Becomes-Ten was about to potlatch. They brought a big box of

Becomes-Ten Gives a Potlatch. Tim Paul drawing, 2008.

blankets out to the centre of the room. Tla-o-qui-aht were handling them. They spread Yellow-cedar robes for the bottom of the pile. The tribes counted up to a hundred. Those were as a pad underneath. Then they started laying out the cotton blankets one on another in a pile a blanket wide. Soon they could not reach standing on the floor. They stood on boxes. A couple of very big Tla-o-qui-aht, Lumpyleg and Collapses-Them, were handling the blankets. The pile became wobbly because it was so high. "Well, stick poles into each side." said the overseer.

They stuck four poles into the floor with their ends sticking up through the roof. The men kept throwing on and spreading out blankets. For a while the tribes tried to count, but they lost count about halfway up. It passed halfway. They went on to the roof side and threw the blankets on from there. It came up to the centre beams. The poles were tied in the middle to keep them from spreading apart. My! They came near the roof boards as they kept piling on.

The blankets went up through the roof. There were still a lot of blankets on the floor. Darn! Now Lumpyleg could not reach standing on the roof. My! High boxes were passed out through the roof. They stood on the boxes on the roof and kept piling it on. Just when they could no longer reach again, the blankets on the floor gave out. This happened when they could no longer reach standing on the boxes.

Lumpyleg slid down. He spoke, "O tribes, do you see now? Becomes-Ten has put things on his rafters to dry. Wonder if he will put my things on the floor. It is said it is now set on the floor. Look, it is sticking out the roof. I can't reach it, as tall as I am."

Na·nitsi·, the Kyuquot chief who had talked before, was shamed. The ropes tied between at the bottom were loosened. The props at the sides

were pulled up. The blankets fell through the roof and scattered about.
From the roof they scattered all over. They were potlatched as they lay
thus on the floor. The many scattered blankets were set before the tribes.
Ten blankets were given to the Kwagu'ł chief, ?Awawati·, and ten to the
'Namgis chief; but the Kyuquot chief was given twenty. They gave six
apiece to the chiefs of different tribes. But the blankets hardly diminished.
The older Kwagu'łs fought for the Yellow-cedar robes, which they valued
highly: they ran out onto the floor.

Thus Becomes-Ten put things on his rafters.

KINSHIP

Kinship and rank were fundamental in the organization of the Whaling
People's society (Drucker 1951:219). Kinship ties, through either male or
female lines of descent, determined where each person fitted into the order
of rank of a group. The particular kinds of relationships also governed social
actions, thoughts and feelings to a great degree, so that, as among many non-
urbanized peoples, Whaling People's society was largely based on kinship.
The names for various relatives – the kinship terminology – can be divided
between those related by blood (or birth) and those by marriage (in-laws).

A brief description of one or two characteristics of the kinship system
may be helpful. It is a generational system (known as "Hawaiian") in that
the generations are emphasized as major lots of relatives, many of whom are
lumped together as the same kinds of named kinsmen. For example, one's
aunts, uncles and parents' cousins are all called *na?i·qs*. Mother and father
each have a distinct name, as would be expected in the parental generation.
In one's grandparents' generation, however, all blood relatives are grandparents (*ts'ani·qs*), including great-uncles and great-aunts. All those in the
grandchildren's generation are grandchildren (*ka·?o·ts*). Great-grandchildren
and great-grandparent generations are similarly named.

The children's generation is divided into child (*t'an'a*), nephew (*wi·?o·*)
and niece (*?a·si·qs*). In one's own generation, siblings are distinguished first
by whether they are older or younger. Cousins are senior or junior to each
other according to the standing of their respective parents. Second cousins
would be named as older or younger according to the age relationship of
the grandparental sibling pair linking them by blood. For brothers and sisters and cousins there were only two basic terms – *m'a·m'i·qs* for the older
one and *y'okwi·qs* for the younger. But additional names exist to label different combinations of siblings distinguished by sex: a pair of brothers (*q'i·k*)
or sisters (*m'a?ah̲*); brothers and sisters together (*h̲achischi* or *ło·tssmo·pchanik*);
sister of a male (*ło·tssmo·p*) or a female (*m'a?ah̲sqiqs*); and brother of a male

Whaling People's Kinship Terminology

	Northern and Central	Southern
Blood Relatives		
father	n'ow'i·qs	do?ow'i·qs
mother	?om?i·qs	?ob?i·qs
child	t'an'a, ?ana<u>x</u>	ya·da<u>x</u>
older sibling, cousin by an older	m'a·m'i·qs	babi·qs (f)
sibling of parent or grandparent		ta·yid (m)
younger sibling, cousin by a younger	y'okwi·qs (f)	y'okwi·qs (f)
sibling of parent or grandparent	qałatik (m)	qałatq (m)
uncle or aunt, anyone called m'am'i·qs or	na?i·qs	hadi·qs
y'okwi·qs by your father or mother		
nephew	wi·?o·	
niece	?a·si·qs	
grandchild	ka·?o·ts	
grandparent	nani·qs	dadi·qs
great-grandchild	tła·yitsqim	
great-grandparent	?oni·qs	tła?oxtagsob
Relatives by Marriage		
husband or wife	?ots<u>h</u>i	yaqs<u>h</u>aqs
secondary wife	yayakpił, m'a?o·ł	
child–in–law, parent–in–law	qwi·?iqs	qwa?aqssa·daqs
and brother or sister of parent–in–law		
spouse's sister, woman's brother's wife	?iyi·qs	
man's wife's sister or his brother's wife;	chi·n'opsiqs	chi?ibsaqs
woman's husband's brother or her		
sister's husband		
a brother's wife or a sister's husband	?i·ktshishtso	?i·kssiqs
all those married to uncles, aunts	?owi·qs	
nephews, and nieces; child of a spouse's		
sibling; step-child; step-parent		
step-sibling	?o?o·witspał	
all relatives of son-in-law, daughter-in-law	kwa·ts<u>h</u>i	
or parent-in-law; parents of spouses of		
uncles and aunts plus their siblings,		
parents, uncles, aunts, grandparents		
and on back		
grandparent of wife or husband;	m'ałt'i	
spouses or grandchildren		

f = female speaker; m= male speaker. From Arima's unpublished field notes, Drucker 1951:277-8, Sapir 1912 12:42-44, Sapir and Swadesh 1939:244-316.

(*q'i·kwa·tssy'i*) or female (*hachimsiqs*). Children could be distinguished as older or younger by adding a qualifier to the word for child: *ta·yi·*, *yaksya* or *m'am'i·qs* for older and *?anox*, *qała·tik* or *y'okwi·qs* for younger, or *?o·?a·ts* for second oldest. (Sapir and Swadesh 1939:249.)

Certain relationships for pairs were distinguished, such as for parent and child (*?aschih*) and for husband and wife (*hitsnop*). Blood-relation terms are readily distinguishable as to generation, relative age and, in some cases, sex. The in-law terms are similarly uncomplicated to the person using them. In the table on the previous page, the term *chin'opsiqs* for husband's brother or a man's brother's wife, for example, from the woman's viewpoint applies to those her husband calls brothers and those married to her sisters; while for a man it means just the wives of his brothers (Sapir 1912 17:44). Some of the term renderings are unfortunately uncertain in the sources.

Certain patterns of behaviour and feeling characterized kin relationships. Parents and children were close, but grandparents and grandchildren were even more warmly linked since children often lived with their grandparents much of the time. Uncles and aunts were like parents, and nieces and nephews could help themselves to their things without getting scolded. There was great familiarity between married adults and their parents-in-law, too. Brothers and sisters were not supposed to be familiar, though, and after about eight years old, a girl was seldom spoken to by her brothers. After marriage, sisters and brothers became less distant though still not very familiar. Brothers and sisters, which include cousins among the Whaling People, could not marry, even if distant cousins. But, if the relationship was so far back that the steps could not be traced, they could marry to get hereditary privileges back into a senior line of descent from a junior line where they had been split off. Discord and unfaithfulness often occurred between husband and wife, mainly because parents arranged marriages, with social rank their prime consideration. Girls were raised well shielded to protect their innocence. Boys, too, were quite inexperienced with the opposite sex.

LIFE CYCLE

To the Whaling People, a person's life began in the womb of a pregnant woman (Boas 1890:39–40, Curtis 1916:41–43, Drucker 1951:118–50). At the life crises, or crucial changes in state, Whaling People observed many protective rituals and made public announcements of the change with ceremonies whose elaborateness varied according to rank. While expecting, a mother observed numerous rules to have an easy delivery and a healthy baby. She could eat or drink almost anything except leftovers and old water, which could make the child stay unborn past its time. She did not pause in doorways because that could prolong birth. Line-tangling activities like weaving, basketry, and cat's cradle could snarl the umbilical cord. To see death or the River Otter harmed the unborn child. The mother generally stayed quiet, and kinswomen did most of her chores.

Birth took place in a small temporary hut near the house, with the woman's mother helping. The cord was cut with a mussel-shell knife. Massage helped expel the afterbirth. Secret family herb medicines might be used to ease delivery. For unusual difficulties, a knowledgeable medicine man might be called. The newborn baby was gently worked to be well formed, arching the eyebrows, for example, or raising the palate, and seeing that the internal organs were placed properly.

For four days following birth, the mother and baby stayed in the birth hut. Broth made from black cod might be given to the mother to stimulate milk production, and drops of dogfish oil given to the infant. In a mat cradle the baby was kept properly positioned with cedar-bark pads, the legs bent and the sides of the head, and the brow, pressed by pads to produce the ideal flattened forehead, at least among the southern and some of the central tribes. In the north, the head was likely wrapped to produce a long, narrow shape. Calves were made to bulge by binding the legs above and below them (Sapir 1921:236). The baby might be given partly dried blubber to suck (Curtis 1916:40).

After those four days of post-birth confinement, the afterbirth, wrapped in shredded cedar bark, was buried, to the accompanyment of ceremony to improve the child, such as singing special songs to make him or her a good singer, or including a chisel or adze to induce woodworking skill. The ears were pierced, as well as the nose, at least for a girl; the noses of boys were pierced later. Ear and nose piercing might be delayed by a chief until he could stage a potlatch for the occasion. At or just after the ear piercing, at a small feast to announce it, the child received the first of its many names. After 10 days, among northern groups at least, the baby was transferred to a wooden cradle big enough to be used for about three years, and the mother came out of seclusion.

For a year the mother continued to avoid certain foods that might be harmful to her nursing infant. Through infancy and childhood, secret family rites and medicines were frequently used to gain health, strength and special qualities. Twins were believed to be closely associated with the Salmon spirits. Since the abundance of salmon depended on the special care of twins, their birth involved strong prohibitions and prolonged isolation – one to four years – in a remote camp for the twins and their parents. (Boas 1890:39-40, Curtis 1916:41, Drucker 1951:127-28, Jewitt 1815:173-74.)

Childhood

Children were brought up with a great deal of verbal instruction emphasizing correct social behaviour and ritual knowledge. The children of chiefs were told to be kindly and helpful, never arrogant, and to take care of their people with feasts and generosity to gain their affection and loyal support. When someone said anything mean, they were not to quarrel but just walk away. Children of commoners were told to play carefully with the children of chiefs, helping and never quarrelling or fighting. Children were encouraged to be peaceful, responsible and industrious. Bad behaviour was corrected not by physical punishment but by a talking-to, typically about the shame such behaviour brought to the family. Family traditions, consisting of reviewing hereditary rights at length, were used to teach the child where they originated. Little stories of current happenings taught them about social relations and the sorry consequences of mistaken actions. Practical demonstration was also used to teach. Parents, uncles, aunts and grandparents imparted technical skills. Older children also communicated basic skills like swimming, canoemanship and the use of weapons. As puberty approached, boys started going along with their fathers on fishing, hunting, trading and other expeditions, while girls were kept indoors as much as possible, learning womanly tasks like cooking, basketry, and robe and mat making. The first animal killed by a boy or the first berries or clams gathered by a girl were celebrated by a feast in honour of the child.

But play was the main occupation of children. Imitation of adult activities was common, and there was a great variety of games (Drucker 1951:444-52). There were play feasts and potlatches, Wolf Ritual performances, dances, shamanizing, archery, spearing, slinging, stone throwing, hoop-and-dart, tops, shuttlecock, ring-and-pin with the humerus (arm bone) of a seal, cat's cradle, native dice, *lahal* (a bone or stick game), hide-and-seek, tag, tug-of-war, mock war, and dolls. There was much to do outdoors, and a lot of time was spent by and on the sea, playing with canoes (Sapir 1921:243).

Puberty

Puberty was a major event for girls. A girl's first period was the occasion for her parents' greatest potlatch, as grand as possible according to rank and wealth (Boas 1890:40-42, Curtis 1916:42-43, Drucker 1951:137-44, Sapir 1913, Sapir and Swadesh 1955:243-53). The specific observances of the girl's puberty rites varied with family and tribe. In a typical central Whaling People's ceremony, four to ten great torches of cedar splints, standing for the months of taboo to be observed, were held in a row outside the house with the girl in the centre between a pair of dancers in masks representing the mighty thunderbirds or whales. Four times, four men fetched water in dishes to spill at her feet in symbolic purification. She then went inside into seclusion at the rear wall behind a screen that was of boards with a painted design for the chiefly and of mats for commoners. For four days she sat there fasting. Girl friends kept her company, singing *t'ama* songs that had improvised verses and were very popular. The torches were put out and given, with gifts attached, to certain guests who had the right to receive them. Family songs, dances, and games were staged. *T'ama* songs were sung with improvised lyrics of sexual fun and making requests for specific gift items. Often the requests were known in advance so they could be fulfilled immediately. Others were delivered later during the several days of celebration, often with extra items added. Smaller gifts were distributed to the guests generally. Feasting and announcement of the girl's new name ended the potlatch at which other relatives might change names as well.

The girl's seclusion ended with purifying bathing, typically in a deep pool of a creek, and hard scrubbing with bundles of hemlock twigs. Pebbles might be dropped as a magic rite for easy childbirth in the future. The puberty ceremony, among central groups at least, might be followed immediately by the Wolf Ritual to initiate the girl and other suitable children into its society, adding another week to the celebrations. Lighter seclusion, with restrictions, continued for a number of months during which the girl wore special hair ornaments decorated with rows of dentalia shells and interwoven with Mountain Goat wool, if she was from the chiefly class. The girl did not eat fresh fish or game, possibly to avoid contaminating the primary food resources. She did not touch her hair or body with her hands but used a comb or a scratching stick. Venturing outside, she kept a cape about her hair. She rose first and retired last. At the end of the long period of restrictions, a feast was given and perhaps also a potlatch. Following her puberty rites, the girl, especially if she were a chief's daughter, kept largely indoors under supervision and practised quiet, demure conduct until marriage.

Boys had no special puberty rights but as they began adult pursuits they became subject to rigorous training rituals including fasting and not sleeping. Youths and young men tended to be overshadowed in tribal life by the dominating mature men. They generally were apprentices and assistants in economic and ceremonial activities.

Names

A person had a number of names through life, most before maturity as new ones were assumed at feasts and potlatches through the sponsoring efforts of the parents who sought good social standing for their child. Names were inherited through ancestral lines of descent through males or females. The origins of these usually grandiose names involved detailed explanations; many came in dreams about power-giving spirits. The history of the previous owners of the name was known and the new owner tried to live up to the glory that their ancestors had brought to the name, especially if it was a high-ranking name.

Tom Sa·ya·ch'apis, a Tseshaht man who was Edward Sapir's primary informant, changed his name five times (Sapir 1921:23-34). His first name, given at birth, was a nickname made up on the spot with no ceremonial significance. Still as a small child, at the potlatch mourning his deceased father, he took the name Tł'in'itsawa ("Getting Whale-skin"), a name that had originated when a chief of a subdivision of the tribe made it up for his son, remembering that little boys used to come for slices of skin when his whales were towed ashore. Next, at a feast given by his grandfather, Tł'in'itsawa took his boyhood name, Haw'itkomotłi (Having-chiefs-behind). This name originated with a great-great-grandfather who received it in a dream from a spirit whale. This ancestor had much success whaling and had become very rich, leaving the other chiefs behind. The next name, Konnoh (Wake Up!), also came from an ancestor's dream while he trained for whaling power, and was assumed at a naming feast given by his Ditidaht grandfather when the boy was about 10. At a potlatch he gave before marriage, Konnoh took another young man's name, Na·we·ʔi·k (Come Here!), the command given by a spirit whale in a dream to his mother's father. Finally, at his greatest potlatch for his daughter's puberty, Na·we·ʔi·k became Sa·ya·ch'apis ("Stands-up-high-over-all), a name eight generations old that a chief had obtained while doing ritual training for wealth power. This name originated from a dream in which the Sky Chief spirit appeared and said, in the ironic manner of spirits: "Why are you sleeping, Stands-up-high-over-all? You are not really desirous of getting wealthy, are you? I was about to make you wealthy and to give you the name Stands-up-high-over-all."

Marriage

Marriage was an alliance of families rather than a union of the bride and groom alone (Drucker 1951:286, Sproat 1868:97). Girls married at about 16, sometimes younger, and boys at 20 or older, although later in the 19th century boys too were marrying at about 16 (Brabant 1926:84). It was not uncommon for girls as young as 8 to have their bride price paid by chiefs who wanted to marry them before other chiefs did, but such child brides remained with their parents until about 16 (Koppert 1930b:49-53). Virginity was prized and guarded between puberty and marriage by close supervision. Still there was secret courting with whispering through cracks in the walls of houses at night and even stealthy visiting (Curtis 1916:65).

Chiefs commonly had more than one wife, because they could afford to make repeated bride-price payments (Drucker 1951:301, Mozino 1970:32). For his first wife, a chief had to choose a woman in the direct line of descent of a chief of equally high rank and acceptable to his group. She became the head wife for whom later wives were supposed to work. Having more than one wife earned prestige and indicated wealth, but it often made for an unhappy household full of friction, though co-wives who were sisters did not tend to quarrel as often. When a wife died, it was common, though not compulsory, for her sister to take her place in the marriage; similarly, if the husband died, a brother might take his place.

Marriage was arranged by the parents or other guardians of a couple marrying for the first time, the youngsters supposedly being ignorant of the proceedings. Chiefly parents (and some commoners) betrothed their children, mostly for the pledging blankets in the period after European contact or, in earlier times, furs and other valuables. The bride price for a girl was well known, at least in blankets. A betrothed man could offer the bride price year after year, for three years, after which it was either accepted, ensuring marriage, or rejected. If rejected, the betrothal was cancelled, the betrothal pledge was forfeited by the girl's family, and there were bitter feelings. Betrothals were generally firm, but some were broken when a greater chief or, in more recent times, a rich non-aboriginal man later came after the girl. It was also possible to cancel a betrothal by mutual agreement, and then, when the betrothed were of high-ranking families, the pledged blankets were ceremoniously cast, from canoes, one by one, into the sea.

The marriage ceremony varied in form, degree of elaborateness and the richness of the gifts exchanged, according to rank and to whether the marriage was a first one or not (Drucker 1951:287-303). For a first marriage without a preceding betrothal, the boy's father would send a marriage proposal party with an able speaker to present the suit. When there was a choice available between two or more suitors, rank was the primary factor in gaining the consent of the girl's father. But a chief with an only daughter might prefer a suitor of slightly lower rank, because his son-in-law would come to live in his house so that he could keep his dear daughter at home. For the chiefly, at least, it was the custom for the girl's side to resist entering the proposed marriage at first. The suitor's side then had to repeatedly send marriage parties.

Once the proposal was accepted, the prospective groom's father gathered his group together at a feast to announce the impending marriage, plan ceremonies and perhaps ask for help in meeting the bride price, though contributions were usually volunteered. For the marriage, the groom's party typically came by water to the bride's house, even if it was in the same village. A pair of big canoes, joined together with planks, provided a floating stage for ceremonial display (Boas 1890:42). Approaching the shore, the groom's party sang its chief's marriage songs and displayed other prestigious rights, such as masked and costumed dances representing powerful supernatural beings. Thunderbird, Whale and Wolf were favourite ceremonial representations. The speaker for the party stood on the beach and after each right was performed, he praised the great ancestry of the groom. He orated loud and long, often for hours. He traced the ancient relationships between the families. Finally he called out the name of each recipient for the bride price, which was given in the bride's house, in parts, to her group. As a rule, the bride price was refused at first and returned to the beach. For up to four days the groom's party might be kept waiting outside on the beach, continuing to sing, orate and offer the bride price until, at last, the bride's father relented, and through a speaker told the spokesman for the groom's party to stop talking, indicating his acceptance.

Then there was a ceremonial suitor's test with the bride's group using two to four of their marriage privileges or rights designed for the purpose. These tests were usually games or contests of skill, strength or courage, such as running a gauntlet of flaming torches, enduring sitting by a fire made blazing hot, climbing a greased rope, walking a horizontal pole that was swinging freely at one end, or carrying a very heavy stone. The groom's side might have to get past a line of strong men who barred access to the bride's house (Boas 1890:42). The winners of the contests received prizes (after European contact, usually blankets or money). There could be arrangements made to let the groom win. The torch gauntlet, for example, was parted when he finally made his run after others had failed.

A feast and a potlatch distribution of gifts from the bride's side to the groom's followed. The bride, dressed in ceremonial finery, danced formally for the groom's party. She was then either taken to her new home, or delivered later if her puberty observances still had to be finished or her dowry was not complete. When the bride reached her husband's home, her new in-laws danced, feasted and heaped gifts upon her. If the groom was of a chiefly family, he or his father endowed the bride with rights to territory, natural resources and ceremonial privileges, like potlatch seats, names, songs and dances. Commoners were often loaned privileges by their chief for use in marriage ceremonies. A dowry was furnished by the bride's family at the marriage or when the first child was born. Contributions to the dowry were made by kinsmen who had received parts of the bride price. A chief's daughter was given various hereditary privileges to be passed, eventually, on to her children. In case of childlessness or divorce, such rights reverted to her family. Exchanges of gifts, principally food, continued to be made from time to time between the two groups allied by marriage.

Elopement, or the marriage of older couples that was not their first, of course, was legalized by much simpler ceremony. A few of the man's kinsmen or friends went to the woman's family to give a small amount of blankets or money, usually without any performance of ceremonial privileges. The bride's side gave no dowry, though a few gifts would be given in return.

Divorce was a simple matter of separation – the wife was either sent back to her family or she left voluntarily (Curtis 1916:67). If the marriage had been one where the groom had gone to live with the bride's family, he would return to his group. The goods exchanged at marriages that had broken up were not returned, but hereditary privileges were. Where the children went, whether after a divorce or a death of a husband, was a problem because both sides would want to keep them. The children usually sided more with the people who raised them, so the claim of the father's side was often stronger. If the wife died, the children remained with their father's group without much question, since they were usually already there. Most divorces were caused by childlessness, though, so did not involve a problem about where children would go.

Another frequent cause of divorce was incompatibility. Unfaithfulness could usually be smoothed over, unless it was persistent. Couples were told not to be jealous when there was adultery. A Spanish observer in the late 18th century noted more severe consequences for adultery with a chief's wife. If the adulterer was a man of rank, he was banished, and if a commoner, he was killed. The woman was whipped (Mozino 1970:43). Faithfulness was a highly regarded virtue, and early European visitors among the Whaling People noted the virtuousness of the women. Women slaves, who were sometimes offered for prostitution, were an exception. Later, in the 19th century, when men went off for half a year at a time to hunt fur seals commercially in the Bering Sea, casual extramarital relations were more prevalent. Stable marriages were admired but most people had more than one mate over a lifetime.

Death

At death the life principle, located in the heart, stopped and the soul, located in the brain, left through the top of the head as a tiny shadowlike double of the person. The soul eventually became a ghost or an owl, at least in later 19th-century belief (Drucker 1951:156, Sapir 1921:366). Before that time, it was believed that the souls of chiefs, of persons killed in battle and of good men who had always prayed to the Sun and Moon, went to the land above, where it was always fine, and the souls of the rest went to the poor underworld (Boas 1890:45, Curtis 1916:44, Mozino 1970:28, Sproat 1868:209-14). Those who had been decapitated in war had their faces on their chests in afterlife. At death, the spirits of several dead relatives came to escort the soul to the afterworld. The dead ate mainly Spring Salmon and charcoal. They stayed in dwellings like those in life, and each tribe of dead was located beneath its living counterpart. A soul thus lived on, having the spouse who was the foremost one in life, having spirit children and continuing to age until eventual expiry (Curtis 1916:44).

Cause of death, other than physical reasons like old age, severe injury or drowning, could be from several kinds of illness caused supernaturally by disease-objects that had entered the body, loss of the soul, possession by a spirit or evil magic spells (Drucker 1951:205-06). The aged and those who had long been ill, were sometimes abandoned far from the village (Sproat 1868:256-57). Autopsies were performed when witchcraft was suspected as the cause of death. Also the fetus was removed from a woman dying in advanced pregnancy. This was done for the father's protection since he too would die if something so closely connected to him was left in the corpse (Drucker 1951:149-50).

Whaling People disposed of a corpse quickly, because they feared death. They buried the chiefly in a box or sometimes a canoe, and commoners in a simple wrapping of mats or old blankets in a shallow grave covered with sticks and stones (Mozino 1970:29, Sproat 1868:259). But by the late 19th century they were putting all their dead in boxes or canoes and placing them in a tree, on posts, in a cave or on a prominent point (Drucker 1951:147-49). Small islands were often special burial places. Twins and deformed infants who died, and their parents as well, were given special burial, laid out on mats with a covering robe at the entrance of a cave as though sleeping in bed. The body of person who committed suicide in a deadfall set for a bear was wrapped and left there after the logs were cleared away. A corpse in the house was taken out through the side wall by removing a few planks, not through the entrance else the souls of the young might follow it (Brabant 1926:59). If the corpse was transported to the burial grounds by water, it was towed in a separate canoe. Those who handled it would bathe before returning to the village.

Mourning ceremonies for chiefs were elaborate, including a potlatch, but simpler for commoners. At death, or even before it came, the women wailed and lamented for hours. Near relatives blackened their faces, wore poor clothing, cut their hair short, to just under the ears for men and shoulder length for women, ate little, and walked with a stick as if very weak (Curtis 1916:44). The personal property of the deceased went to the eldest son who chose what he wanted and distributed the rest to his brothers, sisters and other relations. The belongings of a childless man went to his wife, and those of a childless woman to her sister or other close relative. An unmarried woman's belongings went to her mother or close relative, an unmarried man's to his parents or the family he lived with last. When a chief was near death, the tribe might gather in his house to hear a speaker recount his great achievements during life. His personal effects might be distributed to recipients in order of their rank (Sproat 1868:261-62). If a dying man wanted to take his belongings with him to the afterworld, then his family would burn them after his death – this often meant burning the house as well as considerable other property (Drucker 1951:150, Sapir 1921:366). Various valuables might be deposited with the dead. One chief, at the beginning of the 19th century, was buried with 24 prime Sea Otter pelts in his box (Jewitt 1815: 136).

For persons of high rank, a memorial post was erected that bore a painted crest or a carved figure representing a notable quality of the deceased (Spro-at 1868:260-10). For a leading chief, the memorial could be an elaborate set of large painted wooden sculptures, like the Thunderbird and Whale monument to M'okwina, one of the later chiefs (see page 215). A hunter might have a carving of the animal he most often pursued put on a pole or in a canoe by his grave (Curtis 1916:43). After a chief was buried, two or four songs of mourning were sung in his house and a feast was held at which his heir announced his assumption of the chiefship. A potlatch was held later, after the necessary preparations such as the amassing of goods and the invitation of other tribes. Property was distributed and announce-ments were made, such as the planned destruction of the dead chief's big ceremonial canoe, the shelving of certain of his ceremonial privileges for a year or more, or forever, and the prohibition on using his name, as well as words containing elements of it, for a year or two. In due time, the succeed-ing chief removed the name taboo and suspension of privileges, again with potlatches. Lower-ranked chiefs and well-to-do commoners who died, had a feast given for them at which gifts were given only to the chiefs. Their names were not formally banned, but their use was avoided for a time, espe-cially in the presence of those who had been close to the deceased person. A chief's death might be honoured, as mentioned before, by killing his slaves or people of other tribes with a sense of compensating retaliation. When a chief lost someone special, like an eldest son, he often sent warriors to kill and cause sorrow in another tribe to alleviate his own (Curtis 1916:43).

WHALING PEOPLE'S ACCOUNTS OF SOCIAL LIFE

The above description barely outlines the social life of the Whaling People. Their own accounts afford a livelier insider's view. They focus on specific happenings and persons, in all their complexities, so outsiders would require many stories to gain a comprehensive picture of Whaling People's existence (see Sapir and Swadesh 1939, 1955). Here, we provide two accounts of mar-riages as examples of the Whaling People's viewpoint (Sapir and Swadesh 1939:137-139, 177). Both are much concerned with the hereditary rights that are ceremonially displayed and transferred between the groom's and bride's parties. These privileges, called *topa·ti*, are at the heart of Whaling People's social organization. Many specific details are mentioned in the following accounts, both of which are about Tseshaht marriages, yet they actually cover only the essentials of the proceedings.

In the first account, Tom Sa·ya·ch'apis wants to marry a girl in his own tribe, but arranges for his Ditidaht relatives to act for him. "Uncles" includes relatives of Tom's parents' generation, whether or not they are related by blood. The Ditidaht speaker calls Tom "son", but this is only rhetorical. The songs would be sung by the teller, Tom Sa·ya·ch'apis.

Tom Marries

"Uncles," said I to the ten Ditidaht chiefs, "you are to woo for me."

"Very well" said the Ditidaht chiefs, my uncles.

Twenty went together to woo. The one whose name was Koayik spoke: "Listen to me, O chief. The one who desires to woo you is my tribesman. He is my son, half Ditidaht and half Tseshaht. Consequently you are not to say 'I wonder why he has another tribe wooing for him.' Indeed, he is my son and the son of all the ten chiefs here on your ground. You will take my thought, O chief, since you have had this ceremony for a long time and will always be addressed in this way when you have a daughter by people taking her away. Since you are a chief who never casts out suitors when addressed in this way, take my thought, O chief, for you have this sacred ritual in this place where I am now speaking. Let your mind become favourable for you are always that way if you are a chief. Take pity on me and look on this *topa·ti*, here on the ground, your *topa·ti* for this *topa·ti* of yours has been stepped within. I have ten fires as a *topa·ti* and I have the lightning-serpent."

I now finished wooing. My *topa·ti* remained on the ground there for four days. [All this time Tom was camping with the Ditidaht.] Then the father gathered together absolutely all of his relatives of the Tseshaht tribe. The Tseshaht tribe accepted the *topa·ti*.

"Come and take the *topa·ti* back there," said the father of the girl.

The Tseshaht brought back the *topa·ti* and arrived at my residence.

"Very well, perform your ritual, his *topa·ti*. Start the marriage ceremony tomorrow," said the Tseshaht band.

I assembled my relatives at night. I took the Waninath band and I took the Nashasath and I took the Maktliath. I got my songs ready. At daybreak, boards were pulled down and war canoes were boarded over with the boards. The people got onto two canoe platforms. We rounded the point.

"*Hiyayyanga, hahahanga,*
My lightning-serpents face each other on the beach
When I marry from tribe to tribe.
My lightning-serpents glide about
When I marry from tribe to tribe." [Serpent mask dances in.]

Listen to me, O chief, the one who desires to woo you is my tribesman.
Tim Paul drawing, 1983.

They took off their head-masks there in the house. The Lightning Ser-
pents took off their robes. They piled their robes and head-masks together.
All came outside. I took up another song [sung with swaying dance]:
"*Hi hi he … haha …*
I have ten abalones."
I took up another song [sung with changing masks dance]:
"He has feathers on his head, our chief.
Ho … ahayya … hoho ahayya …
walah imtlats hamalikala himtlats yaokshlala.
Hayya … haho hoho…."
[Sung with Thunderbird dance:]
"Thunderer *yai heheyo….*"
Four times they did it and then they stopped. There were four *topa·tis*
of mine when I married Witsah. Then the father of Witsah took his *topa·ti*,
called springy-device. This was a long sapling this big around. There was
oil with the sapling. My people since I was the one marrying got on it.
They would go so far and then fall to the beach when the sapling bent. It
was not long before one of my people made it, walked it without falling down. I obtained the *topa·ti* as mine. Another *topa·ti* was brought out
and set up on the beach; it consisted of a board on the beach. My people
began throwing at it to find out who could throw hard enough to split it.
A strong one split it. The *topa·ti* became mine.

Captain Bill's Marriage

Walk-down-at-intervals [probably Captain Bill's older brother] acted as
wooer. He went to Yohwaytsa of the Burntfront sept [lineage group] to
ask for his oldest daughter. Her name was Keas. Then he wooed again.
He put up his wooing *topa·ti*, which stood erect on the beach and looked
like a man with feathers on both sides of his head. It was returned to him.
He wooed again. They came back again and said, "Come and get the girl
now!"

All the men, women and children began the ceremony of getting the
girl. They performed a *topa·ti*. The *topa·ti* represented the Moon. Another
topa·ti was Thunder along with Lightning Serpents. Still another was a
Whale. There were three *topa·ti*s. Then they performed for us who had
performed first. They had four fires [torches held an inch apart] which
one tried to get through. None got through except Mentioned-by-name
and Braided-hair. There was another *topa·ti*. Two sticks were set up like this
[converging at the top] on the ground with a rope in between fastened
to the two poles sticking up from the ground. A man Kills-them-before-
they-come-out got out of a canoe and took hold of the rope. The owner
of the *topa·ti* told him to try to reach the top of the poles by climbing the
rope hand over hand. Kills-them-before-they-come-out took hold and
pulled on the rope. As soon as he started lifting himself the *topa·ti* broke.
He succeeded. [Breaking the *topa·ti* is considered equivalent to meeting
the test in the regular way.]

Another was a painted device made of boards that one tried to get
through. The boards did like this: came together edgewise at intervals.
Yohwaytsa the owner of the *topa·ti* said that it represented the sky cod-
fish who is said to be called Sky-cod. Attacking-from-overhead and
Distending-nostrils made it. Thus they finished the tests and obtained the
girl. Our marriage payment consisted of thirty blankets. Later the father
brought the dowry gift. He enumerated dam-traps on the river for cohoe
and also funnel-traps for Dog Salmon and Tyee [Chinook] Salmon.

The salmon traps mentioned at the end of the account of Captain Bill's
marriage as the dowry from the bride's father are rights of great material
value. They would be inherited by the children born to the couple.

Long verbal instructions were frequently given to educate the young.
A good example is the advice given by Tom Sa·ya·ch'apis to his grandson.
Alex Thomas, who recorded it, regarded it very highly. Here is part of Tom
Sa·ya·ch'apis's instructions (Sapir and Swadesh 1939:185, 187, 193, 195,
197), illustrating the ideal conduct recommended for being successful in
Whaling People's society by secret ritual and being good to others.

Yohwaytsa the owner of the topa·ti *said that it represented the sky cod-fish who is said to be called Sky-cod.* Tim Paul drawing, 1983.

Tom Gives Advice to his Grandson

Don't sleep all the time. Go to bed only after having drunk water, so that you will wake up when you need to urinate. Eat once at midday, then go to sleep with that much food in you so that you will not sleep soundly. As soon as everybody goes to sleep, go out and bathe. Further, if you go for a walk in the daytime, go looking for a stream far away. Rub yourself with yew wood so that you will not be shamed by your fellow youths; for you would be shamed if you were not manly, if only your fellows were manly. Work your mind all night taking up one thing after another to decide what you will strive for, whether you should learn woodworking or sea-mammal hunting, or become bold in whaling or in the accumulation of wealth.

If you want to become very wealthy, as I was in my prime, don't sleep with many coverings, for you might then sleep too soundly; indeed you will if you have many covers on. When you come in while cold, hold a cedar stick in your hands, for it is said ghosts are afraid if one is holding a stick.... When day comes, be sleeping in the house with your face hidden, even though you will again be active at night. In that way, your fellows do not know and think you are a sleepy-head.

Rub your hands, make all the branches [rubbing medicines] and every little thing tell you what to use when your occupation becomes known to you, so that you may become a getter of many birds, so that you may get many by snaring, so that you may be a marksman in shooting, so that you may get many in trapping. They say that a young man who just waits for the right time does not get anything. He succeeds only if he has the Wolf Ritual spirit from the start and trains for various little things while growing up....

Do not lose account of your mind as long as you are a person. Sit against the wall in the house working your mind, handling it in such a way as not to forget even one thing, that you may not wish to do evil, that you may not mock an old man, that you may not mock an old woman. Take up the orphan child who has no mother or father and say, "Dear little fellow!" Take him to your home and feed him well so that he will think highly of you. The children to whom you do so remember you when they grow up. Then they will help you. If you come to the beach with a canoe-load of wood, they will start unloading it for you and they will help pull the canoe up on the beach. Take to lousing the little orphan child. Take to lousing the little old man warming his back on the ground; he will then give you advice and important secret lore.

Give aid to the one handling something alone. Carry moving goods for the one who is moving or the one who is packing things alone or boarding over canoes, so that he will think well of you, so that he will have you as chief, so that he will not speak ill of you, so that he will not curse you; for it is said that people curse after one if one is bad, so that he does not reach the peak of life (living out the full span). A person who wants to be bad never reaches the peak. Take in the pitiable-looking old person. Say as you take him in, "Come, my good fellow, that we may eat together!" Be willing to do everything so as to be well off and not poor, so that old people may come to you at once when you bring in different kinds of fish in your canoe, desiring to eat it.

Do not make yourself important. Anyone who makes himself important is not manly. Gather mussels and sheep's-feet, gather clams, gather many sea-cucumbers, gather abalone and sea-eggs, so that your neighbours will have you as chief. It only requires an energetic person to cook it as food. People have as chief the one who looks after them. All one needs is a way of cooking the food, because they will eat enthusiastically the various shellfish of the rocky sea bottom if they are cooked; even that which looks bad when raw has a good taste when cooked.

Do not desire to do a rash thing with a girl, to want to take hold of her, for you might cause her parents to be ashamed.... Do not want to be a lover of the wife of a married man, for he might curse you because of it. Do not follow the young man who is a bad bully. You might do what he wants you to do, for that is his nature, while you have another mind, since you are a chief, that you may be a good chief, that you may be respected; for they will then also be that way to you. What your neighbour has brought home in his canoe he will likewise give you. The one who has brought food in his canoe and wants to do so will invite you alone; for it is the law of the Indians to return kindnesses to the one who looks after them. Then the other chief who is not so treated feels badly.

If your neighbours begin to fight and wrangle, and the other chief is unable to separate them and to make them stop fighting, then you step between them, make for the middle of the crowd where they are fighting. Speak gently, using a kindly voice. Say, "Now stop, O chiefs, stop, stop!" Say, "O chiefs" to both sides, that they may heed you when you say in a gentle voice, "Now stop!" Use a kindly voice so that you may be good, so that your neighbours may consider you good. Then start talking, saying, "Now you will become good toward each other, for you are neighbours to one another, for you are chiefs."

I would say in advising her, if I had a girl, that she should also be willing to pick all kinds of berries and fruit, so that you may say to the old people, "Come and eat!" so that they may say to you, "Come and eat — the princess has a lot of fruit in her house," so they may say of you, "The princess has brought home a lot of fruit in her basket." Learn everything, all there is of weaving work, for you will not take your mother along when you are made a slave [married] by someone; so that you may make a man of your husband, even though you should marry someone who is not manly, for I would be ashamed if you made him unmanly.

Learn to do every kind of weaving work. If you see a man, speak kindly to him even though he be a stranger, so that he may not swear at you. They say that girls are always sworn at if they are silent when spoken to. If a person enters your house while you are weaving, let your work basket go. Take a good mat and have him sit on it. Don't hesitate because you happen to have clean hands. Say that you will wash your hands. When you are through cooking, let him eat.

When you marry into a family, look after them, so that you will likewise be looked after. When you get up, go at once and get wood and start the fire. Say, "Come and eat!" and feed the ones among whom you have married. Then, when you have finished feeding them, wash your hands and take up your work....

Further, let me bring to you advice as to men's things. Be a carpenter, be a maker of canoes, for you would not be manly if you had to go about the beach seeking to borrow something in which to go out to sea. Be a maker of spears and paddles, be a maker of bows and arrows, be a maker of bailers, be a maker of herring-rakes and scoop-nets for herring, for it would not be manly to lack them when you came to need things of that sort of order to get fish by net-fishing in the season of net-fishing in this river, when the season for Sockeye Salmon comes, when the season for Coho Salmon comes in the fall, when the season for Steelhead comes in winter, when the Silver Salmon come into season in the spring.

Chapter 4
The Long Past
of the Whaling People

HISTORY BEFORE WRITTEN RECORDS

History, in the true sense of a string of events in the lives of humans, has happened whether or not it was recorded in writing. As long as some kind of record exists – written, oral tradition or archaeological remains – history is known, to a varying degree, by the nature of the record. Since, like most of the peoples of the world, the Whaling People lacked writing, the bulk of their history, before the arrival of Europeans, can only be known through traditional remembrances extending back perhaps a few centuries, and archaeological evidence that goes back several thousands of years but lacks details on specific events and individuals.

The long past of the Whaling People is largely available to us only through the archaeological record. From 1982 to mid 1995 the number of recorded sites went from 270 to 1,264, of which only 34 sites were excavated and were subject to minor testing. Major excavations were at Yuquot, Hesquiaht, two Toquaht sites and Shoemaker Bay at the head of Alberni Inlet. Eleven sites were excavated in the traditional territory of the Makah, but only Ozette and two Hoko River sites were extensively excavated. The entire coast from Cape Cook to Nootka Sound is largely unknown and there are only site inventories south of Barkley Sound with some limited excavation around Nitinat Lake. The oldest dated site in the territory of the Whaling People is Yuquot at 4,200 years before present (McMillan 1999:47-104).

From the evidence furnished at Yuquot and other sites, a long cultural history has been pieced together that, more or less, represents what happened over several thousand years. At Yuquot the basic information came in the form of some 5,000 artifacts and other material – bone, antler and shell – indicating resource utilization, and all placed in time by their location in four strata of deposits dated by the C14 or radioactive carbon method. The evidence indicates "a single culture evolving conservatively for more than 4,000 years" (Dewhirst 1978:12).

Although there is no indication of any earlier different culture or people, archaeological investigation is still at an early stage there, so the possibility cannot be precluded. At the moment, however, the history of the Whaling People, before written records, is divided into several periods (Dewhirst 1978:13–17; and see McMillan 1999:131–39), as follows:

1. The Early Period, 2200 to 1000 BCE, had tools like pecked and ground stone blades for chisels or adzes, stone hammers, bone wedges, bone awls, stone abraders and sandstone saws that, taken together, suggest a wood-working technology as sophisticated as in recent times. Fishing is also indicated, but the salmon, so important in life of the Whaling People today, may have been less abundant before 3000 BCE, or less easily and constantly available (Fladmark 1975:195–208). But such a condition concerning salmon would have been a factor only for the earliest beginnings of the Whaling People's culture, likely before 2200 BCE, a date obtained at Yuquot without going as far back as the beginning of the deposits. Whale bone occurs in this period, but whether the whales were hunted or simply found beached is not determined. At its earliest, the life of the Whaling People might be characterized as "a shoreline culture with heavy reliance on nearby forest resources and marine oriented toward small inshore fishes and birds" (Dewhirst 1978:18).

2. The Middle Period, 1000 BCE to 800 CE, shows much the same assemblage of tools. In addition, a cedar-bark shredder of whale bone is present as an important indication of the use of shredded cedar bark for clothing and other purposes typical to the Whaling People. The main pursuit was fishing for salmon, cod and small inshore fishes like snappers, rockfish and perch. An important supporting activity was hunting sea mammals, though with harpoon heads that neither toggled nor had socketed bases as they had later. The harpoon-head type is not thought to be suited for whaling and, although many artifacts are made of whale bone, the bone could have come from drift whales. Most artifacts are made of bone or antler from land animals, indicating that deer and elk were often taken.

3. The Late Period, 800 to 1790 CE, shows an increasing maritime orientation. Fishing continued as the primary pursuit with more refined and specialized hooks. Harpoon heads for sea mammals and salmon changed to the toggling, socketed "female" form in recent use. Many sea mammals were hunted. It may be that during this period whaling was invented by groups forced to live outside on the open coast all year round for lack of rights to inside places, as oral tradition states. The last has been summarized by Drucker (1951:99):

In brief, it is conceded by most of the tribes that the art of whaling originated at the old village of Tsaxsis, on the outside of Nootka Island, and
at Tatcu, outside of Esperanza Inlet, where it was an indispensable part of
the food quest. There are no important salmon streams in either vicin-
ity, so the former inhabitants are said to have depended on whaling for a
livelihood as the other groups dwelling on the inlets depended on salmon
fishing. The art diffused to the other tribes gradually, principally through
intermarriages with the Tsaxsis and Tatcu chiefs, and came to be a symbol
of chieftains' greatness rather than a basic subsistence source.

4. The Recent Period, 1790 to present, is, of course, dominated by contact with Europeans and the resulting profound changes, better known
through written records, including those made of native recollections.

WARS

The Whaling People's oral traditions relating to historical events have a lot
to say about wars. Terrible as they are, wars mark change, particularly in
social and political relationships, and insofar as history, in general, is a record
of change, it tends to be much concerned with wars. Although quite gentle and non-violent in ordinary peaceful life, the Whaling People became
bloodthirsty in war, seeking to annihilate the enemy in surprise massacres
and take trophy heads and slaves. There was a typical pattern to Whaling
People's warfare the features of which can be described in order of their
occurrence (Drucker 1951:332-44, Swadesh 1948).

The most frequently given reason for war, in recorded accounts, is revenge (Swadesh 1948:86). Raid and counter-raid followed each other as in
a feud. Attacks could extend to those helping or inciting the enemy. Retaliation also resulted from murder, stealing, enslavement of a relative, rough
treatment and insult, to which Whaling People were highly sensitive. Some
affront could usually be invoked by a chief bent on war to arouse his people
against another group. As in all group actions, chiefs and war chiefs took the
initiative.

A deeper major reason for war was to gain land. Groups that did not own
good salmon streams might try to gain one by force. In a time before Europeans arrived, when the people of Ucluelet Arm decided to get a salmon
stream, they first sent a party to visit their neighbours to decide, after feasting
around, who had the best salmon. Then they attacked the Nam'int?ath people and exterminated them, taking their territory with its fine salmon (Sapir
and Swadesh 1955:362-67). The Ahousaht also exterminated their Otsosat
neighbours early in the 19th century to get Dog Salmon streams (Drucker
1951:344-53). Invading up the Alberni canal, the Tseshaht evidently killed

off the Ts'o·ma?as?ath to take the Sockeye-rich Somass River (Sapir 1912).
The Makah of Cape Flattery, also after Sockeye streams, took over Nitinat
Lake for a period, apparently long before Europeans arrived, according to
Chief Charles Jones Sr.

Plundering was done on raids, but the gain of portable goods was not
a prime reason for going to war. Neither was the taking of heads a cause
for battle, although the leading warriors tried their best to get these awful
trophies of their prowess. On the other hand, slave-taking was the reason
for two attacks by the Ucluelet, who wanted them for buying guns (Sapir
and Swadesh 1955:373-78, 413-40). A motive for warfare that may appear
strange, arose at times from the idea that when a chief or his child died,
the bereaved followers should kill someone to accompany their leader as a
death companion (ch'ichm'o) and to make others have to mourn, too. They
might then kill one or more slaves on the beach or attack another group.
Betterment of rank, to become a head chief through killing an incumbent,
was sometimes a reason for chiefs of secondary rank to start a war.

But the Whaling People waged most of their wars for economic reasons,
even if revenge seemed the most apparent cause of hostilities.

The weapons used in warfare were heavy yew lances or pikes, about
two metres long, with fire-hardened points, light cedar spears about three
metres long with a bone point, thrown at close range (Koppert 1930a:105),
bows and arrows, and slings with a woven spruce-root pocket for the stone.
Chiefs and war-chiefs used a whale-bone club (ch'it'o·t) shaped like a short
sword and a stone skull crusher with a conical point. War chiefs wore body
armour of two or three layers of thick elk hide wrapped around the torso
and laced down the side. They also often wore the skin of the head of a wolf
or bear as a fierce-looking headdress. All warriors blackened their faces with
charcoal and tied their hair into a topknot, using a hemlock twig and sharp
bone pins to hold it in place.

Since the sea dominates the world of the Whaling People, some warfare
happened on the ocean, yet detailed records of such fighting are scarce. Fortunately, one good account exists describing a great canoe battle between
the Ahousaht and Tseshaht in Barkley Sound, apparently in a time before
European contact, because the account mentions no guns. In the account,
the Ahousaht fleet has 49 long canoes (p'inw'at), 10–12-metre whaling and
transport canoes, sometimes used for raiding, along with one supersized or
"White-face" war canoe (Tl'itso·t). This number may seem too large, but
it is in line with an estimated 10,000 strong confederacy including the
Qiɫtsama?ath of east Vargas Island and Qwatswi?ath of Bedwell Sound. The
Ahousaht were apparently bent on expansion even before their early 19th-
century takeover of Otsosat territory, for their original home of west Vargas
Island has only small salmon-spawning streams producing a few Cohos but

no Dog Salmon of the fall that dry well to be a winter mainstay (George 2003:45–46). The battle in Barkley Sound takes place on the return voyage of the Ahousaht from a venture somewhere farther on down the coast (after Sapir and Swadesh 1955:353-5).

A Naval Engagement

Ahousaht just passing by beheaded a Tseshaht. He was fishing with hook for small cod at Ch'ito·kwachisht ("Edgewise on Water"). They killed him, chopped off his head and took it along. He had set out from Hots'atsswił ("Drift Back" [Dicebox Island]) where the Tseshaht were living.

Right away the Tseshaht got angry. The Ahousaht consisted of 50 canoes travelling at sea. The Chief of the Tseshaht planned it. "Use what you know you have, warriors," he said.

One who knew that sort of thing dived into the sea at a place stocked with mud sharks. Another went to a lake stocked with ghosts and dived in. They continued so long as the Ahousaht were away in the down-coast direction. They prepared house posts made of yew, adzing the ends. They are for camping on the way to a new place and are nicely adzed along their length. They gathered the shoulderblades of whales. Those who were short of shoulderblades gathered beating boards intended for the bow of the canoe; what they called beating boards were the ones on which the people of old used to drum. They made Yellow-cedar blankets to be used as shields spread crosswise at the bow when approaching the Ahousaht. The Tseshaht did not sleep nights praying for victory.

"Don't you shoot all at once, let them shoot first," he planned. "You'll approach from both sides. Some of you will be among the rocks of T'oqwa·s ("Something-on-it" [Turret Island]) and some at ʔA·tsam'osh [an islet northeast Effingham Island] You will paddle along slowly in approaching."

And there the rascals appeared round the point at Ch'imataqsoł [Cape Beale]. They [the Tseshaht] were on the lookout on the top of Hots'atsswił hill. The Tseshaht dragged their long canoes (p'inw'ał) into the water. The war party went through into Ho·m'o·w'a [Effingham Island]. Some of the Tseshaht formed an ambush at T'oqwa·s and some at ʔA·tsam'osh. The Tseshaht did not have many canoes. There were only 40 canoes in their war party. Nevertheless they went at the 50-canoe fleet of the Ahousaht. They did so as soon as they left shore at ʔA·yapiyis ("Many Between Beach"). They were paddling slowly, the way they had planned it.

One of the Ahousaht spoke: "Stop!" he shouted. "Form a whetstone!" Ropes appeared from their canoes and were stretched along under each canoe at the bow and at the stern.

Another Ahousaht spoke: "Let's be a whetstone, Ahousaht, let's be a

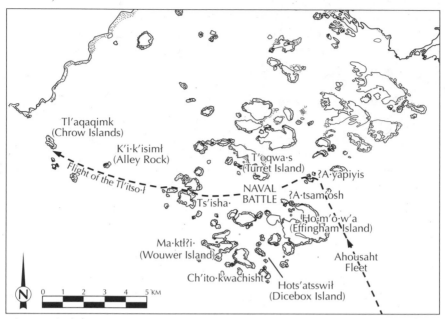

The attack and escape route in the navel battle.

whetstone. Let's not let the approaching war party paddle between us." –
meaning when they were tied together.

They tied themselves together and really pulled it together securely
with the ropes. My, the Ahousaht shot! The bunch at the other edge also
shot. They shot against the wall of whale shoulderblades. The points of the
arrows were breaking to pieces. The Tseshaht continued paddling gently
along. They were making the Ahousaht use up their arrows, that was why
they were moving along gently. My, by the time they got close the arrows
flew far between. Some of the Ahousaht had run out of arrows.

"Now then!" said the Tseshaht, "Now shoot!"

They shot. At the same time they started moving swiftly. They came
close to one on the edge. They took their sharpened yew wood. My, they
speared at the Ahousaht long canoe at the edge! My, the Ahousaht sank!
Their vessel broke to pieces. Then they rammed another canoe. My, it
too broke to pieces! When four canoes had broken up at both ends the
Ahousaht were in an uproar. The Tseshaht shot. The Ahousaht men fled
toward their centre. They were unable to return the fire because their
arrows had given out. Their canoes began sinking, caused by themselves,
because a great many people were running from both ends into other
canoes. The Ahousaht swimming about in the sea were quite a spectacle
like things moving on the water with arrows stuck in. In the centre was a

Returning with the trophies. Tim Paul drawing, 1983.

"White-faced" canoe (*Tl'itso·t*) manned by 20 Ahousaht. The people running to canoes and sinking them were close to the White-face.

Those in the White-face realized that the many in flight were near
them. They could not paddle away because they were tied securely together in the whetstone.

"Cut it loose," said the chief of the crew.

At once they cut the rope at both ends. Those in the White-face
paddled out. Another vessel, just a whaling canoe, paddled out. My, all the
canoes sank! The Ahousaht drowned. Those that had paddled out were
all but grabbed at the stern. The two canoes were nearly caught. Some
Ahousaht died without wounds, simply by being crushed under many
people.

Ni·nisp'atwas with his vessel pursued the two that had escaped. He
went after them staying at the same distance but not getting closer. He was
after a crew of 10. Ni·nisp'atwas also had 10 in his crew. There were 20 in
the crew of the White-face. Ni·nisp'atwas pursued them through the pass
at Ts'isha·. He reached the island called K'ik'isimł [Alley Rock, 5 km east
of Ucluelet Inlet] and passed it. They paddled out to sea from K'ik'isimł.
Those in the White-face were now close to Tl'aqaqimk ("Bush Covered"
[Chrow Islands, about 2 km southeast of Ucluelet Inlet]). And there the
rascal remembered that his warrior's amulet was stuck in his headdress.
Ni·nisp'atwas, the rascal, stood up.

"Hey! Your head will be stuck up on a pole with mouth agape by the power of the Supernatural Porcupine, hey!" he said, casting a spell.

The Ahousaht only looked behind. Their paddles remained poised in the air. They [Ni·nisp'atwas's men] simply beheaded them when they pulled up alongside. They died because he said that to them.

One canoe survived, the White-face with 20 in the crew. The other 49 long canoes, with 10 in each canoe, were lost. They [in the White-face] came drifting sidewise around the point, with everyone crying and wailing, to the place from which they had set out. The passages at Ho·m'o·w'a, Ts'isha· and Ma·kł?i· ("Higher Than Others" [Wouwer Island]) became all blood because many people had died. The Tseshaht could not eat, because all the fish – cod and red cod – had filled themselves with human flesh. They were unable to eat big mussels, sheep's feet (ts'e?nwa [Goose-neck Barnacles]) and small clams because all the sea was with blood.

The Tseshaht have two songs that tell of the time the Ahousaht floated weeping round the point at the place called ?A·ho·s from which they had set out.

"Weep coming round the point for a while," says the song, "Say, when the Ahousaht are a war party." That's the whole of it.

And another song: "Now come along and be a war party against me, so I may do to you as I did to the Ahousaht for I allowed none of them to go home."

The Ahousaht fared better in the post-contact period in a long war with the Otsosat (see page 148).

After the Sea Otter traders arrived in 1785, guns became the favourite weapon of the Whaling People. Heavy charges of powder and shot made the muzzle-loading flintlocks deadly in the close-quarter engagements.

War was decided on formally in a meeting of the men, often held outdoors, perhaps to keep plans secret from women married in from other groups who had relatives among the enemy. Chiefs seeking war spread inflammatory propaganda beforehand. At the meeting, the chiefs or war chiefs (who were next in rank) made speeches denouncing the enemy for assorted offenses and calling for revenge. Although the top-ranked chief was supposed to decide whether or not to go to war, chiefs of lesser rank often swayed opinion. A dominant chief with a strong following often decided the matter. War chiefs typically voted in favour of war.

As they did for other undertakings, men prepared for fighting with ritual bathing. They sometimes also engaged in practical training, like assault charges and practice landings on beaches. But most attacks were planned to be a complete surprise, with the warriors stealing into houses at night to strike down designated individuals in their sleep. Detailed intelligence of the enemy's disposition, down to where the leaders and best warriors slept, was gathered through preliminary visits or from neutrals who visited. Tribesmen with relatives might be sent to spy, but this could be dangerous; such "spies" might also warn their relatives. War chiefs also scouted an enemy village by observing it undetected from the woods. When possible, allies were enlisted to muster a force of overpowering superiority.

The favourite attack – in the dark before dawn, when the enemy slept deeply – usually succeeded as long as the surprise was complete. A daylight charge up the beach usually faltered under defensive fire. Open assaults may have been more successful before guns, though, because the high, wide prows of traditional war canoes made excellent shields against arrows and sling stones. Whether by night or day, the attack was often made from more than one direction, but the problem was to coordinate the divided forces to strike simultaneously. Wolf howls and bird cries were used as signals but often one element attacked before the others. Diversionary tactics were also used to lure the enemy into ambush or to draw fire to waste enemy ammunition (as described in "A Naval Engagement"). Complicated plans tended to fail. A successful method was deception, such as pretending to be on a peaceful marriage visit and suddenly striking down the poor hosts with knives and clubs that had been carried hidden under robes. A few engagements occurred on water, usually when men in war canoes ambushed or overhauled a few fishermen in small canoes.

Alert watchmen were the best defence and were posted when news came of a possible attack, but sentinels seemed not to remain alert for long and were usually asleep when the attack came, often after a deliberate delay by a clever commander. Other defence measures included the thick planks of house walls that were proof against arrows and musket shot, inaccessible refuge sites on steep-sided hills or islands, and palisades. Traditions tell of heavy logs set to roll down on attackers when ropes were cut, and of deadfalls across paths the enemy might use, but such measures do not appear common, at least in more recent warfare.

A successful attack resulted in the deaths of many enemies with only a few for the attackers. Those who fled from their houses would meet warriors waiting outside the entrances. Any who escaped as far as the woods met a force waiting to ambush them. Attackers of a small group tried to hunt down all members so none survived to go for help. The victorious attackers loaded plunder onto their canoes and destroyed what they could not take by burning it in the houses and smashing the enemy's canoes. War parties often had young men who did not fight but ran around looting and taking slaves. Women and children were enslaved, but usually not men, because they were likely to kill their captors when an opportunity presented itself. A few men might be captured just to be cruelly killed later. It was amusing to make a chief or war chief beg for his life and debase himself for the promise of being spared, only to be killed. Brave men disregarded the taunting captors and sang a war or spirit song to the end.

The Whaling People beheaded their slain enemies "by three dexterous movements of the knife, from the back of the neck" (Sproat 1868:187). They did not take scalps. Returning to their village, the warriors held the heads up in their canoes while, on shore, the people raised a loud welcome, singing and drumming furiously on the house planks. Landing, the war chiefs danced on the beach with the heads, singing victory songs and boasting. Some even licked the blood. The heads were put out on a rock at the end of the village beach for four days, then hidden in the woods. Groups around Barkley Sound set up the heads of the defeated on poles. The body of an attacker that remained with the enemy was often mutilated and perhaps hoisted on a pole on the beach and insulted. This fierce violence in war contrasted with mild peacefulness in ordinary social life, even for a war chief (Drucker 1951:343-44). War had a unifying aspect in making groups come together in tribes and confederacies for greater mutual strength, but it also destroyed people. And those related to both sides in a conflict suffered torn loyalties. War contributed to the plunge in population in the turbulent period after the coming of the Europeans, but it virtually ended about the middle of the 19th century when Vancouver Island became a British colony and Her Majesty's gunboats brought Pax Britannica to the Whaling People.

The nature of warfare, its scale and intensity, is best appreciated from actual instances. This example describes a major war in which the Ahousaht of Vargas Island killed off the Otsosat around Flores Island in a series of engagements on both land and sea early in the 19th century. The war began a year or so after the 1811 capture of the Tonquin (see page 171) and lasted about 15 years (Bouchard and Kennedy 1990:240). This account is a slightly modified version of the original recorded by Philip Drucker (1951:344-53). We have made some corrections, mostly based on Bouchard and Kennedy (1990), for clarity and ease of reading.

The War Between the Ahousaht and Otsosat

The Ahousaht Seek Dog Salmon Through Marriage

Up to the early decades of the 19th century, the Ahousaht owned only the outside beaches and foreshore of Vargas Island and a small area across Calmus Passage below Catface Mountain. They owned no important Dog Salmon streams, and, it is said, often suffered privations on this account. They resolved to obtain from the Otsosat a wife for Hayo·pino·ł, the chief second in rank to the head chief.

The Otsosat were a powerful tribe whose chiefs owned rich fishing grounds not only on Flores Island but also up Herbert, North and Shelter arms and Sidney Inlet. They were probably a confederation of several local groups who assembled at Ma·qtosi·s in the winter. The Sidney Inlet people are often referred to as a separate group, the Manhousat.

At length a marriage was arranged for Hayo·pino·ł with the daughter of an Otsosat chief. Despite this formal alliance, the Otsosat did not let the Ahousaht fish for Dog Salmon – it appears that the bride's father, in giving the dowry, did not include any fishing rights in his Dog Salmon streams. Hayo·pino·ł quarrelled with his wife that fall, and she returned to her home.

The Start of Hostilities

The following spring, Hayo·pino·ł sent some young men to bring his wife back. Her father refused to let her return. The young men, offended, broke the tips of their paddles on the way home and reported on arrival that the Otsosat had not only refused to send the woman back, but had treated them roughly and broken their paddles. Hayo·pino·ł was much angered. He chanced to find two Otsosat men on Twins Islet and killed them both.

Their kin, when their canoe drifted in, knew at once on whom to lay the blame. The head chief of the Otsosat sent six war chiefs out to seek revenge. When they found seven Ahousaht men cutting cedar poles for drying racks for herring eggs, they killed and beheaded all of them, then displayed the heads from their canoe while paddling back and forth in front of the Ahousaht village.

Peace-making

All the Ahousaht assembled in their chief's house. Only Hayo·pino·ł, of all the chiefs, still wanted to wage war. The first chief, M'okwiña, was against war at any cost, because his mother was Otsosat. He prevailed, insisting that the tribe move to Kwatso·wi·s (on Deep Pass), and then he sent word to the Otsosat that his people wanted peace. To ensure the peace, the two groups began making arrangements for the Ahousaht war chiefs to marry Otsosat women.

One Ahousaht war chief felt slighted in these arrangements and, during a visit to the Otsosat, slipped off into the woods near the village, circled around to the back of the houses and was just lining up his sights on an Otsosat chief when two Otsosat warriors who had seen his stealthy departure shot and killed him. Enraged at his attempt at treachery, they dragged his body down to the beach. The other Ahousaht visitors knew nothing of the dead war chief's plans, and were quite unprepared. The Otsosat set the corpse up by driving a yew stake up its anus and the other end into the sand. They slashed open the belly so that the guts fell out onto the sand,

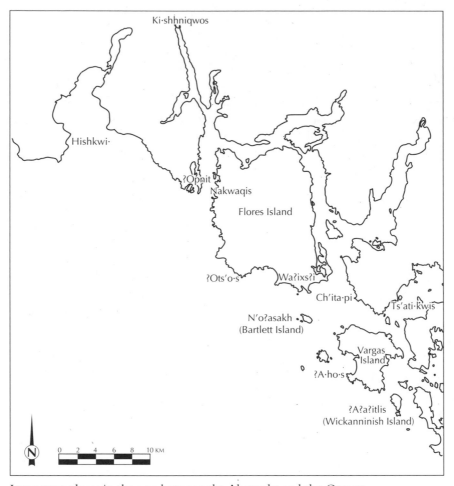

Important places in the war between the Ahousaht and the Otsosat.

and cut off the chief's private parts and tied them to his nose through the perforation in the septum. M'okwina ordered his people not to fight (most of them were unarmed).

The Ahousaht Declare War, the Otsosat Strike First

The Ahousaht returned to their village and held another meeting. Some chiefs still spoke against war – it would cause hard times, for fishermen would not dare go out. Hayo·pino·ɫ lay on the floor covering his head with his blanket. When the others had finished speaking, he rose to his feet and addressed M'okwina.

"Where is your younger brother?" (The Ahousaht, being a small group, were all closely related, and their chiefs addressed each other as siblings).

"Did he have a decent burial when he died? No, he's still out there on the beach, propped up on a stake, with his guts all over the beach. You can do what you want to. I am going to make war if I have to do it alone, hiding by myself in the bush like a wild dog to kill every Otsosat I can catch."

Then the war chiefs Tłihisim and Qami·na stood up singing their war songs and calling for others to go with them. All but M'okwina's immediate family offered to go. So they sent word to the Otsosat that they were coming to fight.

In reply, the Otsosat sent a war party out in their war canoes. They cut off a party of seven Ahousaht fishermen, killed them and displayed their heads to their relatives. (This now made the score 14 dead to 2, a rather inauspicious beginning for the Ahousaht after their declaration of war.) The Otsosat considered attacking their enemy by a mass landing on the beach, while displaying the latest collection of heads, but deferred it because the racks for drying herring roe formed an obstacle that would give the Ahousaht time to establish a defence. They never got another chance quite as good.

The Ahousaht Train for War

Hayo·pino·ł selected 40 young men, and began a period of ritual training that was to last eight months. They remained abstinent this whole time. During the waxing of the moon, they climbed Catface Mountain (Ch'ita·pi), where they sang war songs and prayed for success. Hayo·pino·ł would stand singing while the young men threw dried leaves and gravel (representing buckshot) at him. They also did more practical sorts of training, practising landings on hostile beaches and going through manoeuvres in which they shot at each other with blunt, untipped arrows. One version of the war states that during these mock skirmishes one of the young men could not dodge an arrow that came at his face with enough force to go clear through his cheek and into his mouth. His comrades-in-arms laughed hilariously, and a Tla-o-qui-aht man who was watching shook his head and said, dourly, that it was a poor way to prepare for war.

Hayo·pino·ł's mother, a Nutchatlaht woman, seems to have been the party's chief adviser in magical protection, for she gave them numerous medicines to make them invulnerable. When they were ready, she had them send a half Otsosat messenger with the false news that the Ahousaht were giving up the war, and were moving away from their village at Ts'ati·kwis. The tribe moved instead to the village site on Deep Pass (also called Ch'ita·pi). Some Otsosat scouted Tsati·kwis and found it abandoned.

The entire Otsosat tribe moved to their sites along the outside of Flores Island, to begin fishing for halibut. An Ehattesaht relative of the Ahousaht came by and saw them there, and carried the word to the

Ahousaht. Hayo·pino·ł himself is said to have scouted the foe and found a large camp of them on Bartlett Island (*N'oʔasakḥ*). He assembled his men for a last dry run, and that night they launched their war canoes.

The Ahousaht Attack on Bartlett Island

Off the southeast tip of Bartlett Island (the Otsosat camp was on the northwest tip), the canoes drew up in a line and Hayo·pino·ł called for Qami·na to proceed up the west side and attack, while he and the other chiefs went around to the eastern side of the island. His plan was to capture many woman and children as slaves. Qami·na was put out, for he felt that he would have to carry the brunt of the attack, but he went anyhow.

Qami·na launched his pre-dawn attack in the dark and led his party through the channels until he found the Otsosat men sleeping in their canoes (to make an early start for the fishing grounds). The war canoes laid alongside the fishing craft and began killing and beheading the sleepers.

One fisherman awoke as his companion was being slain, and seeing no escape possible, said, "Be careful don't kill me. I'm Tsiłtsiḥok of the Tla-o-qui-aht."

The warriors called one of their party who was half Tla-o-qui-aht. He looked at the man in the canoe and said, "He is Tsiłtsiḥok, the Otsosat."

So they killed him. They caught another young man, who told them, "Now you don't have to worry, for you have got the principal Otsosat war chief. I am Qimishtop."

He was really Qimishtop's younger brother, who hoped to stall the attackers long enough for the real Qimishtop to escape. While they killed him, his brother the war-chief dove into the water and began to swim to Flores Island. But one of other canoes overtook him, and the warriors in it speared him in the water as though he were a seal.

Only one of the fishermen escaped: he swam to Flores Island (about 2.5 km), and ran along the beaches warning the rest of the Otsosat, who all assembled at ʔOts'os, near Rafael Point. Qami·na's party seems to have spent some time pursuing Otsosat who took to the water. Finally they assembled at the camp with 78 heads. The chief's party came down from the woods back of the camp with only two slave women, who they killed on the beach.

Only one of the Ahousaht force was wounded, one of Qami·na's men who got a spear through the throat. Qami·na pulled out the spear, and they tried to stop the bleeding with herbs and medicines. The wounded man's brother fainted, watching him, and Qami·na stood over him and said, "Don't faint, sit up like a man. We're fighting the Otsosat now."

At day-break the war party displayed the 80 heads to the Otsosat. The war chiefs of the Otsosat danced on the beach to show they were not afraid. Both forces were apparently careful to keep out of range.

On their way home the Ahousaht encountered a Tla-o-qui-aht chief returning from Nootka Sound. He seemed to have thought the Ahousaht were on one of their practise runs for he said to them, mockingly, "Let's see what you caught last night."

Qami·na stood up holding a head in either hand, and one in his mouth, and the other Ahousaht chiefs held up heads and spat on them. The Tla-o-qui-aht sat down in his canoe and covered his face with his blanket for shame. He was friendly to the Otsosat and was sure the Ahousaht could not win the war. He turned back to the Otsosat village. There, lying-to off shore, he had his war chief call out, "Otsosat, show me how many fighting men you have left."

The Otsosat warriors came down to the beach. There were still many of them: according to who's telling the story, either 400, 600 or 800.

The Otsosat Attack Fails at ?A·hos, Vargas Island

The Tla-o-qui-aht hated the Ahousaht, so he went ashore and assembled the Otsosat chiefs, and said, "I'll give you a place on Wickaninnish Island (?A?a?itlis) to hide your war canoes."

He anticipated an Ahousaht move from Ch'ita·pi, and he was right. When the war party returned, the Ahousaht moved to ?A·hos on the outer side of Vargas Island, expecting a retaliatory attack to be aimed immediately at Ch'ita·pi. The Otsosat made their plans, and moved a large force stealthily to ?A?a?itlis, where they hid. They selected four young men, gave them pitch torches, and landed them on the southeast tip of Vargas Island. The four were to cut through the woods, and watch till the Ahousaht men set out in their canoes, then rush the village and burn the houses.

Nearing ?A·hos in their canoes, the Otsosat war party first tried to cut off some Ahousaht fishermen who had shoved off just before they came around the point. This seems to have been another missed opportunity, because the Ahousaht apparently did not expect an attack so soon at ?A·hos and were unprepared. Several Ahousaht on the beach saw the Otsosat canoes but thought they were a Tla-o-qui-aht whaling party. They watched them for some time in the dim light of early morning until they realized that the canoes were in pursuit of the fishermen who were frantically paddling for their lives.

Hayo·pino·ł had eight loaded muskets in his canoe, but as he was launching it to go to the rescue, M'okwina tipped it over. Hayo·pino·ł recovered his muskets and set out, drying them as his crew overhauled the Otsosat. Meanwhile, the Otsosat had overtaken one or more canoes, killing several men and pulling two women into the war chief's craft. The Ahousaht pursuit came up. Hayo·pino·ł opened fire (he had someone reloading for him). He followed the big canoe with the captive women, picking off the occupants one by one. By mischance he killed one of the women. The Otsosat had ordered the other woman to plug the shot holes in the canoe, which she pretended to do, but really let the canoe take water.

Meanwhile, on shore, the four young men with the torches, who were supposed to create a diversion and demoralize the counterattack, had got lost in the woods. The Otsosat force gave up the attack and scattered, taking flight in earnest. The Otsosat's complex operation might have worked had the young men not got lost. The main force was to make a feint to draw a counterattack, incidentally knocking off the fishermen. When the houses started burning, they expected the counterattack to waver, with some canoes turning back to shore, and in confusion the Otsosat would be able to strike decisively.

Hayo·pino·ł continued pursuing the crippled canoe. When there were but four men left he shouted to the captive woman to jump into the water. She did so and Hayo·pino·ł passed her, calling to the canoe following him to pick her up. Hayo·pino·ł closed in on the canoe and finished off its occupants. As he came alongside, an Otsosat man who lay feigning death leaped up with a spear and hurled it point blank at Hayo·pino·ł. But the chief's uncle thrust out a piece of elk-hide armour as a shield, deflecting the spear. Then Hayo·pino·ł killed the last man in the canoe.

The other Ahousaht pursued the remaining Otsosat canoes with no success. The fleeing canoes swung outside the islets, and in trying to cut them off, the Ahousaht lost ground among the reefs and islets flanking Flores Island, so their foe escaped, beached their canoes, and ran along the beach to warn their people.

The Ahousaht Attack on Flores Island

The Ahousaht made a fire on the beach to dry their guns, and made plans. They resolved on an all-out frontal attack on the Otsosat to press the advantage of their victory. They knew the Otsosat would be assembled expecting them.

The war chiefs told them not to falter under any circumstances. "If you see your elder brother die, don't stop or go back; leave him and close the enemy. Don't run straight. Run up the beach dodging and zigzagging."

So the force proceeded to the village where the Otsosat were gathered, a place called Waʔixsʔi. When they beached their canoes, an Otsosat sharpshooter began to pick them off from a hiding place in a tree, and the rest of the tribe, in the houses, were holding their fire, so the charge bogged down. A party of Ahousaht went around behind the houses, where they fired, shouted and blew wolf whistles, but the Otsosat refused to be stampeded.

The Ahousaht chiefs devised a new scheme. Two volunteers ran along the beach to draw the enemy fire, and the Otsosat wasted many shots firing at them. Others dashed up to each house before the defenders could reload, squatted with their backs to the walls and lifted the house boards, wrenching them loose to expose the defenders. A fire party opened fire as soon as the boards came away. Most of the men who ripped the boards loose were shielded by the boards that fell on top of them. The plan worked – the Ahousaht shot all the people they could see in the houses.

The Otsosat were not done yet, though, and began to rally. Chief M'okwina of the Ahousaht, broke from cover and ran the length of the beach to a vantage point on the far end, where he threw himself down happy to find himself intact. (The pressure of Ahousaht public opinion seems to have finally impelled him to take an active part.) To the chief's surprise, a young slave he had brought with him flopped down beside him, having followed him under the enemy guns. He asked the slave why he would risk his life this way and the boy answered, "because if you had been killed, your people would have killed me anyhow." A group of Otsosat now counterattacked, trying to drive the Ahousaht off the beach. M'okwina shot three of them, breaking up the attempt. Finally, the Otsosat burst out of the backs of the houses and fled into the woods. The Ahousaht burned and looted the houses, and then departed. They had lost just four men and had a number of wounded.

Raid and Counter-Raid

The Otsosat held a meeting. Some were in favour of abandoning their territory on the outer coast, which they thought would stop the fighting. But those who had lost close relatives insisted on carrying on. They moved to Nakwaqis on the west shore of Flores Island. From there, after a time, they sent a war party to Ts'ati·kwis, where they found and killed eight Ahousaht men and one woman.

The Ahousaht resolved on immediate retaliation. They sent scouts to Nakwaqis, who returned reporting the Otsosat were all there, and had set deadfalls along all the trails leading to the site through the bush, so the beach was the only possible approach. A sizeable party landed on the beach one morning at dawn. The Otsosat must have had sentinels out who gave warning, for the attack was met and driven off. No Ahousaht were killed, but a considerable number were wounded. It's unknown what damage they inflicted on the Otsosat.

Meanwhile, Tliho·małni, the Otsosat war chief who had killed the

Ahousaht chief then set his body on a stake and disfigured him, died of a wound received in the fight at Waʔixsʔi (he seems to have been the sniper in the force). Relatives at Clayoquot told the Ahousaht where the body was buried. They found it and brought it home, announcing that Tlihoˑmałni was coming to visit, set it up on the beach on a stake driven up its anus, and disfigured it amid a general feeling of satisfaction.

The Otsosat had retreated to a place called ʔOpnit (on the east side of Openit Peninsula). Ahousaht scouts reported it was palisaded and surrounded with deadfalls. They did not relish the idea of another frontal attack, so they carried on a war of attrition, watching for and picking off fishermen from time to time. Meanwhile, they laid claim to and began using the various fishing stations of the Otsosat. It is not clear just how these were parcelled out among the Ahousaht chiefs. Hayoˑpinoˑł got the places at Herbert Arm because he had personally killed the entire family of chiefs who had owned it, but it also seems that the first chief, M'okwina, got a lion's share of the remainder because of his rank, even though he had been opposed to the war and had taken little part in it, except for the attack on Waʔixsʔi. He may also have claimed these places by virtue of his kinship to the Otsosat chiefs.

After some time, the Ahousaht seem to have become careless. The Otsosat survivors, who were still numerous, were living up at the head of Shelter Arm and on the Megin River. They fitted out four big canoes. Only three or four men paddled in each canoe, while the rest hid in case they met a foe. They did meet a Tla-o-qui-aht man and told him they were going outside after clams. That night they attacked an Ahousaht village, killing many, among them the third chief, Kwatyiˑtsmałni. But they made the grievous error of hacking the chief's wife to bits – she was a Tla-o-qui-aht woman.

The son of Kwatyiˑtsmałni fled to Tsatikwis, where he informed Hayoˑpinoˑł of the raid. Hayoˑpinoˑł was as eager for trouble as ever. He and Qamiˑna assembled a force and proceeded directly to the Otsosat village on Megin Lake. In a surprise attack, they killed many of the enemy, and took alive a chief of rank equal to that of the slain Kwatyiˑtsmałni. They told him they would spare his life if he performed certain degrading actions. He did so, and after ridiculing him, they clubbed him to death.

In the fall both tribes got ready to dry salmon. The Otsosat began to come out of their refuges, and the Ahousaht caught and slew a number of large parties of fishermen.

Tla-o-qui-aht Involvement

And now new troubles were in store for the Otsosat. The Tla-o-qui-aht relatives of chief Kwatyiˑtsmałni's wife resolved to avenge her slaying. In the spring, a large party of them proceeded in small canoes with their women to ʔOpnit, where they found a large camp of Otsosat. The Tla-o-qui-aht said they were on their way to H̲ishkwi to purchase dried fish, because their stores had run short. They spent the night feasting and visiting with the Otsosat.

Early in the morning, the leader of the Tla-o-qui-aht climbed on the roof of one of the houses and shouted, "Tla-o-qui-aht women, get up now to cook our breakfast!"

This was the signal that had been arranged. The warriors fell on their unsuspecting hosts and butchered the entire camp.

On their way home the avengers passed the Ahousaht village and displayed the heads they had taken. They shouted, "Look, Qami·na, here are some of the wild ones you couldn't catch!"

Qami·na came down to the beach to reply, "I haven't given up pursuing them. I am resting a bit. I'm going to war again and will kill all the rest of them."

Last Attacks and the Fall of the Otsosat.

Qami·na now seems to have taken the initiative and organized a war party. The vengeful Hayo·pino·ł, if he did not aid Qami·na, at least put no obstacle in his way. Qami·na's war party found a group of Otsosat at a place called Ki·shh̲niqwos in Sidney Inlet. The warriors crept up close to the houses under cover of darkness, and as they lay peering in through the cracks in the walls, scouting the situation, they heard a young Otsosat say, as he hefted a spear he was making, "I'd like to see that great Qami·na. I'd run this into his guts and take his head."

This was too good a cue to miss. Qami·na bounded in the doorway shouting, "Here I am! Now go ahead and kill me!"

The young man dropped his spear in fright and Qami·na killed him, while his force swarmed into the house and killed all the Otsosat, except for a few who bolted into the woods. They took some captives, among them a chief who owned the west shore of Flores Island from Rafael Point to Nakwaqis.

Returning to Ahousaht, they brought the young chief out on the beach, and called on M'okwina to come down and kill him, so that he would be owner of this territory. M'okwina refused, for the young chief was a kinsman of his. Qami·na sang his war song, then brained the young Otsosat. He then claimed the beach line. But later, the Ahousaht gave the salvage and sealing rights to this area to the Tla-o-qui-aht, probably to the chiefs who instigated the treacherous attack on ʔOpnit.

By now there were only a few Otsosat left. Some of them moved away, going to live with kin, either at H̲ishkwi, or down around Barkley Sound

(they no longer dared to go to Clayoquot). A few assembled in a fortified
site on a knoll, and let it be known they were in an impregnable position,
and that they planned to assemble the scattered warriors and attack the
Ahousaht. Hayo·pino·ł looked the situation over. He seems to have profited by past experience. He mapped an operation with alternative plans
of attack. The primary plan, which they tried first, was the obvious one of
landing on the beach and rushing the position. This did not come off, for
the Otsosat fort commanded the beach too efficiently, and the slope was
too steep for an effective charge. The Ahousaht were unable to establish a
beachhead.

Hayo·pino·ł withdrew his forces and proceeded with the alternative
plan. He sent marksmen to places some distance on either side of the
fort on the high hill behind it. Then he detailed a party of axemen to fell
the biggest trees on the hill behind the fort. Several trees fell but caused
only minor damage to the fort, which the defenders were able to repair,
but finally one huge tree came crashing down and stove in the whole
rear wall. The tree itself is said to have killed several Otsosat; the marksmen killed many more. M'okwina once more took an active part in the
war, most likely to vindicate himself in his people's eyes after his refusal to
murder his kinsman. He distinguished himself in this battle by picking off
an Otsosat chief at 100 metres – a remarkably long range for the weapons
of the time, cheap trade muskets crammed full of buckshot. Only a few of
the Otsosat managed to escape through the woods.

This ended of the war. Practically exterminated, the Otsosat no longer
offered a threat to the Ahousaht, who took the territory, and soon came
to be one of the important tribes of the coast. The few surviving Otsosat
scattered among other tribes,

The last incident, some time after, occurred when Qami·na, while on a
visit to Barkley Sound, encountered a man named ?Ani·s, one of the four
Otsosat who had been sent to burn the village at ?A·ho·s. Qami·na seized
the man and brought him to Ahousaht. In the morning, he had some men
bring the captive to the beach, while he stood on a house roof and called,
"Ahousaht, come out, I have something to show you."

When the people turned out, Qami·na told them they had a visitor,
?Ani·s, who once had planned to burn their houses. They began to mock
?Ani·s, but he stood silent, refusing to plead or to perform degrading acts
for his life. An Ahousaht threw a stone, hitting him in the head and killing
him. The Ahousaht spread the story that he had died of shame and fright.

The Ahousaht people who recounted the history of this war perhaps
do injustice to the war chief Qami·na's energy and Hayo·pino·ł's military
genius, because they attribute their victory to superior fire power. Though
the Ahousaht were a much smaller group than the Otsosat, they had more

firearms and ammunition, which they had obtained from their relatives, the Mowachaht. Hayo·pino·ł's Nutchatlaht kinsmen also helped them on several occasions.

Chief Earl Maquinna George, the perceptive Ahousaht historian, provides more details of the war's aftermath (2003:50-52):

Before the Otsosat Nation was completely exterminated, some fled south. They showed up in places like Tacoma and Seattle in Puget Sound on the American side, and on the outer coast, on the Olympic Peninsula, at Neah Bay. In later years they showed up singing songs, the same songs that came from their tribe. So, the Ahousaht knew that they had survived and pursued some of them as far as Neah Bay. They told the Neah Bay people, the Makah, "You give us the Otsosat people. If you don't, we'll kill you, too." So the Neah Bay people killed the Otsosat refugees and gave the heads to the Ahousaht. The Neah Bay people feared the Ahousaht.

Through this war the Manhousat people who were living in Hot Springs Cove and Hisnit between Hesquiat and Hot Springs Cove were spared, although they were part of the Otsosat Nation. The Ahousahts spared them on account of the many close relationships between the tribes. In return, the Manhousat gave up all their rights and the land on that side.

Much of the traditional land holdings of the Ahousaht date from this war. Access to many important resources – good cedar trees, salmon streams, herring spawning beds, and whales and seals – resulted from this war.

THE COMING OF THE EUROPEANS

History, in the narrow sense of written accounts of past happenings, begins for the Whaling People only in the last quarter of the 18th century, when the Europeans arrived. The written records carry European and American points of view, of course, and reflect their interests and concerns. They give much reference to the native peoples, their ways and the dealings with them, but at the same time, the observations are selective and sometimes reveal a misunderstanding of the Whaling People, as may be expected when peoples with such differing cultural backgrounds meet. The First Nations side of the story of contact is oral, of course, and poorly known. Even if the written records are interpreted in the light of general knowledge of Whaling People's lives, native history still remains only partially known and essentially written from a foreign viewpoint. Keeping in mind this basic slant in the historical record, we briefly review the earthshaking and dire consequences of the coming of Europeans for the Whaling People.

The first European to visit the territory of the Whaling People was Juan de Fuca, a Greek pilot in the service of Spain whose actual name was Apostolas Valerianos. Juan de Fuca sailed north from Mexico in 1592 in a caravel to search for the mythical Straits of Anian that were thought to cut through North America. According to the uncertain but fascinating record taken from him in Venice by an English mariner, Michael Lok (1906:415-21), Juan de Fuca entered the strait now named after him, noting the rock pinnacle of Fuca's Pillar at the entrance at Cape Flattery. Also named after him is San Juan Harbour on the north side of the entrance to the strait. "He went on Land in divers places," writes Lok, "and ... saw some people on Land, clad in Beasts' skins." Juan de Fuca may have met some Whaling People among other natives, but he gives no more details, and the first certain instance of European contact comes almost two centuries later.

In early August 1774, the first well-documented contact between Whaling People and Europeans occurred when the Spanish explorer Juan Jose Perez Hernandez, in the frigate *Santiago*, dropped anchor at the entrance to the inlet he named Surgidero de San Lorenzo ("Roadstead of St Lawrence"), now known as Nootka Sound (Cook 1973:54-65). Perez was on his way back to Mexico from a voyage north to counter reported Russian expansion and had already contacted the Haida at the north end of their islands. Three canoes of Whaling People approached while the *Santiago* was still several kilometres offshore but did not make contact. After Perez anchored off Friendly Cove at the entrance of Nootka Sound, three canoes came in the evening but kept their distance. Contact was established at dawn the next day, August 9, and the momentous event has been recorded by Father Tomas de la Pena (1891:132) on board the *Santiago* in his diary:

> The crew began to get the long boat over the side, in order to go ashore. While this was doing there arrived fifteen canoes with about a hundred men and women. We gave them to understand that they might draw near without fear, and presently they came to us, and began to trade with our people what they had brought in their canoes, which consisted only of the skins of otter, and other animals, hats of rushes, painted and with the crown pointed, and cloths woven of a kind of hemp, having fringes of the same, with which they clothe themselves; most of them wearing a cape of this material. Our people bought several of these articles, in exchange for old clothes, shells that they had brought from Monterey and some knives.... In the possession of these people were seen some implements of iron and copper.

Then the wind picked up, and the *Santiago* was getting blown ashore because the anchor was not holding. Perez hurriedly cut his anchor chain and sailed away. But the fateful relations with Europeans had begun, and within a century they would completely upset the traditional life of the

Whaling People. The Mowachaht thought the *Santiago* was a floating house, a *mamałn'i*, and Europeans have ever since been known by this name among the Whaling People.

The iron and implements possessed by the Mowachaht were likely obtained by trade through intermediate groups. The copper may have been local copper. Iron might have been more recent, coming from Spanish California or from the Russians in the Aleutians, if not English fur traders east of the Rockies. Shipwrecks and driftwood from Asia could have also provided some iron. Whatever the source, iron tools must have aided woodworking from some time before direct European contact. Perez's expedition furnished fresh iron in knives, cloth clothing and albalone shells (from Monterey) of the prized beautiful blue not found to the north. The native side exchanged cedar-bark robes, hats and furs, including those of Sea Otters, which was not fully appreciated by the Spaniards. Sea Otter fur became highly valued as a result of the next visit of Europeans four years later.

On May 29, 1778, British Captain James Cook arrived in in the calm waters of Mowachaht territory after following Perez's directions. His ships, *Resolution* and *Discovery*, were soon surrounded by over 30 Mowachaht canoes. He first called the inlet King George's Sound, but soon changed this to Nootka, thinking it to be the native name because of a misunderstanding explained by Estevan José Martinez (I.H. Wilson in Mozino 1970:67): "Captain Cook's men, asking by signs what the port was called, made for them a sign with their hand, forming a circle and then dissolving it, to which the natives responded 'Nutka'." *No·tkak* or *no·txak* means "circular, spherical" (Sapir and Swadesh 1939:276). Of the historic day when the British first arrived among the Whaling People, several eyewitness accounts exist, thanks to the passion for keeping journals in those times. James King, second lieutenant of the *Resolution*, wrote (Beaglehole 1967:1394):

> The first men that came would not approach the Ships very near &
> seemed to eye us with Astonishment, till the second boat come that had
> two men in it; the figure & actions of one of these were truly frightful;
> he worked himself into the highest frenzy, uttering something between a
> howl & a song, holding a rattle in each hand that at intervals he laid down,
> taking handfuls of red ocre & birds feathers & strewing them in the Sea;
> this was follow'd by a Violent way of talking, seemingly with vast difficulty
> in uttering the Harshest, & rudest words, at the same time pointing to the
> Shore, yet we did not attribute this incantation to threatening or any ill
> intentions towards us; on the contrary they seem'd quite pleas'd with us;
> in all the other boats, someone or other act'd nearly the same as this first
> man did.

King also described the famous Chief M'okwina, which means "stone" (Beaglehole 1967:1394):

One boat larger than the rest had as we suppos'd a Chief in her, or at
least a man whose dress & manners were singular; he stood upright in the
middle of the boat, & upon a plank laid across to be more conspicuous;
the naked parts of his body & arms were painted with a red, & his face
with a whitish paint, his head was wildly ornament'd with large feathers.

This M'okwina has become a well-known historical figure since he was
a top-ranking chief at Friendly Cove when it was the focal point of the
Spanish-English struggle for dominance in the northeastern Pacific and
since he seized the American trading vessel *Boston* whose armourer or
blacksmith, John Rodgers Jewitt, became his slave for three years and left a
vivid first-hand picture of the chief (Jewitt 1807, 1815).

Unlike Perez, who only stopped overnight and left without landing, Cook
stayed for a month overhauling his ships and interacting with the people.
From the hospitable reception given by the Mowachaht, Cook named Yuquot, the place of their summer village, Friendly Cove. The journals of the
expedition provide the first extensive description of the Whaling People.
Much trading went on, of course, and the main native product exchanged
was fur, including over 300 Sea Otter skins. Here is a small part of the fine
early description of the Whaling People by Captain James Cook to indicate
the outlook of the European as contact between the two peoples began
(Beaglehole 1967:312, 321-23).

They are a docile, courteous good natured people, but very passionate and
quick in resenting what they look upon as an injury, and like most other
passionate people as soon forget it. I never found that these fits of passion
went farther than the parties concerned either with us, or among themselves, the others never troubled themselves about it, nay often with so
much indifferency as if they did not see it. I have often seen a man rave and
scould for more than half an hour without any one taking the least notice
of it, nor could any one of us tell who it was he was abusing. In these fits
they act as if they wanted words to express their passion. At other times
they are commonly grave and silent and are by no means a talkative people.
In trafficking with us, some would betray a navish disposition and would
make off with our goods without making any return, if there was an opportunity, but in general the most of them acted with different principles.
Their passion for iron and brass and indeed any kind of metal was so strong
that few could resist the temptation to steal it whenever an opportunity offered. They were not, like many of our friends of the south sea islands who
rather than be idle would steal any thing they could lay their hands upon
whether it was of use to them or no, these touched nothing but what was
valuable in their eyes. Linen and such like things were perfectly secure and
might and did hang out ashore without any one to look after them night
and day, so little did they value either our clothes or cloth....

As to edge tools I never saw any other than a chisel and a knife, both of iron; the chisel is a long flat piece of iron, fitted into a handle of wood, a stone serves for a mallet a piece of fish skin for a polisher. I have seen some of these chisels that was eight or ten inches long and three of four inches broad, but in general they were smaller. The blades of the knives were crooked some thing like a pruning knife and what we could call the back was made the edge of the knife. The most of them were about the breadth and thickness of an iron hoop and were certainly of their own forming and helving. Iron, which they call *Seekemaile*, a name they also give to Tin and all white metal, seemed to be neither scarce nor plenty with them, but we could never learn how or where they came by it. Some account of the Spaniards having visited this coast was published before I left England, but it could not all come from them; it was too common, in too many hands and too well known for them to have had the first knowledge of it so late as the year 1774 or '75. Indeed one cannot be surprised at finding iron with all the Nations in America since they have been so many years in a manner surrounded by Europeans and other Nations who make use of iron, and who knows how far these Indian Nations may extend their traffic one with another....

Copper, which they call *iaio'pox*, a name they also give to brass, was the only metal except iron we saw among them; this, if we did not mistaken them, is found in-country, but it must be very scarce as they had but little of it.

Of the Government and Religion of these people, it cannot be supposed that we could learn much; there are such men as chiefs who are distinguished by the name or title of *Acweeks* and to whom the others are in some measure subordinate, but I believe the authority of each extends no farther than over the family to which he belongs. These *Acweeks* were not always elderly men from which I concluded that this title came to them by inheritance.

I saw nothing that could give us the least insight into their Religion, unless the figures before mentioned, called by them *Kulmina*, were really idols as some imagined, but as they frequently mentioned the word *Acweek* when they spoke of them they might probably be Monuments of some of their ancestors, and even in this case they may pay them some kind of adoration. But all this is mere conjecture, as may well be supposed, for we never saw any kind of homage paid them and we could gain nothing from information, as we had learnt little more of their language than to ask the names of things and the two simple words yes and no.

Was I to name them as a Nation I would call them *Wak'ashians*, from the word *Wak'ash*, which they frequently made use of, but rather more with the women than the men; it seemed to express applause, approbation and friendship; for when they were satisfied or well pleased with anything they would with one voice call out, "*Wak'ash Wak'ash*".

THE SEA OTTER DECADES

The Sea Otter trade flourished from 1785 to about 1825 and, as for other post-contact periods, the details come from the European side alone. The Spanish, British and Americans all took part and their complicated records give only limited mention of the Whaling People, giving the impression that this period was mainly a European-American affair.

Sailing on from Friendly Cove, Captain Cook came to his untimely end in Hawaii. His expedition carried on and, in China, discovered that the Sea Otter pelts from the Mowachaht fetched high prices. Word leaked out and the Spaniards were the first to follow in the trade, but with furs from California. Not until 1785 did the first commercial Sea Otter trader reach Friendly Cove. Captain James Hanna came from China aboard the *Harmon*, an English merchantman of only 60 tons.

The different tone of the trader's attitude to the native people was strikingly demonstrated in the special salute accorded on the *Harmon* to M'okwina when he visited. Hanna set off gunpowder under M'okwina's chair. Later, to avenge the insult to their chief, the Mowachaht attacked the little ship in open daylight, but the assault by canoes was repulsed by gunfire. The two groups re-established a trade relationship, mostly because of the Mowachaht's desire for civilized products, like iron for tools. Hanna took his haul of Sea Otters to China where he sold it for more than 20,000 Spanish dollars, then a tremendous sum (Cook 1973:101).

He came again a year later, along with several other British traders licensed by the East India Company. One of these traders, James Strange, performed acts of British possession on the coast that would have hardly been welcomed by the native inhabitants had their intent been understood. He landed sailors that were sick with scurvy at Friendly Cove and had them start a little gardening for the first attempt at agriculture on the west coast of Vancouver Island. He also left his surgeon, John Mackay, to winter with Chief M'okwina. Mackay had with him a musket and two pistols, insisted upon by M'okwina. Strange had convinced the natives that only a European could use a firearm by overloading a musket and having poor M'okwina fire it to his painful surprise (Strange 1928:33). Mackay had a hard winter, being made to adopt native ways, even to taking a wife and suffering through a food shortage along with the Mowachaht. When picked up by Captain Barkley, the first trader in the following year, Mackay had no European clothing or firearms.

As the Sea Otter trade suddenly blossomed, contact with the *Mamaɫn'i* (Europeans) and their ways quickly intensified with new developments each year, particularly at Friendly Cove. Chief M'okwina profited by his constant association with Europeans and grew in power in relation to other chiefs of the Mowachaht confederacy, while the Mowach'ath as a group became richer and stronger. The Tla-o-qui-aht also profited from this contact, with Wi·kinanish, their leading chief, supplying the most Sea Otter pelts. Both groups received the particular attention, for instance, of the enterprising John Meares who, with William Douglas commanding a second ship, arrived in 1788 hoping to establish trading forts. His ships brought along 50 Chinese, mainly craftsmen like smiths and carpenters (Meares 1967:2–3). Also aboard was M'okwina's brother, Quelequem, returning from China as the first world traveller of the Whaling People.

At Friendly Cove, Meares constructed a palisaded two-storey building and a schooner, the *North West America*, with the permission of M'okwina, who watched with great interest. Meares sailed south, trading and exploring well past Cape Flattery, visiting Wi·kinanish in particular and also meeting the aggressive Makah Chief Tatoosh of the cape. Later he sent a longboat to trade into Juan de Fuca Strait but at its entrance, in Port San Juan, the Pacheedaht attacked, wounding three men with arrows (Robert Duffin in Meares 1967: App. 4). Evidently the Pacheedaht were allied with the Cape Flattery groups who were at war with Wi·kinanish's Tla-o-qui-aht, whose influence extended as far as but not over the Pacheedaht.

Meares lent firearms to M'okwina for a successful attack on neighbours to the north, the muskets being returned with ammunition exhausted. He wrote a valuable early description of the Whaling People, including their political groupings and rough population figures. He also reported cannibalism being practiced by some chiefs, the accredited example being M'okwina; this was abhorred by the Europeans and likely soon declined (see McDowell 1997). Meares's verbal picture of the grand house of Wi·kinanish suggests the mightiness of the Tla-o-qui-aht at the time (1967:138–39):

> On entering the house, we were absolutely astonished at the vast area it
> enclosed. It contained a large square, boarded up close on all sides to the
> height of twenty feet [six metres], with planks of an uncommon breadth
> and length. Three enormous trees, rudely carved and painted, formed the
> rafters, which were supported at the ends and in the middle by gigan-
> tic images, carved out of huge blocks of timber. The same kind of broad
> planks covered the whole to keep out the rain; but they were so placed as
> to be removed at pleasure, either to receive the air and light, or let out the
> smoke. In the middle of this spacious room were several fires, and beside
> them large wooden vessels filled with fish soup. Large slices of whale's
> flesh lay in a state of preparation to be put in similar machines filled with

water, into which the women, with a kind of tongs, conveyed hot stones from very fierce fires, in order to make it boil – heaps of fish were strewed about, and in this central part of the place, which might very properly be called the kitchen, stood large seal-skins filled with oil, from whence the guests were served with that delicious beverage.

The trees that supported the roof were of a size that would render the mast of a first-rate man of war diminutive, on a comparison with them; indeed our curiosity as well as our astonishment was on its utmost stretch, when we considered the strength that must be necessary to raise these enormous beams to their present elevation; and how much strength could be found by a people wholly unacquainted with mechanic powers. The door by which we entered this extraordinary fabric, was the mouth of one of these huge images, which, large as it may be supposed, was not disproportioned to the other features of this monstrous visage. We ascended by a few steps on the outside, and after passing this extraordinary kind of portal, descended down the chin into the house, where we found new matter for astonishment in the number of men, women and children who composed the family of the chief, which consisted of at least eight hundred persons. These were divided into groups, according to their respective offices, which had their distinct places assigned them. The whole of the building was surrounded by a bench, about two feet [60 cm] from the ground, on which the various inhabitants sat, ate and slept. The chief appeared at the upper end of the room, surrounded by natives of rank, on a small raised platform, round which were placed several large chests, over which hung bladders of oil, large slices of whale's flesh, and proportionable gobbets of blubber. Festoons of human sculls, arranged with some attention to uniformity, were disposed in almost every part where they could be placed, and were considered as a very splendid decoration of the royal apartment.

The skulls would come from warfare, in which the Tla-o-qui-aht excelled. Meares found them less influenced by Europeans than the Mowachaht and more industrious. He noted in mid June (1967:149): "At break of day, without regard to the weather, the village was always empty; the men were employed in killing the whale, hunting the Sea Otter, or catching fish, and the women were in the woods, gathering berries, or traversing the sands and rocks in search of cray and shellfish." In trading ability they were outstanding as well, with Meares admitting (1967:148), "In all our commercial transactions with these people, we were, more or less, the dupes of their cunning." The Sea Otter trade produced good profits for both sides while it lasted.

Off Cape Flattery, Meares was met by many canoes of Makah who were "of a much more savage appearance" and visited by Chief Tatoosh, "so surly and forbidding a character we had not yet seen" (1967:153). Yet the fierce warriors, about 400 of them, sang a pleasing song in unison for Meares and his men.

In the fall of 1788, as Meares left, the first American traders, John Kendrick and Robert Gray, arrived to winter in Nootka Sound. The Mowachaht were in their winter village far inside the sound. The Americans, backed by Boston merchants, became known as *Postin?ath* and the British *Kincho·ch?ath* (King George men). The Spanish came from Mexico to affirm their claim to the North Pacific and, in May 1789, Estévan José Martínez anchored in Friendly Cove, which he had visited with Juan Perez in 1774. Soon after, ships backed by Meares arrived to establish trading colonies, only to be seized by Martínez. As the Spanish and British clashed, the Mowachaht moved several kilometres away. Martínez built a fort and set up two batteries of cannons. He seized several British ships, including one commanded by James Colnett. Chief Quelequem, M'okwina's brother who had been close to Meares, protested from a canoe, shouting at Martinez on his quarterdeck, calling him *p'ishaq* ("bad") and a *k'apshitł* ("thief"). The hot-tempered Spaniard reacted sharply and later recorded it in his diary entry for July 13, 1789 (Mozino 1970:75): "Irritated by such slanderous (degrading) words, I took a rifle ... and aiming it, I misfired. One of my sailors who saw this took another and fired it, from which shot Keleken [Quelequem] died."

The incident shocked the Mowachaht. M'okwina moved away to stay with Wi·kinanish. In the fall the Spanish left, recalled to Mexico, but returned in 1790 under Francisco de Eliza. A garrison of 75 soldiers arrived, under Captain Pedro Alberni, who developed a good farm with assorted crops, livestock and poultry. Alberni also won back the friendship of M'okwina, who had returned, by having his troops sing a song flattering the chief (Mozino 1970:78). Relations improved, and when the very hospitable Juan Francisco Bodega y Quadra came as commander in 1792, M'okwina and other chiefs became regular dinner guests and vied for his esteem. That year the Spanish also occupied Núnez Gaona (Neah Bay) for four months, erecting a fort, but relations with the Cape Flattery people were not friendly. When an officer alone in the woods was killed, the Spaniards retaliated by destroying an approaching canoe with a cannon shot. Violent incidents mounted between the Whaling People and the traders, whether Spanish, British or American, straining relations. But the Sea Otter trade flourished.

The acquisition of guns changed the lives of the Whaling People. One notable early supplier of firearms was an American, Captain John Kendrick of the *Lady Washington*. In 1791 he traded muskets to buy rights to pieces of land for trading purposes because, unlike Spain and England, the United States had no imperial claim in the region. He furnished more than 200 muskets to Chief Wi·kinanish of the Tla-o-qui-aht for territorial rights around their main village at Opitsat (Mozino 1970: 16,71). He also

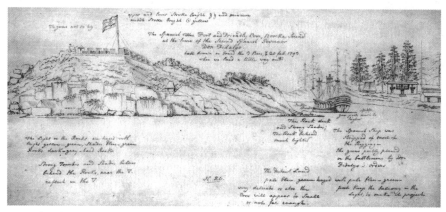

Spanish Fort and Command House, Yuquot, August 15, 1792.
Sigismund Bacstrom drawing; RBCM PDP01329.

supplied the Mowachaht with firearms for rights to several places around
Nootka Sound. The Mowachaht and Tla-o-qui-aht used their new weapons
to become two of the most successful groups in the warfare of the period.
They passed on guns to their allies who, in turn, succeeded in war. Warfare
appears to have been heightened by the acquisition of firearms during the
last decade of the 18th century and the first half of the 19th, a glorious period for the well-armed groups, but terrible for their enemies without guns,
many of whom were virtually exterminated.

Europeans introduced even more deadly menaces to the Whaling People – new diseases for which the natives lacked resistance. Venereal diseases
were introduced by around 1790 and even if not fatal could contribute to
population decline when they caused sterility (Archer 1973:27-28). There
must have been repeated deadly epidemics that have gone unrecorded. The
population crashed precipitously following contact with Europeans and
Americans as among so many other native peoples in the New World. Between 1775 and 1881 the northern and central Nuu-chah-nulth lost two-
thirds of their population (Boyd 1990:145). So-called civilization was hardly
a blessing.

Sea Otter traders reported several attacks against them by the Whaling
People. In February 1792, Wi·kinanish threatened to attack Kendrick's as-
sociate, Captain Robert Gray, in the fortified building the American traders had erected opposite Opitsat village (Howay 1925:294-5). The summer
before, Gray's Hawaiian cabin boy had deserted and the captain had imprisoned a chief, lured aboard his ship *Columbia*, to exchange for his servant.
After the threat from Wi·kinanish, Gray reputedly destroyed Opitsat by cannon fire before leaving. Returning in late May, Gray repulsed an attack on

the *Columbia* in Nasparta Inlet, as described by John Boit, the young fifth mate (Howay 1925:296):

> At 10 in the evening, a number of large canoes full of People, came into the Cove. They halted near some rocks about pistol shot from the Ship, and there waited about ten minutes, during which time all hands was brought to arms, upon deck in readiness to receive them. Soon after a large War Canoe, with about 25 Indians, paddled off for the ship. We hail'd them, but they still persisted, and other canoes was seen following, upon which Capt Gray order'd us to fire, which we did so effectually as to kill or wound every soul in the canoe. She drifted along side, but we pushed her clear, and she drove to the north side of the cove, under the shade of the trees. 'Twas bright moon light and the woods echoed with the dying groans of these unfortunate Savages..

Cannons kept the Europeans and Americans in their ships superior to the Whaling People in their canoes. When a hostile native party masked its intentions and surprised a ship's crew in hand-to-hand combat, it could win. In the Sea Otter-trade period such successful attacks were carried out twice by Whaling People. Native captures of ships caused much excitement, and both victories by Whaling People were celebrated for generations afterward.

On March 22, 1803, Chief M'okwina captured the *Boston*, an American trading vessel, at Yuquot. The armourer and the sailmaker survived to serve as useful technicians for the Mowachaht. The armourer, John Jewitt, in his unvarnished account (1807:3-4), clearly describes the attack and the immediate precipitating circumstances:

> We arrived at Nootka Sound the 12th of March, 1803, all in good health, and anchored five miles [8 km] above the village in twenty-five fathoms [45 metres] water, muddy bottom. On the 13th the natives visited us and brought a plenty of fresh salmon, which we purchased for fish hooks, &c.; on the 14th our people were on shore getting wood and water for the ship. The natives visited us with a number of canoes round the ship. On the 15th Maquina, the chief, came on board to dine with the captain. After dinner the captain made him a present of a double-barrel musket, with which he was much delighted and went on shore.
>
> Our people were employed as usual until the 19th when the chief came on board with nine pair of ducks as a present to the captain, and told him that the double-barrel musket was not a good one, and that he had broken the lock. Captain Salter was very angry, called him a liar, took the musket and threw it down into the cabin and called for me to know whether I could repair it. I told him it could be done. The chief returned to the shore very angry and the captain took no more notice of what had happened.

Boston Cove, about 1914. Edward S. Curtis photograph; RBCM E-00858.

On the 22d the chief came again on board, looked much pleased, had a mask over his face and a whistle in his hand, seemed to be very happy and asked the captain when he should go to sea; "Tomorrow," replied the captain. "Why don't you go to Friendly cove and fish, there is a plenty of salmon there," said the chief. The captain spoke to Mr Deliewser, and they agreed it would be a very good plan to get a stock of fresh salmon to carry to sea. After dinner the captain dispatched the jolly boat with Mr Deliewser and nine of the people. The steward was on shore washing the captain's clothes; the sail maker was in the main hatches at work upon the sails; I was in the steerage cleaning muskets. About one hour after the boat was gone, the captain told Mr Ingraham to hoist in the long boat, saying there was a sufficient number of the natives on board to help to pull at the tackle falls to hoist her in. When they had got the boat half way up, the natives seized every man at his tackle fall, and likewise the Captain, threw him over the quarter deck, and killed every man with his own knife taken out of his pocket, and cut off their heads and threw their bodies overboard.

Hearing a noise on deck, I went and got my musket, and ascending the stairs was caught by the hair of the head, by three of the natives. One of them struck at me with an axe and cut my forehead, but having short hair, their hands slipt and I fell down the steerage. The Chief, observing it was me, told them all not to hurt me, for that I was an armourer and would be of great service to him. He ordered his people to shut over the hatch. I lay in a most deplorable state; being very weak in consequence of the loss of blood from the cut I received.

After they had taken the ship they sent canoes off to murder the men that were in the boat, which they soon did and brought their heads, which amounted to twenty-five, on board, and placed them in a right line on the quarterdeck. I remained below four hours, when the Chief called me on deck and told me that I must be his slave and work for him and he would spare my life, to which I of course assented. The Chief led me on the quarter deck and told me to look at all the people's heads that were placed in a line, at which sight the reader can better imagine what were my feelings than I can describe them.

Previous offenses against the Mowachaht by other traders to Yuquot were part of the reason for M'okwina's attack. According to Jewitt (1815:111-12), the chief noted a Captain Tawnington's theft of his furs while he was away, Martínez's killing of four chiefs, and Captain Hanna's deadly firing of canoes for the theft of a chisel. The *Boston* carried 3,000 muskets and fowling pieces, according to Jewitt (1815:14). Within a few days of the capture of the *Boston*, canoes came visiting from about 20 other Whaling People tribes to share in the spoils. At one feast M'okwina gave away over a hundred muskets, enhancing his prestige by his grand potlatching (Jewitt 1815:41-45). No doubt the captured arms and ammunition made the Mowachaht and their allies invincible in war. At the same time ships came to avoid Yuquot as a place no longer friendly. An unexpected side result of the capture of the *Boston* was Jewitt's invaluable historical account.

Eight years later, in 1811, another American trading vessel, the *Tonquin*, from John Jacob Astor's enterprise on the Columbia River, was captured, apparently by the Tla-o-qui-aht. Except for an interpreter who brought the news to Astoria, there were no survivors. Published accounts vary in detail, but Washington Irving's (1836:64-69) is perhaps the best.

The *Tonquin* set sail from the mouth of the river on the 5th of June. The whole number of persons on board amounted to twenty-three. In one of the outer bays they picked up, from a fishing canoe, an Indian named Lamazee, who had already made two voyages along the coast, and knew something of the languages of the various tribes. He agreed to accompany them as interpreter. Steering to the north, Captain Thorn arrived in a few days at Vancouver's island, and anchored in the harbour of Neweetee, very much against the advice of his Indian interpreter, who warned him against the perfidious character of the natives of this part of the coast. Numbers of canoes soon came off, bringing Sea Otter skins to sell. It was too late in the day to commence a traffic, but Mr M'Kay, accompanied by a few of the men, went on shore to a large village to visit Wicananish, the chief of the surrounding territory, six of the natives remaining on board as hostages. He was received with great professions of friendship, entertained hospitably, and a couch of Sea Otter skins was prepared for him in the dwelling of the chieftain, where he was prevailed upon to pass the night.

In the morning, before Mr M'Kay had returned to the ship, great numbers of the natives came off in their canoes to trade, headed by two sons of Wicananish. As they brought abundance of Sea Otter skins, and there was every appearance of a brisk trade, Captain Thorn did not wait for the return of Mr M'Kay, but spread out his wares upon the deck, making a tempting display of blankets, cloths, knives, beads and fish-hooks, expecting a prompt and profitable sale. The Indians, however, were not so eager and simple as he had supposed, having learned the art of bargaining and the value of merchandise from the casual traders along the coast. They were guided, too, by a shrewd old chief named Nookamis, who had grown grey in traffic with New England skippers, and prided himself upon his acuteness. His opinion seemed to regulate the market. When Captain Thorn made what he considered a liberal offer for an otter skin, the wily old Indian treated it with scorn, and asked more than double. His comrades all took their cue from him, and not an otter skin was to be had at a reasonable rate.

The old fellow, however, overshot his mark, and mistook the character of the man he was treating with. Thorn was a plain, straightforward sailor, who never had two minds nor two prices in his dealings, was deficient in patience and pliancy, and totally wanting in the chicanery of traffic. He had a vast deal of stern but honest pride in his nature, and, moreover, held the whole savage race in sovereign contempt. Abandoning all further attempts, therefore, to bargain with his shuffling customers, he thrust his hands into his pockets, and paced up and down the deck in sullen silence. The cunning old Indian followed him to and fro, holding out a Sea Otter skin to him at every turn, and pestering him to trade. Finding other means unavailing, he suddenly changed his tone, and began to jeer and banter him upon the mean prices he offered. This was too much for the patience of the captain, who was never remarkable for relishing a joke, especially when at his own expense. Turning suddenly upon his persecutor, he snatched the proffered otter skin from his hands, rubbed it in his face, and dismised him over the side of the ship with no very complimentary application to accelerate his exit. He then kicked the peltries to the right and left about the deck, and broke up the market in the most ignominious manner. Old Nookamis made for shore in a furious passion, in which he was joined by Shewish, one of the sons of Wicananish, who went off breathing vengeance, and the ship was soon abandoned by the natives.

When Mr M'Kay returned on board, the interpreter related what had passed, and begged him to prevail upon the captain to make sail, as, from his knowledge of the temper and pride of the people of the place, he was sure they would resent the indignity offered to one of their chiefs. Mr M'Kay, who himself possessed some experience of Indian character, went to the captain, who was still pacing the deck in moody humour, represented the danger to which his hasty act had exposed the vessel, and urged him to weigh anchor. The captain made light of his councils, and pointed to his cannon and fire-arms as a sufficient safeguard against naked savages. Further remonstrances only provoked taunting replies and sharp altercations. The day passed away without any signs of hostility, and at night the captain retired as usual to his cabin, taking no more than the usual precautions.

On the following morning, at daybreak, while the captain and Mr M'Kay were yet asleep, a canoe came alongside in which were twenty Indians, commanded by young Shewish. They were unarmed, their aspect and demeanour friendly, and they held up otter skins, and made signs indicative of a wish to trade. The caution enjoyed by Mr Astor, in respect to the admission of Indians on board of the ship, had been neglected for some time past; and the officer of the watch, perceiving those in the canoe to be without weapons, and having received no orders to the contrary, readily permitted them to mount the deck. Another canoe soon succeeded, the crew of which was likewise admitted. In a little while other canoes came off, and Indians were soon clambering into the vessel on all sides.

The officer of the watch now felt alarmed, and called to Captain Thorn and Mr M'Kay. By the time they came on deck, it was thronged with Indians. The interpreter noticed to Mr M'Kay that many of the natives wore short mantles of skins and intimated a suspicion that they were secretly armed. Mr M'Kay urged the captain to clear the ship and get under way. He again made light of the advice; but the augmented swarm of canoes about the ship, and the numbers still putting off from shore, at length awakened his distrust, and he ordered some of the crew to weigh anchor, while some were sent aloft to make sail.

The Indians now offered to trade with the captain on his own terms, prompted, apparently, by the approaching departure of the ship. Accordingly, a hurried trade was commenced. The main articles sought by the savages in barter, were knives; as fast as some were supplied they moved off, and others succeeded. By degrees they were thus distributed about the deck, and all with weapons.

The anchor was now nearly up, the sails were loose, and the captain, in a loud and peremptory tone, ordered the ship to be cleared. In an instant a signal yell was given: it was echoed on every side, knives and war-clubs were brandished in every direction, and the savages rushed upon their marked victims. The first that fell was Mr Lewis, the ship's clerk. He was leaning, with folded arms, over a bale of blankets, engaged in bargaining, when he received a deadly stab in back, and fell down the companionway.

Mr M'Kay, who was seated on the taffrail, sprang on his feet, but was instantly knocked down with a war-club and flung backwards into the sea, where he was despatched by the women in the canoes.

In the meantime, Captain Thorn made desperate fight against fearful odds. He was a powerful as well as resolute man, but he had come upon deck without weapons. Shewish, the young chief, singled him out as his peculiar prey, and rushed upon him at the first outbreak. The captain had barely time to draw a clasp-knife, with one blow of which he laid the young savage dead at his feet. Several of the stoutest followers of Shewish now set upon him. He defended himself vigorously, dealing crippling blows to right and left, and strewing the quarterdeck with the slain and wounded. His object was, to fight his way to the cabin, where there were fire-arms; but he was hemmed in with foes, covered with wounds, and faint with loss of blood. For an instant he leaned upon the tiller wheel, when a blow from behind, with a war-club, felled him to the deck, where he was despatched with knives, and thrown overboard.

While this was transacting upon the quarterdeck, a chance medley fight was going on throughout the ship. The crew fought desperately with knives, handspikes, and whatever weapon they could seize upon in the moment of surprise. They were soon, however, overpowered by numbers, and mercilessly butchered.

As to the seven who had been sent aloft to make sail, they contemplated with horror the carnage that was going on below. Being destitute of weapons, they let themselves down by the running rigging, in hopes of getting between decks. One fell in the attempt, and was instantly despatched; another received a death-blow in the back as he was descending; a third, Stephen Weekes, the armourer, was mortally wounded as he was getting down the hatchway. The remaining four made good their retreat into the cabin, where they found Mr Lewis, still alive, though mortally wounded. Barricading the cabin door, they broke holes through the companionway, and, with the muskets and ammunition that were at hand, opened a brisk fire that soon cleared the deck.

Thus far the Indian interpreter, from whom these particulars were derived, had been an eye-witness of the deadly conflict. He had taken no part in it, and had been spared by the natives as being of their race. In the confusion of the moment he took refuge with the rest, in the canoes. The survivors of the crew now sallied forth, and discharged some of the deck guns, which did great execution among the canoes, and drove all the savages to shore.

For the remainder of the day no one ventured to put off to the ship, deterred by the effects of the fire-arms. The night passed away without any further attempt on the part of the natives. When the day dawned, the *Tonquin* still lay at anchor in the bay, her sails all loose and flapping in the wind, and no one apparently on board of her. After a time, some of the canoes ventured forth to reconnoitre, taking with them the interpreter. They paddled about her, keeping cautiously at a distance, but growing more and more emboldened at seeing her quiet and lifeless. One man at length made his appearance on the deck, and was recognised by the interpreter as Mr Lewis. He made friendly signs, and invited them on board. It was long before they ventured to comply. Those who mounted the deck met with no opposition; no one was to be seen on board; for Mr Lewis, after inviting them, had disappeared. Other canoes now pressed forward to board the prize; the decks were soon crowded, and the sides covered with clambering savages, all intent on plunder. In the midst of their eagerness and exultation, the ship blew up with a tremendous explosion. Arms, legs, and mutilated bodies were blown into the air, and dreadful havoc was made in the surrounding canoes. The interpreter was in the main chains at the time of the explosion, and was thrown unhurt into the water, where he succeeded in getting into one of the canoes. According to his statement, the bay presented an awful spectacle after the catastrophe. The ship had disappeared, but the bay was covered with fragments of the wreck, with shattered canoes, and Indians swimming for their lives, or struggling in the agonies of death; while those who had escaped the danger remained aghast and stupified, or made with frantic panic for the shore. Upwards of a hundred savages were destroyed by the explosion, many more were shockingly mutilated, and for days afterwards the limbs and bodies of the slain were thrown upon the beach.

The inhabitants of Neweetee were overwhelmed with consternation at this astounding calamity, which had burst upon them in the very moment of triumph. The warriors sat mute and mournful, while the women filled the air with loud lamentations. Their weeping and wailing, however, was suddenly changed into yells of fury at the sight of four unfortunate white men, brought captive into the village. They had been driven on shore in one of the ship's boats, and taken at some distance along the coast.

The interpreter was permitted to converse with them. They proved to be the four brave fellows who had made such desperate defence from the cabin. The interpreter gathered from them some of the particulars already related. They told him further, that, after they had beaten off the enemy, and cleared the ship, Lewis advised that they should slip the cable and endeavour to get to sea. They declined to take his advice, alleging that the wind set too strongly into the bay, and would drive them on shore. They resolved, as soon as it was dark, to put off quietly in the ship's boat, which they would be able to do unperceived, and to coast along back to Astoria. They put their resolution into effect; but Lewis refused to accompany them, being disabled by his wound, hopeless of escape, and determined on a terrible revenge. On the voyage out, he had repeatedly expressed a pre-sentiment that he should die by his own hands; thinking it highly probable that he should be engaged in some contest with the natives, and being resolved, in case of extremity, to commit suicide, rather than be made a prisoner. He now declared his intention to remain on board of the ship until daylight, to decoy as many of the savages on hoard as possible, then to set fire to the powder magazine, and terminate his life by a signal act of vengeance. How well he succeeded has been shown. His companions bade him a melancholy adieu, and set off on their precarious expedition. They strove with might and main to get out of the bay, but found it impossible to weather a point of land, and were at length compelled to take shel-ter in a small cove, here they hoped to remain concealed until the wind should be more favourable. Exhausted by fatigue and watching, they fell into a sound sleep, and in that state were surprised by the savages. Better had it been for those unfortunate men had they remained with Lewis, and shared his heroic death: as it was, they perished in a more painful and protracted manner, being sacrificed by the natives to the names of their friends with all the lingering tortures of savage cruelty. Some time after the death, the interpreter, who had remained a kind of prisoner at large, effected his escape, and brought the tragical tidings to Astoria.

Sea Otters became so depleted that the trade practically ended in the sec-ond decade of the 19th century. Though the odd pelt continued to be taken, trading ships stopped coming. With that interest gone, world commercial attention no longer focussed on the Whaling People, and there was a lull in European and American interest for several decades. The people remained independent and traditional life continued vigorously despite the undoubt-ed onset of the great decline in population due to disease and intensified warfare. Civilized technological introductions, like abundant metal tools and firearms, brought some changes, but these were incorporated well enough into the lives of the Whaling People so that it enjoyed a general continuity. Small schooners continued to trade along the coast. Fort Victoria, found-ed in 1843 by the Hudson's Bay Company, was outside Whaling People's territory but was visited, especially by the nearby southern groups. The first half of the 19th century might be regarded as a "contact-traditional" phase, when the lives of the Whaling People continued essentially as before, with adjustments made to elements introduced from the outside world.

COLONIAL DEVELOPMENT
AND LOSS OF INDEPENDENCE

In the second half of the 19th century British colonial development began on Vancouver Island, which led to the passing of independence and vigour for native life on the west coast. Because of the Cariboo gold rush in 1849, with its sudden influx of outsiders (largely American), the British established the Colony of Vancouver Island to extend its influence over whole island. The new colonial government considered the Whaling People troublesome because of their warlike habits, so it imposed a political order backed by naval gunboats. The population of the Whaling People was already much reduced by introduced diseases, making the tribes much weaker than in the initial stages of European contact. The Nuu-chah-nulth seemed to have escaped the major smallpox epidemics of the mid 19th century, but an outbreak in 1853 spread from the Makah to the Pacheedaht (Boyd 1999:302). The devastating 1862 outbreak was not recorded among them, but in 1875 smallpox was reported from Barkley Sound, Hesquiat, Nootka Sound and Kyuquot. Oral traditions collected in 1964 from Chief Louis No·kmis at Bamfield refer to a "before 1875" smallpox outbreak in Barkley Sound (Arima et al. 1991:212).

British domination of the Whaling People developed in stages from the mid 19th century, generally without opposition, although native sentiment opposed it. But this development was not entirely without conflict, which indicates that a fundamental clash of interests existed. In 1859, William Bamfield, a trader who operated around Barkley Sound, was made the first Indian agent for the west coast. Three years later he disappeared, perhaps accidentally, perhaps not. European settlement of the land did not develop extensively on the west coast because of its general unsuitability for farming, but in the Alberni Valley, inland at the end of an inlet, a British settlement became established in August 1860, with the arrival of two armed vessels, *Woodpecker* and *Meg Merrilies*, manned by about 50 men under Gilbert Malcolm Sproat (1868:1-4). His account of how he forced the Tseshaht to move, recorded in the following conversational exchange, throws into sharp relief the confrontation between European and native interests:

> Near a pretty point at one side of the bay, where there was a beach shaded by young trees, the summer encampment of a tribe of natives was to be seen. Our arrival caused a stir, and we saw their flambeaux of gunsticks flickering among the trees during the night.
>
> In the morning I sent a boat for the chief, and explained to him that his tribe must move their encampment, as we had bought all the surrounding land from the Queen of England, and wished to occupy the site

of the village for a particular purpose. He replied that the land belonged
to themselves, but that they were willing to sell it. The price not being
excessive, I paid him what was asked – about twenty pounds worth of
goods – for the sake of peace, on condition that the whole people and
buildings should be removed next day. But no movement was then made,
and as an excuse it was stated that the children were sick. On the day following the encampment was in commotion; speeches were made, faces
blackened, guns and pikes got out, and barricades formed. Outnumbered
as we were, ten to one, by men armed with muskets, and our communica-
tions with the sea cut off by the impossibility of sailing steadily down the
Alberni Canal (the prevalent breeze blowing up it), there was some cause
for alarm had the natives been resolute. But being provided, fortunately, in
both vessels with cannon – of which the natives at that time were much
afraid – they, after a little show of force on our side, saw that resistance
would be inexpedient, and began to move from the spot. The way in
which these people move their encampments will be described further
on. Two or three days afterwards, when the village had been moved to
another place, not far distant, I visited the principal house at the new
encampment, with a native interpreter.

"Chiefs of the Seshahts," said I on entering, "are you well; are your
women in health; are your children hearty; do your people get plenty of
fish and fruits?"

"Yes," answered an old man, "our families are well, our people have
plenty of food; but how long this will last we know not. We see your ships,
and hear things that make our hearts grow faint. They say that more King
George men will soon be here, and will take our land, our firewood, our
fishing grounds; that we shall be placed on a little spot, and shall have to
do everything according to the fancies of the King George men."

"Do you believe all this?" I asked.

"We want your information," said the speaker.

"Then," answered I, "it is true that more King George men" – as they
call the English – "are coming: they will soon be here; but your land will
be bought at a fair price."

"We do not wish to sell our land nor our water; let your friends stay in
their own country." To which I rejoined: "My great chief, the high chief of
the King George men, seeing that you do not work your land, orders that
you shall sell it. It is of no use to you. The trees you do not need; you will
fish and hunt as you do now, and collect firewood, planks for your houses,
and cedar for your canoes. The white man will give you work, and buy
your fish and oil."

"Ah, but we don't care to do as the white men wish."

"Whether or not," said I, "the white men will come. All your people know that they are your superiors; they make the things that you value. You cannot make muskets, blankets or bread. The white men will teach your children to read printing, and to be like themselves."

"We do not want the white man. He steals what we have. We wish to live as we are." [...]

A civilized settlement was now formed almost immediately in their midst, and the natives stared at the buildings, wharves, steam engines, ploughs, oxen, horses, sheep and pigs, which they had never seen before.

The superior power, when provoked, of the King George men was demonstrated not long after, in 1864. An Ahousaht chief, Cap-chah (possibly *Kapcha·*, "the water spirit"), captured a small trading schooner called the *Kingfisher*, killing its crew of three then plundering and burning it in the old style. Soon after, Rear-Admiral Joseph Denman was despatched with HMS *Sutlej* and HMS *Devastation* to Ahousaht territory around Flores Island. The British called the capture of the *Kingfisher* a crime and the attackers murderers, but the Ahousaht generally resisted the authority of British gunboats — this affair typified the basic confrontation between the colonists and the Whaling People. Denman first went up North Arm behind Flores Island in the *Sutlej* to "Sik-tok-kis" village to demand the surrender of the 12 principals thought responsible for the attack on the *Kingfisher*. The natives in the bush would not answer the landing party, but one man who came down to speak was captured for questioning. The *Devastation*, under Commander John Pike, went to Herbert Arm where all communication was again refused, and a large group in war paint fired on the ship and its boat.

Having found out from the captured man the whereabouts of those who attacked the *Kingfisher*, Admiral Denman then proceeded with punitive actions, including a land strike, described in his despatch to the governor of Vancouver Island (Sproat 1868:198-200).

On the 3rd, I proceeded up Herbert Arm to Moo-yah-kah, and sent the *Devastation* to Sik-tok-kis, Obstruction Inlet and Shelter Arm, with orders to destroy the canoes, houses, &c., but not to fire on the natives unless resistance were offered. Commander Pike was not able to find the village in Destruction Inlet, but he destroyed Sik-tok-kis and those in Shelter Arm, and found in each of them letters, accounts and other property belonging to the *Kingfisher*.

I sent Friday [his interpreter] into Moo-yah-kah under the ship's guns. A number of Indians came down and held a palaver with him on the beach; he told them that I promised not to fire on them if they delivered up to me all the men concerned in the affair of the *Kingfisher*, three of whom I knew were there. Friday, on his return, brought a message from the Indians saying, that if I wanted the men I might come and take them, if I destroyed the village they would soon build it up again, and that if I attempted to touch the canoes they would shoot every man who came near the shore.

I then ordered a heavy fire to be opened on the village, and on the surrounding bush, to clear it, and sent in the gigs to complete the destruction of the village under cover of the ship's guns, and those of the heavy boats.

Notwithstanding these precautions, several musket shots were fired at the boats, but were instantly silenced by the boats' guns, which replied to them with admirable precision.

Having brought away twelve canoes, I returned to Matilda Creek, where the crime had been perpetrated, and the *Kingfisher* sunk, and next day I ordered the remains of the village, which had been abandoned and dismantled, to be fired.

The *Devastation* had, on the 5th, been ordered to destroy the villages of Cap-chah in Cypress Bay and Bedwell Arm, and to bring away his canoes. The boats were fired on, and Cap-chah himself was seen at the head of his men in Cypress Bay, dressed in one of the blue jackets that had formed a part of the *Kingfisher*'s cargo.

Finding that all these measures had failed to bring the Ahousahts to terms, I was obliged to strike a yet more severe blow, directed against Cap-chah himself in such a manner as to impress the Indians more deeply with the idea of our power, and with the impossibility of escaping punishment due for such atrocities against unoffending White traders.

On the morning of the 7th of October, forty seamen, and thirty marines, with one Ahousaht and six Khal-oh-quaht Indians, to act as guides, were landed at White Pine Cove in Herbert Arm, under the command of Lieutenant Stewart, the senior lieutenant of this ship.

Lieutenant Stewart was ordered to march across the trail to Trout River (about three miles [5 km]), and to endeavour to seize Cap-chah and any of his people.

The Ahousahts were completely taken by surprise, and they must have been all captured in the temporary huts that they had constructed in the bush, had not the alarm been given by the barking of a dog when our party was within a few yards of them. The Indians had barely time to rush into the thick cover, from whence they opened a heavy fire upon our men, which was returned with such effect, that in a few moments they took flight, leaving ten men dead. Cap-chah himself, who did not fight, was wounded in two places as he ran away.

Denman reported that 69 canoes were destroyed and about 15 men killed, without injury on his side. Having inflicted punishment, he reduced his demand for the surrender of murderers from 12 to 6, although items from the *Kingfisher*, found at every place destroyed, implicated the tribe at large. Denman gave the tribe a month to comply with his new demand, but

Ma·qtosi·s, a village of the Ahousat, 1886.
Frederick Dally photograph; RBCM AA-00837.

at the end of that period he did not return. Because of this, the Ahousaht believed they had won and Cap-chah added to his reputation as the great chief who had defied the King George warships (Sproat 1868:201-02). Since the destruction of the canoes kept them from laying-in the winter food supply, the Ahousaht dispersed to live with friendly tribes until the spring fishing began. They built new canoes and considered the loss of "half a war-canoe" of men inconsequential. So ended the outstanding instance of the use of civilized military force against the Whaling People. Indecisive as it may appear, Denman's punitive expedition in effect marked the end of independent native power on the west coast.

In 1871, British Columbia joined Canada and both governments thought about assigning First Peoples in the province to reserves. The Dominion required that the size of a reserve be calculated on the basis of eight acres (3.25 hectares) per family; the province considered that excessive. In 1875-76, a joint federal-provincial commission was set up to allocate reserves on no fixed basis for acreage. The Nuu-chah-nulth reserves were mostly defined in the early 1880s by a commissioner, Peter O'Reilly, who sought to limit them as much as possible (see Fisher 1977:155, 165, 199-206).

In 1913 another commission was formed to make further adjustments. It found the West Coast Agency to have 150 reserves totalling 12,385.1 acres (5,012.1 ha) for 1,683 persons, giving 7.36 acres (2.97 ha) per capita. It added 14 reserves but cut off 600 acres (243 ha) from a Huu-ay-aht reserve and 240 acres (97 ha) from a Tseshaht reserve, leaving a total of 12,200.25 acres (4,937.27 ha). The reductions were made because the reserves were regarded as being "in excess of the reasonable requirements of the Indians" (Canada 1916 4:851). In the second half of the 20th century, the restoration of such reserve lands had become an issue. More important is the fact that aside from certain limited tracts, such as around Victoria harbour, the land in British Columbia has never actually been surrendered by the First Peoples in treaties. A settlement of the "Land Question" will have to be reached eventually but will take time.

The southernmost Whaling People, the Makah and the Ozette, came under the political sway of colonists somewhat differently than those in British Columbia. On the American side of Juan de Fuca Strait, these groups signed a treaty in 1855 with the US government, represented by Governor Isaac Stevens, ceding their territories except for reservations. The Qw'idishch?a·?tx came to be called Makah in this treaty, because that was the name that Governor Stevens's Clallam interpreter used for them (Colson 1953:76). The Makah Reservation took in several main villages of the region and, at 20,539 acres (8,312 ha; Colson 1953:34), was twice as large as all the Whaling People reserves in British Columbia put together. The Makah population was 654 in 1861, declining to a little over 400 for much of the first half of the 20th century before rising again. A tribal census in July 1999 identified 1,214 enrolled members with 1,079 living on the reservation (Renker n.d.).

FALLING UNDER FOREIGN INFLUENCE

From the middle of the 19th century, the Whaling People have been subjected to ever-increasing European influence and the corresponding loss of their traditional culture. In the last decades of the 20th century, they changed their ways toward those of Western civilization, yet they remain indigenous Whaling People. About the middle of the 19th century, the European claim to the west coast became more than the planting of flags and drawing of map boundaries; they now began to actually take over the country. While most of the west coast was not occupied by homesteaders because of its general unsuitability for farming, the settlement of other areas in the west and the development of towns and cities affected the Whaling People. Increased demand for native products stimulated trade. Employment in the colonial economy also developed.

The production of dogfish oil (from the Spiny Dogfish, a species of shark) developed into a major economic activity about 1850. The oil was used principally to lubricate saw-mill machinery that was then helping to meet the great demand for construction lumber (Swan 1870:32). It could also be burned in lamps. To the natives it was a food (Drucker n.d. 14:137),

although whale and seal oil were more esteemed. The flesh that was left after boiling to produce the oil was made into fish cakes, according to Charles
Jones Sr. Much of the late spring and summer was spent catching dogfish with the sharp-angled hook and harpooning the huge Basking Sharks,
whose liver held much oil. The oil trade brought the Whaling People a
flood of European goods, like blankets, metal tools, guns, flour, pilot biscuits,
beans, rice, molasses and sugar (Jones and Bosustow 1981:27), not to forget
alcohol. Dogfish oil was a leading trade item for the Whaling People over
the second half of the 19th century (Sapir and Swadesh 1939:141, Crockford 1996:37).

Following the decline of the Sea Otter, the fur trade continued on a
smaller scale with deer, elk, and smaller furbearers like Mink and Marten,
being furnished to visiting schooners or at trading posts. Some Sea Otters
were still taken – a Nutchatlaht chief in 1874, for example, displayed 29
skins valued at $2,000, and the Hesquiaht in 1881 got about 17, worth $30
to $90 each (Brabant in Moser 1926:21, 104). For four decades, from the
1870s to 1911, another form of maritime fur trade, fur sealing in the Bering
Sea, became a principal pursuit, and except for five seasons between 1890
and 1895, the Whaling People supplied the majority of sealers employed
in this industry (Crockford 1996:7). Some groups became involved later
than others – the Hesquiaht, for example, began sealing in 1889 (Moser
1926:104). In 1893, ten Makah-owned sealing schooners participated in the
hunt (Murray 1988:156).

Men shipped out on schooners for months at a time (Jones and Bosustow 1981:35), their sealing canoes stacked in racks on board. On the sealing
grounds they hunted through the long summer days, using the traditional
two-pronged harpoon, from the canoes that were equipped with oars, sail
and compass. In the summer of 1884, 17 Hesquiaht men killed 1,400 seals,
getting $2 for each but having to pay for board (Moser 1926). Sealing was
glamorous but dangerous on the foggy and stormy Bering Sea. In about
1905, several schooners went down in a terrible gale, taking away the men
of many Whaling People's families. Whether on this occasion or another, the
small Manhousat group lost most of its men and became integrated into the
neighbouring Ahousaht.

The commercial hunt so depleted the once abundant Northern Fur Seal
that the governments of Great Britain (for Canada), Japan and Russia had
to make a series of agreements to save them from extinction – they finally
banned fur sealing on the open sea in 1911. In 1897 the United States
passed legislation prohibiting Americans from pelagic fur sealing, which
electively blocked Makah hunters from the industry (Whitner 1981:2).

For the Whaling People, their heavy involvement in sealing expanded
their world view. Hunters going to the Bering Sea met aboriginal peoples

of the distant north. A considerable number also visited California, notably San Francisco, and a few even travelled as far as Asia.

The last quarter of the 19th century brought intensified British and American influence upon the Whaling People, including pressures to subordinate and change them. Basic political independence was lost and the foreign ways of European civilization were imposed – and in some cases, willingly adopted – to such a degree that a fundamental break from the ancient whole of traditional life began. The onset of this period, when the Whaling People fell under colonial sway, was aptly marked by a visit along the coast in 1874 by the naval gunboat HMS *Boxer* carrying Superintendent of Indian Affairs Dr I.W. Powel. The Reserve Commission was being set up at the time, which would reduce the territory of the Whaling People to little tracts where they had their houses, along with fishing and hunting stations. Also aboard *Boxer* was a pair of Roman Catholic missionaries, Right Reverend C.J. Seghers, Bishop of Victoria, and Reverend A.J. Brabant, and these would begin the conversion to Christianity (Moser 1926). Aside from the Alberni colony, well to the interior of the island, only four non-aboriginal traders lived in the Canadian sector of the Whaling People's territory. In the American sector, the Makah Reservation was already long established with an Indian Agent and a boarding school.

The Whaling People's population continued to plunge as the deadly new diseases bloomed repeatedly into new epidemics, like the smallpox outbreak noted among the Hesquiaht in 1875 by Rev. Brabant (Moser 1926:39-42). He also records measles and tuberculosis in 1887–88, killing children in particular, and whooping cough in 1898 (Moser 1926:116, 127). Many more unrecorded epidemics no doubt took their toll. Over this lay the more constant population destroying effects of venereal diseases and the debilitating curse of post-contact native life, alcohol (see Foxcroft 1995:239-245). The importance of disease and liquor in undermining the Whaling People can hardly be overstated. Nuu-chah-nulth historian Ki-ke-in (Ron Hamilton), has noted the devastating effects that abuse of alcohol has had (Townsend-Gault 2000:215):

> During the fur-sealing era, numbers of our people went out and got very wealthy indeed, and drank themselves to death. Wasted themselves away.
> Did things with that money that weren't particularly useful, productive, socially redeeming.

Peter Webster (1983:43-44) describes his own struggle with alcohol abuse and his attempts to help his family and community fight against the tragic effects of alcoholism:

> When I became a drunk it was as though I forgot I was in the world. This time of my life is a blank. I simply have no stories to tell about it....
> A sad thing is that even though Jessie and I started late with drinking, I

Manhousat fishermen and sailors from HMS *Boxer* at Hot Springs Cove, September 8, 1874. Richard Maynard photograph; RBCM AA-00546.

feel that most of my children think that we had been drunks since we were children. I now have a hard time with my family trying to help straighten out their lives. I keep telling them of how bad I found drinking. Also remind them of the more than fifty deaths of the people of Marktosis alone since the beer parlours opened to Indians.

Alcohol and drug abuse and attendant suicide by young people continues to be of great concern to the Ahousaht and other Nuu-chah-nulth communities. In July 2007, the Ahousaht community issued ultimatums to people illegally selling alcohol and drugs. They were required to enroll in a treatment program or they would be banned from the community (Lavoie 2007).

Warfare was ended by the establishment of an overruling colonial order that, however distant in the daily life of the Whaling People, was a presence whose awful power, when provoked, might be quickly exerted by sea. With the danger of attacks gone, people could travel more freely and visit new civilized centres for both work and pleasure. Not only did the fur seal hunters go off to the Bering Sea, others went to work in salmon canneries on the Fraser River or the hop fields of Puget Sound. As horizons widened, people broke with tradition in many ways. Things as fundamental as diet and dress changed, often mixing the old with the new. At Hesquiat, Father Brabant noted such changes in 1882 in the following revealing passage (Moser 1926:103):

> Up to a couple of years ago they lived almost exclusively on fish and po-
> tatoes. They availed themselves of the presence of large schools of dogfish
> to make dogfish oil, which they sold to coasting schooners, receiving in
> exchange flour, molasses, tobacco, print-calico and articles of dress. The
> old people who did most of the work objected to the buying of clothing,
> but the young people, especially the women, did not listen to the plead-
> ings of their elders, and invested most of their earnings in the purchase of
> decent wearing apparel. I now made it a rule that no men should come to
> my house unless they wore pants!

When he had first established a mission at Hesquiat in 1875, Brabant had been content to make it a rule that a shirt had to be worn in church (Moser 1926:64).

Missionaries zealously sought to change the Whaling People in matters far more crucial than dress. Brabant has left a good record of the ways he tried to discredit traditional beliefs and observation, being particularly ag-gressive against his prime opponents, the medicine men and chiefs who were the native spiritual leaders. He even organized a native police force to quell opposition, played the younger generation against the conservative elders on issues of conflict, like arranged marriage, and involved Christian equality for all to downgrade the high status of the chiefly (Moser 1926:48, 102, 115). Christianization thus attacked not just the old beliefs and ritu-als but the general social order as well. By the 1890s conversion was well advanced. Catholic missions had been operating at Hesquiat (1875), on east Barkley Sound and at Kyuquot (1880). There was Protestant activity as well, mission schools being established at Nitinat (1893 Methodist) and Ahousaht (1896 Presbyterian).

Traditional native life was suppressed on all fronts. The potlatch, so fun-damental in the workings of Whaling People's society, was attacked by the missionaries, Indian agents and other non-aboriginals, as wasteful, wicked and an obstacle to the introduction of Christianity and civilization among the natives. In 1884 it was officially outlawed, but the law was not enforce-able, and the Whaling People kept on potlatching. More diligently applied were fishing and hunting regulations with patrolling officers. Again such restrictions were widely evaded, but under the new laws, the natives were deemed poachers in using their own ancestral resources. Even the gathering of cedar bark became subject to prosecution as timber companies logged off the land. Particularly devastating was the government's prohibition on use of the salmon weirs that had been so important through the ages in keep-ing the Whaling People free from want. It is said that in the 1890s when the police told the chief of Clo-oose to stop using his hereditary trap in the Cheewat River, he just left it to rot. Even into the second half of the 20th century, First Peoples have been fined or imprisoned for setting nets in their

Summer canoe races in Victoria's Inner Harbour, May 24, 1904. The Nuu-chah-nulth-style 15-metre racing canoes were adaptations of the war canoe. Their beam of less than a metre was just half the width of a war canoe, and they held 11 paddlers instead of the traditional ideal of 20 plus a steersman. These races continue today, but they are now mostly Salish. RBCM A-07202.

rivers. They have been forced to give up their rich patrimony of salmon and other resources of the bountiful west coast.

The 20th century has seen acculturation advance to the point where Whaling People's daily life is highly modernized and their native languages are becoming completely displaced by English. From about the 1890s, Victorian-style family houses began replacing the big traditional communal houses. Livelihood was becoming family-centred as people began to work more for money in the Canadian and American economies. Schooling was introduced to impart civilized learning, often with boarding residence away from home to separate the children from their parents and traditional influence. First to be schooled were the Makah, starting with a day school but, in 1874, going on with a boarding school that isolated the children even more. In 1895 there was a day school again on the Makah Reservation, but older students continued to be sent off to large residential establishments elsewhere.

For approximately 100 years the Canadian government used residential schools to assimilate First Nations children into the larger society and by doing so attempted to eliminate traditional teachings and authority. In 1837 a House of Commons report stated that the needs of aboriginal children would be best served if they were removed from their families. In 1920 "the Indian Act was amended to require that all First Nations children attend a residential school for at least ten months a year" (Buti 2001). Approximately 5,000 Nuu-chah-nulth and Ditidaht children were taken from their homes and isolated in eight different schools in British Columbia. Boarding schools for Whaling People children in Canada included: Christie (1900–1973) and New Christie (1974–83) near Tofino, run by the Roman Catholic Church; Ahousaht (1904–39), run by the Presbyterian/United Church; and Alberni Residential School (1920–73), run by the United Church.

Between 1992 and 1994, the Nuu-chah-nulth Tribal Council inter-viewed 110 former students. They identified several key issues, including: loss of language; emotional, physical, sexual and spiritual abuse; loss of native culture; and loss of self-respect. In 1994, as a result of the research conducted by the Nuu-chah-nulth Tribal Council, the Royal Canadian Mounted Po-lice became aware of 174 victims of abuse at residential schools. See, for example, Art Thompson's eloquent and moving discussion of his traumatic experience at the Alberni Indian Residential School and the negative ef-fects on his life (Black 2000:342-346). Former residential school students identified 102 suspects. In 1995, Judge John Hogarth, in sentencing Arthur Henry Plint, a dorm supervisor and violent pedophile at the Alberni Indian Residential School, stated (Nuu-chah-nulth Tribal Council 1996:viii): "As far as victims of the accused are concerned, the Indian Residential School system was nothing but a form of Institutionalized Pedophilia, and the ac-cused, as far as they are concerned, being children at the time, a sexual terrorist."

Education was not central to residential schools. For example, in 1950 only 10 per cent of aboriginal school-age children had passed beyond Grade 6, whereas 30 per cent of non-aboriginal children had reached that level. Children were only taught for half days, if that, and spent the rest of their time engaged in hard physical work, such as caring for farm animals and doing laundry, basically providing for their own survival (Buti 2001). Using abusive methods, such as punishment for speaking "Indian", these schools produced students fluent in English who were largely estranged from their parents and grandparents because they could not speak their mother tongue, dismissive of their own cultural traditions and ashamed of their heritage. In 2008 Tom Happynook, president of the Nuu-chah-nulth Tribal Council, said (Steel 2008a:1): "Taking children from their homes and sending them off to be raised in institutions by strangers was harmful and abusive and it left deep scars on generations of First Nations people."

In 1998 the United Church of Canada issued an apology to former stu-dents of residential schools, their families and communities (Phipps 1998): "We are aware of some of the damage that this cruel and ill-conceived

Christie School near Tofino, run by the Roman Catholic Church.
RBCM A-07688.

system of assimilation has perpetrated on Canada's First Nations peoples. For this we are truly and most humbly sorry." In 2007 the Canadian federal government announced a compensation package for former residential school students. Called the Indian Residential Settlement Agreement, it includes an initial payment of $10,000 for each person who attended a residential school plus $3,000 for each year attended. The average payment is expected to be $28,000. People who suffered physical and sexual abuse may be entitled to a settlement payment of up to $275,000. The "common experience payment is for loss of language and parenting skills" (*Ha-Shilth-Sa* 2007:34:15:12, 21). But the damage done was more than any monetary payment can compensate for. In 2007, Francis Frank, president of the Nuu-chah-nulth Tribal Council said (*Ha-Shilth-Sa* 2007:34:9:9): "Everyone knows the sad legacy of the schools, and it was far from just educating our people. It was a legalized form of genocide to get rid of the so-called Indian at the time."

As fur sealing ended in the first decade of the 20th century, many aboriginal men turned to commercial fishing as their main employment. In the beginning, the dugout canoes were competitive enough so that outfitting was no problem. Whaling People dominated local salmon fishing in places like Barkley Sound through World War I (Shoop 1972:49). Such economic success ended, however, in the 1920s when the industry grew more competitive over declining fish stocks, with companies consolidating into a few big ones and equipment becoming elaborate and expensive. The 1930s brought the Great Depression with its hard times for almost everyone.

But this decade brought an important positive change for the Whaling People on the American side, when, after three-quarters of a century of suppression, the Makah regained some freedom to manage themselves as a result of the 1934 Indian Reorganization Act of the US Congress, a Tribal Constitution in 1936 and a Tribal Charter in 1937. The Makah were the first in tending to cluster at those reserve villages having the more developed communication links to urban centres, and to then amalgamate with the government-recognized bands of the reserve. The government then dropped the incoming tribes from its official list. This made the Makah a consolidation of several formerly independent villages.

On the Canadian side of Juan de Fuca Strait, the Qwa·ba·dow?a·?atx̱ and Tło·?o·wsa?atx̱ joined the Ditidaht in the mid 20th century. Farther north, past Barkley Sound, the Kelsemat and Manhousaht joined the Ahousaht. The Muchalaht joined their terrible enemies, the Mowachaht, in 1951 and are now known as the Mowachaht-Muchalaht. At the northwest end of the Whaling People's territory the Chickliset amalgamated with the Kyuquot. Traditional groupings were not forgotten as their continued operation in ceremonial affairs shows, but the leading political and economic unit has become the official band or tribe with its corporate interests and dealings with governmental and other external bodies. The Whaling Peoples groups have reformed into "Reserve Tribes" in the 20th century.

Following World War II, fortunes fell again as the commercial fishing industry centralized in Vancouver and Victoria where its processing plants were supplied by larger, refrigerated boats. With few modern boats and keen competitors, the participation of the Whaling People in commercial fishing declined (Shoop 1972:53). As in other poor areas, unemployment benefits and even welfare have become regular features of existence for some. In the 1980s logging continued to provide a good income for many families, but since then the fortunes of the logging industry have declined, producing higher levels of unemployment. On occasion, reserve timber stands are sold, but such transactions furnish only minor revenue, since reserves are small in British Columbia. In the United States the comparatively much larger Makah Reservation has a continuing major source of income from about 8,000 hectares of timber property, ensuring some prosperity.

In the 1980s, although there was talk of land claims in British Columbia, there was no indication that Whaling People's reserves would be increased on Vancouver Island. On the contrary, the previous decade saw the creation of Pacific Rim National Park, showing the federal government's disregard for aboriginal land claims, because the park occupies a great stretch of the all-important coastal strip from San Juan Harbour to Long Beach, almost half the length of the Whaling People's traditional territory. In 2003 an addition of 86.4 hectares to the Esowista Reserve was negotiated with Parks Canada and Indian and Northern Affairs by the Tla-o-qui-aht (Kennedy 2004), but by August 2008, this expansion had still not advanced beyond the planning stage (Dart 2008).

In July 2008, the Amos family of Hesquiaht raised a memorial pole by family member and artist Tim Paul to honour their grandfather, Chief Anayitzachist, and a Mowachaht man named Katkinna. In 1869, these men were accused of murdering members of the crew of the wrecked American barque *John Bright*. They were seized by Royal Marines after their houses were burned and their canoes smashed. Then they were executed by public hanging without fair and proper representation in July of that year. The pole was raised to honour Anayitzachist, who was the chief of the Ho·mi·sath, a group famous as whalers and nicknamed the "Aiehtaka·mła·th" in recognition of their prowess as Sea Otter hunters (see Drucker 1951:236). The pole was temporarily raised at Tofino and then placed permanently at Homiss, the traditional winter village of the Homiss people on the Hesquiat Peninsula north of Estevan Point. The Amos family is seeking an apology from the provincial government. Family members were supported by a large number of friends, including Miles Richardson of the Haida Nation, former Chief Commissioner of the BC Treaty Commission (1998–2004) and Joe Alphonse of the Tsilhqot'in. In 1864 Tsilhqot'in men were hanged for actively resisting the violence of colonial road builders in their traditional territory (*Ha-Shilth-Sa* 2008:35:14:1,3). Ironically, in 1882, Chief Aimé, another ancestor of the Amos family was presented with a gold medal in recognition of the "kindness and humane conduct" of his people following the tragic shipwreck of the barque *Malleville* at Homiss. Two hundred dollars was also given by the American government to be distributed to those who assisted in recovering the bodies of all who had perished (Brabant 1977:97-99, *Ha-Shilth-Sa* 2010:37:2:1,8). The pole was placed at Homiss to remind the provincial and federal governments that the land designated as the Hesquiat Peninsula Provincial Park, established in 1995, is in fact the traditional territory of the Homiss people of the Hesquiaht First Nation.

Still farther north, park development would likely have expanded to historic Friendly Cove were it not for the cool reception the idea received as early as 1977 from the Mowachaht. But in 1997 the Mowachaht-Muchalaht First Nations, as a part of a strategy to have their own history recognized as being central to the establishment of British Columbia, sought through the Historic Sites and Monuments Board to have Yuquot designated as a National Historic Site (Mowachaht-Muchalaht First Nations 2000:11-32).

Other places in Nuu-chah-nulth territory, like the island groups in Barkley Sound, may be under pressure to be used as recreational areas for the general public.

In 1983 a modern treaty process began, establishing negotiations between First Nations, British Columbia and Canada. The vast majority of First Nations in British Columbia, unlike those across most of Canada, did not sign treaties with the colonial powers that came to dominate their territories and lives. In 1993 the British Columbia Treaty Commission was established with the goal of addressing the need to negotiate modern treaties between the First Nations, British Columbia and Canada. In 1994, 13 of the 14 First Nations that compose the Nuu-chah-nulth Tribal Council entered the British Columbia Treaty Commission treaty process. The Ditidaht First Nation, a member of the Nuu-chah-nulth Tribal Council, is negotiating at a separate treaty table with the Pacheedaht First Nation, which is not a member of the Nuu-chah-nulth Tribal Council. In 2000 the Hupacasath First Nation withdrew from the Nuu-chah-nulth treaty table to negotiate independently, reducing the number of First Nations to 12.

On March 10, 2001, the negotiators for the Nuu-chah-nulth Tribal Council, British Columbia and Canada initialled an agreement in principle. Following community consultations and a vote by each community, the agreement was rejected by six of the participating First Nations.

Five of the six groups that approved the agreement in principle – the Huu-ay-aht, Kyuquot-Cheklesath, Toquaht, Uchucklesaht and Ucluelet – joined to form the Maa-nulth First Nations, meaning "villages along the coast". They approached British Columbia and Canada about negotiating a final agreement based on the draft 2001 Nuu-chah-nulth Agreement In Principle. In July and October, 2007, members of the five Maa-Nulth First Nations voted to approve the final agreement. Provincial legislation to ratify the agreement was introduced to the BC Legislative Assembly on November 21, 2007. On November 29, the legislation received Royal Assent.

Seven Nuu-chah-nulth First Nations – the Ahousaht, Ehatteshaht, Hesquiaht, Mowachaht/Muchalaht, Nuchatlaht, Tla-o-qui-aht and Tseshaht – continued to work toward a negotiated treaty with British Columbia and Canada. In 2003 Nuu-chah-nulth leaders expressed concerns about the precedents that would be set by the Maa-nulth Treaty. Among other issues, Nuu-chah-nulth negotiators noted that the hereditary chiefs and their territories "are not recognized in the agreement"; that the forestry agreement is based on a "harvest turnaround period of 100 years, which first of all is not realistic, and secondly turns the forest into a tree farm, not a forest that recognized the interconnectedness of the ecosystem", and that "if we want resources for future generations there needs to be a much greater turn around time". A Nuu-chah-nulth spokesman stated, "There should be a

Nuu-chah-nulth-wide vote if there are implications that affect everyone....
I don't think people should be allowed to sell out the future of their grandchildren." Maa-nulth negotiators responded that the precedents that would
be set will be positive and will not negatively affect Nuu-chah-nulth Treaty
Table negotiations. (Wiwchar 2003a.)

The BC Treaty Commission summarized the provisions within the Maa-
nulth Treaty as follows (British Columbia 2007:23):

> The agreement provides constitutionally-protected self government, a
> lump sum payment of $73.1 million over 10 years, as well as $1.2 million
> annually in resource royalty payments for 25 years and $9.5 million an-
> nually for program funding. The agreement provides 22,375 hectares of
> land including subsurface resources, in addition to the existing reserves
> of 2,084 hectares and allows the First Nations to add to their settlement
> lands through purchases. Two further key sites off treaty settlement land
> will become provincial protected areas. There is one-time funding of
> $47.3 million to fund transition and implementation in such areas as fish-
> eries, parks, public works, governance, and land and resource management
> to be paid over eight years. A further $11.1 million has been provided out-
> side the treaty for capital projects, to purchase commercial fishing licences
> and to prepare for treaty implementation. In addition to the treaty right
> to harvest wildlife and migratory birds for food, social and ceremonial
> purposes, a separate harvest agreement outside the treaty provides com-
> mercial fishing access for salmon, halibut, herring, rockfish, sablefish, crab
> and prawns, as well as allocations for food, social and ceremonial purposes.

In discussing the proposed Maa-Nulth Treaty, George Watts, long-time
former chair of the Nuu-chah-nulth Tribal Council, stated (in *Ha-Shilth-Sa*
2003:30:13:3): "I think there will be a hell of a lot more opportunities after
treaty than we have now." The treaty process has clearly been a challenging
and difficult process for many Nuu-chah-nulth people. In 2007 the Tseshaht asked the BC Supreme Court to delay the ratification of the proposed
treaty by the Huu-ay-aht First Nation because of overlapping land claims in
the Broken Islands in Barkley Sound (*Times-Colonist* 2007; British Columbia 2007:8). On April 9, 2009, the five Maa-nulth First Nations signed the
Maa-nulth Final Agreement with the Government of Canada, which will
allow the treaty to be implememented (Morrow 2009:A4).

In September 2008, the Tla-o-qui-aht, one of the original 13 First
Nations at the main Nuu-chah-nulth treaty table, withdrew in order to seek
an Incremental Treaty Agreement (ITA) with the province (Steel 2008b:1,
7) The remaining 6 First Nations do not intend to seek an ITA with the
province (Lavoie 2008:A1).

According to the Ministry of Aboriginal Affairs and Reconciliation,
an ITA is not a replacement for treaty negotiations, but simply advances

"treaty-related benefits for the First Nations and the province. They are pre-treaty agreements, not final agreements" (British Columbia 2008). Under the terms of the ITA, signed on November 13, the Tla-o-qui-aht will receive 63 hectares of land near the village of Tofino valued at $19.5 million and $600,000 in capacity building funds over the length of the four-year agreement. The terms of the agreement (British Columbia 2008) will not allow the Tla-o-qui-aht to:

> initiate any court action or proceeding to challenge any governmental action associated with a provincial Crown land disposition or land use authorization ... on the basis that the province has failed to fulfil any duty to consult or accommodate in respect of such matter or that any such matter constitutes an unjustifiable infringement of any aboriginal rights or title of the Tla-o-qui-aht.

Some members of the Tla-o-qui-aht First Nations have critized this arrangement (Ogilvie 2008), stating: "As of today, Thursday November 13, 2008, the Tla-o-qui-aht *muschim* are withdrawing their consent to the illegal theft of Tla-o-qui-aht territories through what is known as the ITA."

Seeking "a fair share" of resources to provide for families and future generations the Nuu-chah-nulth First Nations have been unable to reach a satisfactory resolution for access to fishing resources through the treaty process (Happynook 2008). The Nuu-chah-nulth claim they have an aboriginal right to a commercial fishery. But British colonial authorities evoked the "common law doctrine of the public right to fish" that "created an open-access fishery, erasing pre-existing claims of Native ownership" by ignoring the fact that First Nations had successfully regulated the fishery for centuries before European contact. The public right to fish was used as a legal instrument to justify the appropriation of First Nation's fisheries. In the late 19th century the Canadian Dominion Fisheries bureaucrats created a separate category called "Home Consumption of Fish by the Indians" that was seen as a "Native food fishery distinct from commercial fisheries" and later formalized in law as an "Indian food fishery". (Harris 2001:17, 19, 25, 31.)

This fictive subdivision of First Nations fisheries, in colonial officialdom's position does not include "commercial" fish that had always been traded to other First Nations and non-aboriginals. This bureaucratic fiction has continued to be used as a legal instrument, preventing First Nations from selling the fish they have always caught to the general public. Perhaps the most contentious use of this legal position was the $10,000 fine levied in 1988 by a judge of the British Columbia Provincial Court against the Nuu-chah-nulth Tribal Council's NTC Smokehouse Ltd for "buying and selling Indian food fish". The judge cited an 1888 Fisheries regulation that prohibits the sale of "food fish", and because the defendants did not have a commercial license, they were in violation of the law despite the existence of a local Tseshaht by-law allowing for the sale of "food fish" (*Ha-Shilth-Sa* 1988:15:6:1).

Finally, in June 2003, the Nuu-chah-nulth Tribal Council filed a "Writ of Summons" against Canada seeking reconciliation. In April 2006 the trial began but was adjourned in May after the court ruled that only Nuu-chah-nulth nations without overlapping boundary claims could proceed. Eight nations resolved their outstanding boundary issues. An additional three nations continue as plaintiffs in a second phase of the trial. In signing the ITA with the province, the Tla-o-qui-aht agree that they will at the time of signing the final agreement between themselves, Canada and the province under the BC Treaty Commission process "discontinue from the Ahousaht [Nuu-chah-nulth Tribal Council] Fisheries Litigation" in the same way that the Maa-nulth Treaty First Nations withdrew (British Columbia 2008). On February 4, 2008, the trial resumed.

The Nuu-chah-nulth argue that following Canadian Confederation in 1867, the federal government established strategically located Indian Reserves to ensure that the Nuu-chah-nulth could continue their traditional practice of harvesting and trading fish. But in the 20th century, "progressive restrictions on aboriginal harvesting and a complete ban on the commercial sale of fish" (Morrow 2008) has resulted in a drop in the number of Nuu-chah-nulth-owned fishing boats from 200 in the 1950s to fewer than 20 boats in 2003 (Alexander 2003:4).

The Nuu-chah-nulth and other First Nations in British Columbia have been subjected to constant harassment for using their traditional fishing territories, including confiscation of marine resources and even imprisonment. Peter Webster and others were incarcerated for a month at Okalla Prison for refusing to pay the provincial seine tax (Webster 1983:42). Adam Shewish, the hereditary chief of the Tseshaht, was forced to dump clams that he had collected for home use in traditional Tseshaht territory in the Broken Group of Islands, yet Fisheries officials allowed commercial clam harvesters to decimate this same stock. Charles Jones Sr, the hereditary chief of the Pacheedaht, was imprisoned at 80 years of age for allegedly setting a gill net in the San Juan River (Jones and Bosustow 1981:54-55).

In 2009 BC Supreme Court Justice Nicole Garson ruled the "Nuu-chah-nulth First Nations have an aboriginal right to harvest and sell all species of fish found within their territories" (First Nations Fisheries Council 2009). And in June 2011 the BC Court of Appeal agreed with Justice Garson and the Supreme Court of BC's "findings of significant intertribal trade in fisheries products by the ancestors of the Nuu-chah-nulth prior to European contact to establish a commercial right to sell fish" (Growlings 2011). The Court of Appeal has given an additional year for the Nuu-chah-nulth and Fisheries and Oceans Canada to negotiate a fishery that includes rights-based commercial access to the Nuu-chah-nulth (Codlin 2011). This is a major step in the Whaling People's continuing struggle to establish in law their long-standing right to harvest the bounty of their traditional territories.

Despite the far-reaching changes brought about by the *Mamaɬn'i* (Europeans and Americans) in the two centuries since their initial appearance in a "floating house" in 1774, the Whaling People survive on their rugged shores. Their ranked social system continues with hearty feasting, generous potlatching and grand ceremonial displays, albeit less intensely than before. They keep on going as their native selves with a certain toughness, good sense and humour, adapting to the ways of Western civilization in seemingly total fashion, but never really becoming *Mamaɬn'i*. For all the tribulations suffered since the Europeans arrived, the Whaling People have not vanished in body or soul and remain the first people in their ancient homeland. The full rights of national citizenship came very late to First Nations in both Canada and the USA. The Indian Citizenship Act of 1924 gave US First Peoples the right to vote. The Nuu-chah-nulth in Canada did not receive the right to vote provincially until 1949 and it was another 11 years before they acquired the unrestricted right to vote in federal elections (Duff 1965:100).

Chapter 5
Spirit-Filled Realms of Medicine, Rituals, Art, Music and Myths

It can be seen as a strength of spirit that the Whaling People have survived the last 200 years. This strength has been with them for thousands of years and is embodied in their view of the cosmos. The general conception of the universe as a pantheon of spirits, great and small, and the constant ritual training for success in all undertakings through spirit power have already been described. Let us now look at the medicine men and a pair of ritual societies with their ceremonies, art, music and myth, in all of which spirits are intimately involved. Such strong supernatural presence is not surprising, for the Whaling People's world was very much one running on spirit power.

SICKNESS AND CURING BY MEDICINE MEN

The Whaling People's specialists in the supernatural and curing, the medicine men (shamans) acquired their powers through a combination of inherited secret knowledge, encounters with spirits and training in ritual performance. Supernatural contact was the key element. Becoming a medicine man was one of the few avenues to prestige not restricted to those of high rank, and practitioners were mostly of lower rank or commoner status (Drucker 1951:181, Sproat 1868:169). Chiefs lacked the time to play the role fully and, besides, they already had high-ranking status. There were two kinds of medicine men: the "soul-workers" who had the power through spirit encounters to restore lost souls, and the "workers" of the secret *ts'a·yiq* society of the central and southern groups who could handle sickness other than that due to soul loss (Boas 1890:44). Soul-workers almost always acquired power through a quiet quest for a supernatural encounter, although a chance meeting with a spirit was also possible. Such power was not inherited but tended to run in families since a soul-worker taught a younger close

A Tla-o-qui-aht medicine woman. Edward S. Curtis photograph; RBCM E-00873.

relative how to prepare through ritual bathing and what to do to overcome the different spirits encountered. He took his pupil along on ritual excursions to the lonely places where spirits were met.

An unusual sound announced the coming of the supernatural being in a vision, at times after months or years of preparatory bathing with fasting and abstinence from sexual relations. Its power made some individuals faint away for hours, at the same time bleeding from the mouth, nose and ears. During this trance the spirit told of the power bestowed or sang the songs to be used to cure. If found thus unconscious and bleeding, the person was carried home where a medicine man diagnosed and announced the cause. He then set the acquired power properly in the individual to make him into a practitioner. But the person who was ritually well-prepared would withstand the force of the spirit, keep it in sight, make the ritual cry, _ʔiˑ_, and take steps to overcome the spirit to gain its helping power by uttering a special phrase, striking with a stick, or spitting blood from a cut tongue. Thereupon the spirit turned into a bit of foam or disappeared, leaving a token object. It reappeared shortly after to give instructions.

Another way to gain power was through an encounter with a Wolf. This kindly being often gave power in gratitude for the removal of fishbones stuck in its throat or gums. Or a Wolf might simply give power when met and reappear later in dreams. A traditional form of encounter happened when ducking under a fallen tree. Man and Wolf would collide head-on and both be knocked unconscious. With other supernatural beings great danger accompanied encounters because if the person was not ritually clean or failed to take the proper steps at the meeting with the being, he or she was vanquished. The bested person either died on the spot or struggled home only to collapse, limbs rigid and face contorted, and die. Sometimes a medicine man could remove the spirit clinging on the back of the person.

After a successful encounter, the foam into which the spirit turned or the small token object it left, such as medicinal leaves, dyed cedar bark, a rattle or a painted pebble, was stored in a strip torn from the person's blanket, to be preserved as a fetish containing power. Hiding it in the woods, the man (or woman) returned home, but the power about him was still dangerous to others, so for a day or more he stayed away from the houses. Each night the spirit came in dreams to teach diagnosis and treatment procedures, songs, face painting, hair dressing and the wearing of rings of shredded red-cedar bark around the head, arms and legs. All of these practices were thus stamped with the individuality of the particular spirit. Also the power of the budding medicine man was properly set by an established practitioner who, usually for four nights, sang and sprinkled eagle down over him, and scraped his body to gather the power together in the breast. When fixed in this way, the novice made the barking cry of the medicine man – *hai, hai, hai, hai* – indicating publicly that he was becoming one. Or the spirit encounter might be kept quiet and unnoticed until the time when enough confidence was gained through continued dreaming of the spirit or it ordered self-revelation.

A long training by the spirit was followed with practice performances in public in which the novice was told to sing and dance accompanied, for certain songs, by singing and plank-beating housemates. Rattle and tambourine drum were also used (Sproat 1868:170). As the novice sang and danced, he became transported into the supernatural sphere and the instructing spirit became visible. On its wishes, he danced or stopped, danced through the village houses, or went off singing into the forest to bathe ritually and learn curing procedures including the use of medicinal plants. During this training period he wore the cedar-bark ring ornaments of the medicine man that later were worn only when performing. After a few months, or even years, his readiness to open his practice and his medicine man's name were publicly announced on the spirit's instruction at a feast given by the new shaman or his chief. On these occasions, medicine men (of the central groups at least) displayed sleight-of-hand tricks. Well-advertised by his long training performances, and with his songs known thus enabling recruitment of accompanying choruses, when he needed them, the new medicine man waited to be called upon to exercise his particular kind of power. A medicine man also improved his supernatural capabilities by continuing to seek spirit encounters. Meetings after the first one did not require the training performances although the spirits occasionally made the medicine man sing at night.

The medicine man was called in to cure when sickness was beyond treatment by the normal family remedies of herb infusions, massages and songs. Usually a local doctor was called for the poor, but for wealthy chiefs, a renowned shaman was often brought in from a distance (Drucker 1951:202). He came with his assistants who carried his gear in a small box and would help in his songs. He first diagnosed, then cured. Usually he performed at night before enthralled spectators with the patient laid out by the central fire of the house. Intimating that the patient might be beyond recovery, he began to shake his rattle and hum a song to call his helping spirit. A close relative of the patient would offer payment, in furs, blankets, canoes, or money, of no fixed amount but with acceptability to the spirit indicated by the strength of the medicine man's singing. Few shamans could live by fees (Drucker 1951:193). As the shaman sang on, spirits filled the space about him, giving instructions. If powerful, he might see inside the patient and discover what was wrong. Sickness was most commonly attributed to little, live, black disease objects found in the body in cysts full of dark blood. If near the surface, these disease-causers were sucked out together with the bad blood. If deeper, they were dug out by hand, commonly from the belly, upper back, back of neck, or temples. Disease-causing objects, sent or thrown in by evil medicine men – sorcerers – were harder to extract. If sickness was due to loss of soul, commonly to sea spirits like the Salmon, the shaman made a spectacular journey to recover it from the spirit's home under the sea or in some other strange far-off place. Spirit possession by entry into the patient was incurable, causing death or madness. But a spirit clinging to the back might be removed. Another sickness that medicine men could not cure was that caused by contagious magic performed on something that was near the victim. The usual treatment given by a medicine man was vigorous, with hard massaging and violent extraction of disease objects. And all the while, there was loud singing, rattle shaking and plank beating (Drucker 1951:2078; Moser 1926:140; Sproat 1868:255-6).

Sorcery and black magic were done secretly, of course, so it was hard if not impossible to tell who did it. Such evil action was said to be done for revenge, jealousy, spite or gain. Medicine men were hired to kill. They might cause sickness, too, expecting to be called in to cure and be paid. Through their contacts with spirits, the medicine men could get power to send or throw disease objects that were commonly sharpened bits of bone or claws, often tied together in pairs with hair. When such things were extracted in curing or by autopsy after death, there was great excitement and accusations. Certain identification of the sorcerer was not possible, however, without confession. Medicine men might also steal souls. Contagious magic was done by hereditary secret ritual, such as putting something close to the victim together with a corpse. Such action caused lingering incurable illness, like never-healing ulcerous sores. Also known was the poisoning of food with plant substances that made the victim bloat up, turn purplish black, and die with his or her tongue swollen and sticking out (Drucker 1951:21215).

THE *TS'A·YIQ* DOCTORING RITUAL SOCIETY

As an alternative to the regular curing by a medicine man, the central and southern groups had a doctoring ceremonial called *Ts'a·yiq*. This ceremonial was apparently named after the Kwagu'ł term for medicine man but resembled the Coast Salish guardian spirit dance (Boas 1890:46-47, 1897:642; Drucker 1951:215-18, 243; Sapir and Swadesh 1939:107-08). Mainly ritual, the *Ts'a·yiq* involved a minor society composed of patients and others who had dreamed a *Ts'a·yiq* song under the leadership of a medicine man.

When someone was sick, commonly of a lingering ailment of a minor nature but unresponsive to treatment by medicine men, a relative might invite the *Ts'a·yiq* society of the village. Undyed, shredded Yellow-cedar bark was the mark of the society, worn as headbands with long streamers, belts, wristlets and anklets. In the patient's house, starting at the door, each society member in turn sang his or her own *Ts'a·yiq* songs, accompanied by the rest. Each sang with a sobbing effect that was gradually increased until he or she was crying. At this point, the singer sat down.

When everyone around the house had sung, which took some time because some singers had up to five or ten songs, the society members went out and filed round the village to seize initiates, dragging them along by the hair to eliminate headaches. Back inside, each novice was dragged around the house twice. *Ts'a·yiq* songs were then sung in earnest, but the novices kept quiet until they really wanted to sing, meanwhile breathlessly exclaiming *ay ay ay*, the cry for power not to be sickly. Society members had a certain immunity to disease. Then, with the leader and the patient at the head, the group danced around the village, holding up the index fingers and trembling violently.

The ceremonial lasted 10 days among the Opetchasaht at the head of Alberni Inlet (Sapir and Swadesh 1939:108). As a tribal variant among the

Tla-o-qui-aht in the early historic period, the chief did not wait for sickness to occur but convened the society, recruited novices with the parent's consent, and enlisted all the medicine men to create a more orderly, socially-oriented society.

THE WOLF RITUAL

The Wolf Ritual was the principal ceremony of the Whaling People. Called *Tło·kwa·na* in the north and *Tło·kwała* by central and southern groups (the words actually mean "medicine man"), it has become known commonly as the Wolf Ritual or Wolf Dance, after the featured supernatural beings. Secret societies among the Whaling People staged the Wolf Ritual repeatedly through the winter. It was supposed to be a secret ceremony, but everyone in a given place would help stage the event, except for children under seven or eight years old (the age of the youngest initiates) and invited guests from other groups. (Boas 1890:47-52, Curtis 1916:68-98, Drucker 1951:386-443.)

The Wolf Ritual was like a tribal initiation passed through by all. In 1942 Elizabeth Colson (1953:178) determined that every Makah over the age of 50 had been initiated into the *Tło·kwała* as small children. The chiefly and wealthy who could afford the expenses of feasting and potlatching were repeatedly initiated. The details of the proceedings varied locally, but basically the Wolf Ritual was the dramatic re-enactment of a myth in which a young chief is carried off by Wolves to their home in the forest.

A Kyuquot myth recorded by Edward Curtis (1916:94-8) relates the origin of the *Tło·kwa·na*. This account also has many details of Whaling Peoples' attitudes, motives and actions. The hero's meeting with the supernatural Wolves is typical, beginning with prolonged ritual bathing and involving a bargaining for power. The place of the secret whistles and bullroarers in the *Tło·kwa·na* is well explained near the end.

Origin of the *Tło·kwa·na*

At K'atsnimt lived a young chief, Yan'am<u>x</u>om. There was another man who was constantly washing ceremonially in the woods, and Yan'am<u>x</u>om determined to do likewise. So every morning and every evening for two years he washed himself; and gradually he increased the length of the hemlock sprigs that he used in rubbing his body, until they became branches as long as the stretch of his arms. As he washed, he looked at the rising or the setting sun.

One morning while he was drawing a long branch across his naked back, it was suddenly grasped from behind and held. He looked about and

Wolves watch Yan'amxom rub his body with hemlock boughs. Tim Paul drawing, 2008.

saw a Wolf holding the branch between his teeth, and a little way off sat another Wolf on his haunches, watching with his head on one side. When Yan'am<u>x</u>om turned, the Wolf released the bough and trotted away into the woods with his mate. Then the young man laid on the pile of used branches and went home, very happy because he was about to get that for which he had been striving.

On the next day the same thing occurred, and on the following day at sunrise he did not use the hemlock, but merely rubbed himself with water. Then he lay down in the water, waiting to see what the Wolves wished to do with him. Very soon they came out of the woods, and quickly the man closed his eyes, pretending to be dead. One of the Wolves squatted on his haunches, while the other went about the edge of the water, sniffing at every spot Yan'am<u>x</u>om had touched. Then he began to sniff at the man, and nipped his arm. He seized the arm and began to drag him out to the bank; but suddenly he dropped the body, and both Wolves ran into the woods.

Then Yan'am<u>x</u>om was vexed, and said to himself, "Now I will really wash hard!" He rubbed his body violently with hemlock, and remained all day beside the stream, and at sunset he rubbed again with hemlock. Then he went home. Thus also he did on the three following days, and the next morning he lay down in the water, and again the two Wolves came. This time one of them bit him and then dragged him out of the stream. He seized the man by the back of the neck, swung him up on his back, and ran through the woods, followed by his mate. They came out on the beach and trotted on for some distance to Sacha?akot.

As the Wolves trotted along the beach, Yan'am<u>x</u>om became curious to know where he was, and he opened his eyes a very little. The Wolf staggered and almost fell. He turned his head and said hurriedly: "Remain dead! Do not open your eyes yet!" So Yan'am<u>x</u>om quickly closed his eyes and breathed lightly. But again he grew curious, and the same things happened. After a while they came to a small creek, and the Wolf as he crossed threw the man off into the water, where he lay facing the bank they had just left. He opened his eyes and saw that he was a long distance from the place where he had been washing. On the other bank sat the Wolves, wet with sweat and with red tongues hanging out. When they had rested, one of them dragged the man out, swung him up on his back, and trotted away.

Now the Wolves turned into a trail through the woods, and after a time entered the mouth of a great cave. For a long time they passed under the ground, and then at the back of the cave they came to a small hole lined with sharp points of rock. The man was thrown to the ground, and the Wolves crept through. Then one of them took him by the neck to drag him through; but at the hips he stuck fast. Still they tugged and pulled, and with a great effort they drew him through; but his hips and legs were terribly torn by the sharp rocks. They were now in the open.

After a time Yan'am<u>x</u>om heard the sound of many voices, and he thought they were at the end of their journey. The voices became more distinct, and he heard the people saying to one another, "Here is the person we have been hunting." This was the Wolf village, where the Wolves, removing their fur coats, lived in the form of human beings.

The man was thrown down roughly outside the door of a house, and the two Wolves went in. Some young men came out, dragged the man inside, and laid him on some new mats. Still he kept his eyes shut.

"Do not let him lie too long." said a voice. A plank was laid on the floor with one end raised, and under the lower end was placed a wooden dish to catch the blood. For they were going to cut him up and eat him. One of the Wolves with a knife kneeled beside Yan'am<u>x</u>om. "Why," he said, "this animal has fine fur!" For the animal people regarded humans as animals with fur. He placed the point of the knife on the body. Then suddenly Yan'am<u>x</u>om grasped the knife, tore it away from the Wolf, and leaped up. Instantly all the Wolf people dashed for their skins and tried to scramble into them. For the animal people were ashamed to be seen without their skins, and had no power without them. There they stood in the sight of Yan'am<u>x</u>om, some with only one arm covered, others with the skin coats hanging down their backs.

For an instant there was silence. Then the chief spoke to his people quietly: "We had better give these coats to him and get back our knife." So

The young chief is carried off by the Wolves. Tim Paul drawing, 2008.

all the Wolves' coats were piled in the middle of the room, and the chief begged, "Will you give us our knife?" But the man refused to give it up, and the chief said: "All these things you see in this house shall be yours. If you wish to get Sea Otters, you can do so easily. If you wish to hunt seals, you can get many of them. If you wish to hunt whales, you can kill them." But even for these Yan'amxom was unwilling to give up the knife. He kept his eyes fixed on an object hanging on the wall, wrapped in balsam boughs. Then the Wolf chief said: "Give us our knife and you shall have our comb. Then if you have any friend or sister or daughter who wishes long hair, you have only to draw this comb out to whatever length you choose, and the hair will be of that length." Still Yan'amxom kept the knife tightly clasped under his folded arms. "Well then," said the chief at last, "give us our knife and take this *kist'a*." He showed a handful of water. "If you have any friend who is dead, you have only to sprinkle this water on his eyes and face and he will be alive again." But Yan'amxom was not satisfied, and kept looking at the object wrapped in balsam branches.

Then the Wolf chief pondered. At length he turned to his people. "We had better give him what he is looking at, and get our knife." So one of the Wolves took the bundle down from the wall and revealed a stone club as long as a man's forearm. "For our knife," said the chief, "you shall have *mokw'ant*. If you are hunting Sea Otters or seals, or anything else, show this, and when the animal sees *mokw'ant* it will die. If you have enemies, show this *mokw'ant* and when they look upon it they will fall dead." Gladly Yan'amxom gave up the knife and took the stone club.

Now the family of Yan'amxom became anxious about him and when he was not found by those sent to look for him at the place where he had been washing, the people began to mourn him as dead. Then his parents, because this was their only child, moved away from the other people to be alone at Ch'iktłis, while they mourned.

After a year they set out to return to the village. The woman sat in the bow crying, while the man paddled in the stern. As they went, they became aware of the howling of a great number of Wolves on a high mountain, and mingled with the howling was a faint sound like a human voice singing. But so far away was it that they could not be sure it was not a crow, and the man stopped paddling to listen. A lull in the howling made the singing voice plainer, and he urged the woman: "Stop crying and listen! It is not a crow; it is singing!"

The woman ceased her crying, and the singing was plainly heard. Said the man: "You see it is a man's voice! I think it is perhaps our son! Quick, take your paddle; we must get home quickly!" So the woman took up her paddle and they hastened homeward.

On a point of land ahead of them they saw a Wolf, and when they came closer they beheld a great many, hundreds of them. In the midst of them stood a man, their son! He was naked, but around his wrists, ankles, waist, and head were circlets of balsam sprigs. Then they paddled harder than ever, in order to apprise the people of what was coming to them.

When they reached the village the man hurriedly told the people what he had seen, and advised them to prepare their spears for a fight with the Wolves and ropes with which to capture his son. It was not long before Wolves of all colors and sizes appeared on the beach, which was some distance from the hill on which stood the village. A scout was sent to see if this really was Yan'am x̱om, and when he was near the Wolves the man called out to him: "Do not catch me too quickly. You must come down to the beach four times, and then you can catch me. Let some one who knows how to use the harpoon spear me in the arm. Then there will be no trouble."

When this was reported to the people, they embarked in canoes tied side by side, because they were afraid of the Wolves. But some of the old people remained in the village. When for the fourth time the Wolves appeared on the beach, the people in the canoes approached them and a man with a harpoon got out while those in the canoes held the end of the harpoon rope. He threw the weapon and struck Yan'am x̱om in the arm, and the men in the canoes dragged him out to them.

As soon as Yan'am x̱om was struck, the Wolves dashed away to the village and began to tear down the houses and the hill itself. The falling timbers crushed some of the old people, but others quickly made fires of their old clothing, and the human odour drove off the Wolves before they had quite demolished the hill.

Now when other tribes heard about these things, many of them doubted, and from every direction they came to see for themselves. When Yan'amxom knew that they were coming, he made a wooden club in the likeness of *mokw'ant*, which he kept in its wrapping. Then one day the beach was black with large canoes, and Yan'amxom let it be known that he would dance twice on the housetop with the wooden club, but the third time he would dance with *mokw'ant* itself, and those who continued to doubt would pay for their unbelief. So while the visitors sat in their canoes, he danced on the roof, holding the wooden club above his head. Then dropping the wooden club he raised the stone one and tore off the wrappings. Immediately the people fell dead, and the canoes were overturned.

Now Yan'amxom covered his weapon and went to the beach. He dragged out of the water the bodies of those who had not scoffed at him and brought out his *kist'a* (the pot of life-giving water). Those on whose faces he sprinkled it sat up as if awaking from a long sleep; but all unbelievers he left dead in the water.

Then Yan'amxom announced that he would give away presents, and all the people came to his house. The Wolves had told him how to make pipe whistles and tongue whistles and bullroarers, and he made a number of these and showed the members of his family how to use them. At the potlatch, while the people were in the house, his relatives stood outside blowing the whistles and whirling the bullroarers, and the people were amazed and frightened. This was the beginning of the first *Tɬo·kwa·na*.

Now the chiefs of the other five villages of the Kyuquot became very jealous of Yan'amxom and, determined to find out his secrets, they sent men who crept into the house one night, killed him, opened his box, and took out the whistles and bullroarers one by one. But they could not understand these things, and thinking them worthless threw them away. But *mokw'ant* they could not find, because it was kept secreted in the woods in the crotch of a great cedar.

To emphasize the prevalence of the supernatural order during the Wolf Ritual period a number of ordinary life habits were replaced by ceremonial alternatives. For instance ordinary songs, normal personal names, usual words about wolves, gum chewing, hat wearing, basketry and mat weaving were prohibited. Violations of these prohibitions were punished, for example, by mauling and stripping those who said "wolf" (*qwayats'i·k*) instead of the ceremonial word, "crawler" (*sa?ak*). The regular privileges of rank such as graded public seating and chiefly rights to special food items were disregarded. All meals were taken as communal feasts. Rank relationships were displaced, outwardly at least, by association in age-grade clubs loosely organized on a friendship basis and often named, among the northern groups after the imitative dances they performed (Drucker 1951:400-4), or among the central ones after the various tribes (Boas 1890:48, Sapir and Swadesh 1955:112). Usually there were seven age-grade groups: the young, middle-aged and old, for men and women, and the war chiefs. In addition, there were more transitory boys' and girls' club groups to perform certain dances.

But behind this appearance of a different ceremonial order, the regular social order continued to operate, with the Wolf Ritual being basically organized by the rank system. A Wolf Ritual was planned ahead of time, sometimes months before, by a sponsor of rank or wealth in secret consultation with the chiefs. These leading people decided on the proceedings to be staged and chose the main novices whose fathers, on notification, contributed according to their means to the wealth needed for the ceremony. Wolves were played by commoners as inherited privileges of their lineages. Chiefs had rights to have special kinds or numbers of Wolves to appear with their children. They also supplied the whistles and bullroarers for the vital supernatural sound effects. A novice was supposedly taken to the ancestral home of his or her lineage where ceremonial privileges were learned so that they could be claimed and displayed upon return with attendant potlatch distribution of gifts to witnessing guests. In this way the Wolf Ritual was a major means for transmitting hereditary rights and maintaining the ranked social system (Drucker 1951:387-8).

A Wolf Ritual performance, which required a week or more to complete, provided a much-enjoyed spectacle, participant theatre, singing, drumming, dancing, feasting, potlatching and general fun. The initial capture of the novices was variously staged. The principal initiate, commonly the child of the sponsor of the performance, might disappear under contrived circumstances to draw attention to him, then reappear on the beach perhaps to be suddenly seized by the Wolves (see Curtis 1916:70). Often the village was assembled at a feast held for the purpose or as part of other celebrations, notably puberty rites (see Sapir and Swadesh 1955:248). Then the Wolves burst in, perhaps through the rear wall, creating feigned pandemonium, and carried off the initiates. The Crawlers, as the Wolves had to be called, acted vigorously on all fours with a grey or black blanket covering. This cover was traditionally a wolf skin. A carved mask was worn on the brow or a blanket corner projected overhead for the snout. Face, arms and legs were blackened. A few chiefs also used masked kidnappers representing the Grizzly Bear or Wild Man of the Woods, privileges obtained in marriage from the Kwagu'ł. Repeated attacks were made by the Wolves and other fierce creatures to capture the initiates a few at a time. Men pursued them in vain, firing blanks from their weapons in recent times. Some novices were captured unnoticed, leaving torn garments of identification. Parents of the captured were scolded for their carelessness, roughed about and thrown in the sea. Armed parties searched houses at odd hours, creating a disturbance.

The captives, supposedly deep in the forest, were actually in the curtained-off back part of the sponsor's house. Parents and grandparents visited them secretly to teach spirit songs. Age-grade groups staged dances imitating assorted animals, birds, fish, people – real and mythical, even plants and winds. They also put on ludicrous and ribald skits. The capture phase lasted four days and closed with a thunderous mass drumming on planks at night, "calling" the Wolves (Drucker 1951:399-408).

Rescue of the initiates was preferably staged with canoes, both rafted in pairs and singly (Drucker 1951:408-10, Sapir and Swadesh 1955:92-3). The Wolves appeared on a point near the village, four or eight times, usually with varying numbers of novices on each appearance, from none at first to all at the end. The initiates had bloody faces and wore balsam fir branches about their heads, waists, arms and legs. Girls wore balsam capes as well. They signalled what privileges they had obtained. After repeated, excited skirmishes, pretending to be struck dead by Wolves' power, upsetting of canoes and so forth, the novices were seized and taken back to the village. There they went in procession, attended by their rescuers and led by a chief. They entered each house, circling inside, singing their spirit songs, showing dance steps and tokens of other privileges like supernatural quartz crystals with which other groups were invited to potlatches. Among the Tseshaht, novices with quartz crystals made them whistle continually and "threw" them at other children who then became initiates (Sapir and Swadesh 1955:94). The procession ended in the Wolf Ritual house where, after a feast, each novice was publicly presented, sang his or her spirit song, and had a father or grandfather (or if poor, the sponsoring chief) announce the supernatural ancestral home visited, the song learned, his or her new name, and any particular ceremonial instructions to be carried out, like the giving of feasts and potlatches displaying special privileges.

Since the supernatural power of the Wolves was in the novices, they were kept in the Wolf Ritual house of the sponsor for purification by procedures that varied from place to place. Generally there were more village processions, singing of spirit songs and imitative dances for four days. The balsam-branch costumes of the captivity were removed to be burned, ideally at the new moon. The fire was poked with big wooden tongs, having been made among the Mowachaht and Ahousaht earlier in a humorous ceremony before the drumming to call the Wolves. When the balsam costumes were destroyed, the Mowachaht drummed vigorously on planks and shouted four times to drive off the *Tło·kwa·na* Spirit (Drucker 1951:414).

The Ehattesaht shouted similarly. The Kyuquot blew whistles over the heads of the novices. With the Spirit driven off, the ritual proper was over, and the sponsoring chief gave his potlatch, distributing goods and, from the late 19th century, money to witnessing guests and performers. Then followed other potlatches, like those promised by novices at their public presentation, and feasts such as the ones of the age-grade clubs of imitative dancers.

Another Wolf Ritual performance might be given by someone else. Long ago, the post-rescue processing of the novices may have been more prolonged. The Hesquiaht, for example, took the novices through three stages of four days each, with singing, processions, bathing, hair washing and combing, and special dress. On their last night a Wolf danced while white eagle down was scattered, and the Wolf then symbolically disappeared (Drucker 19S1:415-16). The Tseshaht treatment of novices also lasted about 12 days, with much imitative dancing by them after the first four (Sapir and Swadesh 1955:94-114). Their society members, faces blackened with charcoal, drove out the Wolf Ritual Spirit by using special exorcising dances and songs, together with periodic mass drumming. The excitement culminated in the whistling supernatural quartz crystals being taken from the novices by the dancers, thrust in the water outside, and released to fly back to the Wolves, or to circle over the house of the chief giving a succeeding *Tlo·kwa·na* ceremony.

In a performance recorded for the Tseshaht, four fearsome dances followed including a young men's suck dance, with sucking sounds, which contained the mystery of cutting the tongue to make blood flow from the mouth as the Wolves did secretly among themselves, and the crawl dance that featured the evisceration and pretended eating of a dog. The cannibal dance was also bloody, with its biting of selected spectators who were paid for playing their role. Such deliberately awful performances helped turn unappreciative European observers against the Wolf Ritual as something wicked. War chiefs also took part in the superficial "spearing" of arms, thighs, or ribs with skewers or the blades of sealing harpoons. These torturous acts were privileges of the war chiefs, who purposely broke ceremonial prohibitions to be skewered and then were led about by harpoon lanyards while singing spirit songs (Drucker 1951:389-90; Jewitt 1815:120-1). They thus showed off their bravery and disregard of pain. For new initiates, the Wolf Ritual state continued for a year, among the Tseshaht at least, with face blackening and prohibitions of certain foods (Sapir and Swadesh 1955:115).

It might be said that the Wolf Ritual was the spiritual initiation into the life of the Whaling People, a major means of transmitting ceremonial rights and the greatest public entertainment.

ART

The world at large knew little about the art of the Whaling People, compared to that of other Northwest Coast cultures, until recent studies filled that void in art history (see Black 1999 and Brown 2000:273-91). The Whaling People's art appears to be well embedded in their ranked rights or privileges and in their supernatural beliefs. Masks, for instance, are generally parts of more complex ceremonies, displayed along with music, dance, drama and speeches covering myth associations and social meanings. The other parts are art, too, but here we focus on the material representations and decorations, while trying to keep in sight their total reality in real life contexts. Whether carvings, paintings, basketry or other things, art objects were largely owned hereditary rights (topa·tí) depicting supernatural beings who people encountered and acquired power from. In a way, the art of the Whaling People is an illustration of their spirit world.

The sculptural style of the Whaling people has its roots in the ancient "Old Wakashan" tradition shared with their Kwakwala speaking neighbours (King 2000:260-61). Human face masks tended toward flat triangular cross-sections, flat eye areas smoothly blended together with the cheeks below. Painted designs are often bold unconnected geometric shapes, including elements such as feather and star-like designs (Black 1999:80, 100). Eye motifs are often formed from circles, crescents and trigons (here meaning T-shaped elements with three concave sides) that together resemble northern-style ovoids and eyelid forms but in fact are older and antecedent to the latter as part of an ancient proto-Northwest Coast style with very deep roots in the archaeological past (Macnair et al. 1984:42, Brown 1998:62-3, Black 1999:100-101, McMillan 1999:146). These elements can

Thunderbird and Wolf. Dale Croes drawing.

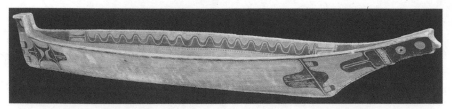

This model canoe shows the graphic style of repeating rectilinear motifs, spirals, dots and zigzag or serpentine lines. RBCM 6600.

be seen in the scroll-work that adorns the headdresses or head-masks representing the Lightning Snake (Hi?itl'i·k) that were worn by Whaling People (Brown 2000:285-6). Two graphic styles have been identified. One has been called a narrative tradition and can be seen in engraved petroglyphs (McMillan 2000:247), the whaling scenes on woven basketry (Black 1999:34, Brown 1998:60), on older wooden painted screens (McMillan and St Claire 1982:14, McMillan 2000:243) and more modern painted cloth curtains (Black 1999:58). The second graphic style focuses on repeating rectilinear motifs, spirals, rhythmic patterns of dots, and zigzag or serpentine lines. This style predates northern Northwest Coast formline art and can be seen on the antler valves of whaling harpoon heads (Newcombe 1907), model canoes and masks (Black 1999:114-17; Brown 1998:63, 2000:280).

House posts of the Whaling People were noted by the earliest European visitors as being carved into figures, in the leading chiefs' houses at least, but the tall, free-standing multi-figured "totem pole" was evidently not a traditional feature. Grave posts, if carved, were of simple design. Beginning in the 20th century, small, many-figured "totem poles" have been produced for sale, and a few larger ones have been erected, notably at Yuquot in Friendly Cove, where Kwagu'ł influence is strong with marriage alliances. The grandest was the so-called Lord Willingdon pole carved in 1913 and presented in 1929 to the visiting Governor General. In the late 20th century the pole fell to the ground.

Among the subjects of Whaling People's art, the Big Whale (?I·ḥto·p) and Thunderbird (Ti·tsk'in), together with the associated Lightning Snake, are prominent as mighty creatures who are the prized inherited rights of the leading chiefs used for ceremonial display. Again and again they are proudly shown on painted screens, inside house figures, and as masks. A fine sculptural example of the Thunderbird with the Whale his prey is the pair of screens in the house of M'okwina made in the second half of the 19th century for a successor to the title and set up at his grave when he died in 1902 (Moser 1926:159). Succeeding figures, carved for the house, show how the west-coast art style changed in this century. Whale and Thunderbird often appear as masked dancers.

A carved central post for supporting beams in a house at Ahousat. RBCM B-01076.

Captain Jack (left) and Chief Napoleon Maquinna (right) pose beside Captain Jack's marriage pole with his son, Benedict, at Yuquot in 1928. The men wear *Xweixwei* masks. Relatively isolated along the west coast of Vancouver Island, the Nuu-chah-nulth have long maintained several important links eastward for cultural interchange. The pole illustrates their link from Tahsis ("gateway") along the Nimpkish River and Nimpkish Lake to the Kwakwa̱ka̱'wakw, whose art influence shows in its carving. Also via the Kwakwa̱ka̱'wakw came the Salish *Xweixwei* masks, re-interpreted here as huge head-top masks, a popular style among the Nuu-chah-nulth. RBCM PN-4656.

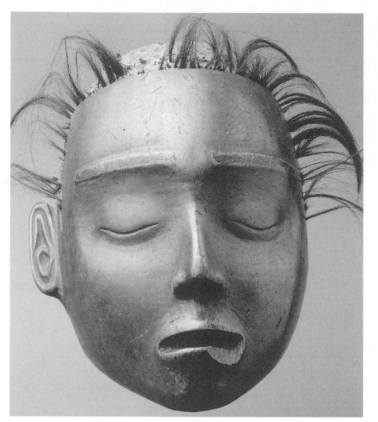

Ceremonial carved wooden head collected on Captain James Cook's voyage of 1778. Isiko Museums of Cape Town AE 2361.
Right: Whale-bone club (*ch'ito·l*). A Tseshaht traditional narrative asserts that this club made them great. Parks Canada X.77.256.1.

Susan Moogk (1980:64) has suggested that in the puberty ceremony an allegory is set up whereby the girl who is becoming a woman is like the Whale, full and rich; and in contrast, the Thunderbird is an allegory of maleness. The large torches of the puberty ceremony are taken to be the Lightning Snake who is worn as a belt by the Thunderbird and at times sent flashing down to earth as his messenger.

These favourite spirits are depicted in various ways. The Lightning Snake could be shown as a crosspiece over a pair of house posts. Tools, like an adze, might have the handle carved into a Thunderbird. The traditional whale-bone war clubs sometimes have the handle carved into what looks like the stylized head of a bird, perhaps of the Thunderbird again. One old club has its hilt carved into a man's head with a serpent-like creature on top. As a part of war costume, a mask-like headdress used to be worn by chiefs and

Whale and Thunderbird, with a symbolic Mount Canuma behind, at the grave of a Chief M'okwina who died in 1902. RBCM AA-00610.

war chiefs. An early observer, John Meares (1967:254) described a mask that accompanied the painted war cloak of elk hide that stopped arrows as "representing the head of some animal; it is made of wood, with the eyes, teeth, &c., and is a work of considerable ingenuity". Meares also noted that men wore masks representing sea mammals, like the Sea Otter. Such masks, while worn on top of the head, still changed the appearance of the hunter. Dramatic staging is important in ceremonial representations of mythical creatures, as in the following example (Sapir and Swadesh 1939:143) of a Whale and Thunderbird display that Tom Sa·ya·ch'apis of the Tseshaaht made for his daughter's puberty ceremony:

> We came around the point at Ho·m'o·wa going along whale fashion in the small canoe and, in the two war canoes, holding spears poised at the one going along in whale fashion. Their whaling spears were poised in the bow. It represented the reputed constant hunter and whaler. There on the bank, perched on a tree, was Thunder. Thunder was there, ready to pounce on the whale representation with his claws. Thus many were my *topa·ti*.
>
> The Whale stopped in the canoe; Thunder stopped and entered the house.

Chiefly whalers' hats with the knob on top (like the one shown on page 32) were often decorated with finely woven silhouettes of whales being

A mid-20th-century representation of Thunderbird in Captain Jack's home at Yuquot. Vancouver Public Library 13442.

pursued by whaling canoes. Other chiefly rain hats had painted designs. As the handicraft market developed late in the 19th century, basketry designs of whales, canoes, thunderbirds, lightning snakes, birds and geometric ornamentation were produced, often in a very fine weave over rectangular wooden forms or round bottles.

The designs were set against a light natural background of dried grass by wrapping dyed strands over the regular elements of the woof at the right spots. At first the colours were obtained from natural substances like black from mud, red from alder bark, and yellow from the root of Oregon grape. Later, commercial dyes were used. These trade baskets were generally small, though some "shopping" baskets reached the size of a large handbag. These fine wrapped twined baskets continue to be made by Nuu-chah-nulth, Di-tidaht and Makah weavers. Wooden bowls and dishes collected as early as the late 18th century sometimes display flat designs cut into the sides and handles carved in the round into heads or figures of humans or animals.

Painted screens, to seclude a girl at puberty or conceal dancers before they emerge in ceremonial display, provide another good field for depicting the Whale, Thunderbird and Lightning Snake. Perhaps because the surface is rectangular, the compositions often contained many rectangular elements. In

Pair of Lightning Snake
headdresses.
Brian Laggat photograph;
provided by Howard
Roloff.

such flat painting, the Whaling People's tendency to emphasize geometrical shapes, like rectangles and circles, is well developed. It was not common, but a few chiefs had a crest design painted on the front of the house, probably a recent practice derived from the Kwagu'ł and more northerly nations. The big canoes for war and ceremonial visits were sometimes painted outside with Whale, Thunderbird, human heads or other figures (Jewitt 1815:86), including the Lightning Snake (Meares 1967:263). War tunics of elk skin had similar representations painted on them (Jewitt 1815:67).

On masks, the painting is a supporting surface ornamentation, the wooden structure itself depicting the usually supernatural bird, animal, human or other form. Many of the masks are worn on top of the head like a headdress. These, in recent times at least, are frequently made of light cedar board bent back from a narrow flat front, if not constructed of separate side pieces making a boxy mask with a cut-out silhouette shape as seen from the side. Some are quite large. Then there are smaller "maskettes" worn on the brow, perhaps derived again from those of the Kwagu'ł or more northern peoples like the Haida and Tsimshian. They are chiefly display rights and might depict crests like the Thunderbird. Face masks are often just held up before the upper part of the face, a cloak or blanket hiding everything below; some have moving parts, like blinking eyes. Masks in the form of a human face might represent ancestors or spirits, such as the Yellow-cedar spirit (*ʔAɫmaqoꞏḥ*), a ghost of a drowned man (*pokmis*), a wealth-giving dwarf, or the wild man of the forest (*Chiꞏniꞏʔatḥ*). Many mask characters have the same counterparts among the related Kwagu'ł people. From the Coast Salish, the *Xweꞏxweꞏ* masked dance, is known to the Whaling People, at least

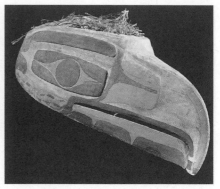

Human face mask (left) and bird mask (one of a pair).
RBCM 16873 and 12038.

around Alberni. Animals are also depicted in masks, like cougars, deer and ducks. Such representations are shown in the age-grade society dances that are a part of ceremonial performances, the principal occasion being the Wolf Ritual.

The Wolf Ritual, the greatest of the Whaling People's ceremonies, features several kinds of Wolves – Crawling, Whirling, Standing and even Swimming Wolf. Each of these Wolf types behaves differently, as their names indicate, and the masks differ (Moogk 1980). Crawling Wolf can have a plain black mask, before coming to be represented just by a blanket with a corner extending overhead for the snout. Whirling Wolf usually has slanting baleen hair and curling lines painted on the sides of the snout. The Standing Wolf mask has generally upright shapes. Such Whaling People's masks have not yet been thoroughly studied. Also, masks used in ceremonial performances with supernatural significance, and items that represent jealously guarded hereditary rights, are not things to be shown too freely. In the following account, Tom Sa·ya·ch'apis of the Tseshaht (Sapir and Swadesh 1939:129, 131) lists the imitative dance rights he owned, and indicates the great number of masks a chief might own. He tells of a particular Wolf Ritual performance in which his father was "bitten away", carried off in the mouths of the Wolves.

> My father, then a little child, was bitten away. In this way the right,
> exclusively mine, of having wolves rush into my house, was obtained.
> No Tseshaht other than my father was bitten away. They then presented

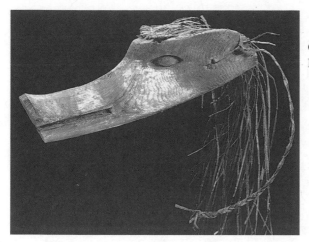

Crawling Wolf mask.
RBCM 10708.

Ts'i·qa· songs and all sorts of Wolf Ritual practices, including different things to imitate in imitative dances during the Wolf Ritual and a ritual for tracing the novices who have been bitten away. In that way were my Hisa·wist'a?at<u>h</u> privileges obtained. I have from this source the swimming of a big wolf. I have a crawling imitative dance. I have a bee imitative dance. I have a sawbill dance. I have a dance-spirit dance. I have a Wolf Ritual crazy dance, a *No·lim* dance, a lover-signalling dance. I have a raccoon dance. I have a *Tsatsi·sk'omts* bird dance. I have a devil-fish dance. I have a Wolf chief's grey blanket. I have all sorts of imitative dances. I have a horse-clam dance. I have an eagle dance. I have a raven dance. I have a red-woodpecker dance. I have a Yellow-cedar Bark Ogre. I believe that is all I have from the Hita·tso?ath.

From the Hisa·wist'a?at<u>h</u> I have these: a *Tsa·tsa·wił* dance, a quivering-in-the-air dance, a river dance – this one, the river dance, has a song, a breakers dance, a day dance, a spring-salmon dance, a killer-whale dance, a wren dance in which the wrens always dig about in the house. All these dances have songs. There is also the spring-salmon dance, a rat dance, a mink dance, a black-oyster-catcher dance. I have the *topa·ti* of representing the sea high up on the beach flooding into the house. There is also a thunder dance with the Lightning Serpent crawling in through the roof. That is as many as I can remember.

In these many dances, the main thing is motion imitating the animal or other subject represented, together with the appropriate song, but masks and other costume items could also be worn to add to the illusion.

House posts and beams were sometimes carved and painted. Beams might represent an animal but carved ones were rare, apparently. Abstract painted patterns symbolizing particular privileges appear to have been the more common way to ornament beams. House posts, when carved, seem

A man named Roberts, from Ucluelet, wearing a Crawling Wolf headdress.
RBCM PN-9402.

to have been mainly human figures, but again representing special rights or supernatural beings. So, the big house built by Sa·ya·ch'apis had its main beam supported in the middle by a monumental figure of the creator of the Tseshaht tribe (Sapir and Swadesh 1939:141). Free-standing figures of the "potlatch welcome" type exist as well, an excellent example being the Huu-ay-aht pair originally at Bamfield and now at the Royal BC Museum (catalogue numbers 2102 and 2103). Another carved figure from Bamfield, mainly a large head on a post by the beach, was said to be for dancing upon as it represented a vanquished foe. Carved figures, which were mostly heads with simplified features on posts, were also used in shrines for secret whaling rights. Others might have been planted at graves. Animal carvings were set at graves, too. Such sculptures may be regarded as art, but their symbolic significance was far more important than any physical aspects we now admire.

The sculptural and graphic traditions of the Whaling People have been kept alive and well by a number of contemporary artists (see Brown 2000:286-90). The best known of these artists are Joe David (see Duffek

Basket makers, probably Annie Atliu and Ellen Curley or Emma George, demonstrating Nuu-chah-nulth weaving techniques at the Louisiana Purchase Exhibition in St Louis, Missouri, in 1904.
Charles Carpenter photograph. RBCM H-04543.

2000:352-62), Ki-ke-in (Ron Hamilton; see Townsend-Gault 2000:203-29), Tsa-qwa-supp (Art Thompson, 1948–2003; see Black 2000:341-51), Tim Paul (see Macnair 2000:363-73), and from the American side, Greg Colfax (see Brown 1998:184-86) and John Goodwin (see Black 2000:345). In the same way that transitional artists among the Haida and Kwakwa̲ka'wakw (e.g., Charles Edenshaw and Willie Seaweed) have been identified as key transmitters of their respective art traditions, artists such as Cheletus (*Chulutuss*), Atlieu, Young Doctor and Jimmy John are recognized as important conveyors of the sculptural and painting arts of the Whaling People into the 20th century (see Black 1999:20, 68, 108-111; Marr 1987:59, 63).

Basketry is also an important component of the art of the Whaling People. In addition to the many well-made utilitarian baskets produced over the centuries, women made finely decorated basketry hats, a number of which were collected in the late 18th century by Spanish, English and American explorers and fur traders. These finely made hats were valuable status symbols worn exclusively by whaling chiefs. In depicting successful whaling hunts with their leviathan quarry securely attached to a line of seal-skin

Wrapped twined tourist baskets, Neah Bay.
Edward S. Curtis photograph; RBCM E-00861.

floats, the hats functioned as positive mnemonic devices (Ki-ke-in in Black 1999:127). Unfortunately we do not know the identity of any of the artists who produced the older hats. It was not until the 20th century – when artists such as Ellen Curley, who was commissioned by C.F. Newcombe to re-create a whaler's hat (*tsiyapoxs*), and Annie Atliu produced wrapped twined basketry for sale – that we began to learn the names of many fine basket makers among the Nuu-chah-nulth, Ditidaht and Makah (Gogol 1981, Dyler 1981, Black 1999:119-31, Laforet 2000).

MUSIC

Whaling People are music lovers. Theirs is mainly vocal, rhythmic with drumming and rattles, often dramatic. In Wolf Ritual performances, whistles and bullroarers are used more for special sound production than as musical instruments. Dance aprons with their rattling beaks of birds and hooves of deer or elk, add rhythmic background sound in ceremonial dances. Although voice is the primary music maker, these others are important (Drucker 1951:106). The traditional drum is a long plank raised off the ground on short sticks and beaten with hardwood billets. On occasion the house planks themselves served as drums. More specially designed is a long narrow open box, raised at one end in a sling for resonance and beaten with the fists padded with cedar bark. The now common big round "tambourine

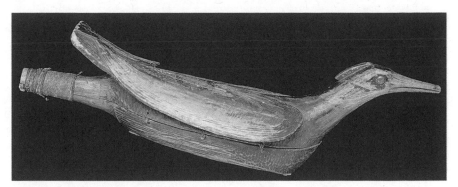

Bird rattle. RBCM 2132.

drum" with one skin head was acquired only in the 19th century (probably in the second half, together with the *lahal* gambling game) with songs accompanying it (Drucker 1951:445).

Rattles are made of three kinds of material. Wooden rattles are usually carved in the shape of a bird, perhaps a duck. Those made of whale baleen or Mountain Sheep horn were steamed and folded double around a wooden handle. The scallop rattle has large shells strung on wooden hoops. Rattles often have supernatural associations particularly when used by shamans.

Whistles come in various shapes and sizes. A very small type is concealed in the mouths of novices in the Wolf Ritual. Larger whistles sometimes have reeds. There are also multiple whistles producing different tones. The bull-roarer, a small board whirled on a string, sounds like an earthquake. For a thunderous noise, rocks are rolled inside a long box. But these sound-effects represent supernatural sounds and are not considered music.

The Whaling People's fine singing was appreciated by Europeans as early as Captain Cook's visit in 1778. James King, Second Lieutenant of the *Resolution*, noted in his journal the Whaling People's exceptional appreciation (among the peoples so far met by the expedition) of European music (Beaglehole 1967:1394-95):

> The greatest number of the Canoes remained in a cluster around us till
> ten o'clock, & as they had no Arms & appeared very friendly, we did
> not care how long they staid to entertain themselves, & perhaps us: a
> man repeated á few words in tune, & regulated the meaning by beating
> against the Canoe sides, after which they all joined in a song, that was
> by no means unpleasant to the ear. A young man with a remarkable soft
> effeminate voice afterward sung by himself, but he ended so suddenly &
> unexpectedly, which being accompanied by a peculiar gesture made us all
> laugh, & he finding that we were not ill pleased repeated his song several

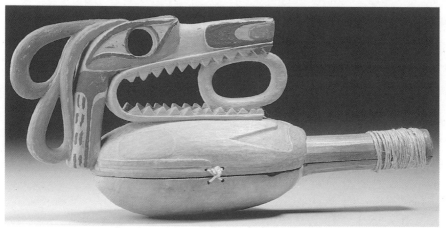

Serpent rattle. Iris and B. Gerald Cantor Center for Visual Arts, Stanford University, 8646.

      times. As they were now very attentive & quiet in listening to their diversions, we judged they might like our music, & we ordered the fife & drum to play a tune; these were the only people we had seen that ever paid the smallest attention to those or any of our musical instruments, if we except the drum, & that only I suppose from its Noise & resemblance to their own drums; they Observed the Profoundest silence, & we were sorry that the dark hindered our seeing the effect of this music on their countenances. Not to be outdone in Politeness they gave us another song, & we then entertained them with French horns, to which they were equally attentive.

In 1786, a trader found that his cymbals and a song he made up were extremely popular at Friendly Cove (Strange 1928:26-27).

    Music must be heard, of course, rather than talked about, but Helen Roberts and Morris Swadesh noted certain distinctions and practices in their excellent study of Whaling People's songs (1955 :203-29). Each highborn family has one or more master singers, male or female, who performs at public performances during feasts and potlatches. From an early age, a child with a talent for singing is trained by a master singer. This involves much prayer, fasting and memorizing. Medicines are given for a good voice and memory. Each family has its own songs for different occasions to be sung only by the family owning them, although the whole tribe might know them. Songs are inherited at birth by the eldest boy. Younger brothers have their own sets of songs but these are not the very formal *ha·tsḥoła* songs with their associated masks that belong to the eldest. On the other hand, the eldest son is not required to bear the burden of being a master singer in addition to his other duties as a leader. The master singer leads off the songs with the rest joining in immediately. He beats the time with a fan of white eagle feathers held between the fingers. Before a potlatch he, or a family delegate, goes around to tell the people what the gathering's songs will be, say, two or four sung in order. The night before, the people gather in the house of the potlatch giver to practise under the direction of the master singer who begins by indicating the beat with his arm, from one to six beats, the first five short, the last one long. For certain songs there is part singing ("split voice"), usually practiced first. Only men or only women might sing, some low and some high, for two parts. Men might sing in two parts while women add a higher third part, or third and fourth parts. Even six-part singing is done. Sometimes the drum beat is made to lag just a little behind the singing. There is often a characteristic rhythmic pattern in which a cluster of short notes is followed by one or more long tones and then another cluster of short ones that might end on a weak beat. It is common for the pitch to rise gradually during the song. A novice is taught to start with a low natural voice, then to sing higher and higher, as he grows used to the words, up to his full pitch. Songs are sung in as high and loud a voice as possible. Tunes can range over an octave but progress by small intervals for close-knit melodies with a variety of turning movements. Most songs are plain without extra parts, like introductions or interludes, and are divided into two or three phrases. The phrases are often made up of six measures. The measure tends to be evenly sub-divided, giving a smooth rhythm. Changes occur in all these features during most songs.

Whaling People sing many kinds of songs (no·k). T'ama· songs are informal and social, some ceremonial and some familial. They are sung at potlatches, often to request gifts or to make fun of people. New words can be made up to old tunes. Tama· songs seem prettier than most others. Another informal type of song is kwi·kwa·ła, the lively dance songs. Ha·na?a are gambling songs that are usually sung four times or end as soon as a correct guess is made. These three types of songs are sung in chorus, sometimes in parts, and are accompanied by drumming or the beating of sticks on planks. Ts'a·yiq are doctor songs performed solo with stick-beating and dancing. Novices initiated into the Ts'a·yiq doctoring society and filled with its spirit can sing the songs at once without practise. The voice is high pitched and choked, with a sad quality making everyone feel like crying. Ha·tsho·ła are formal wealth-display songs. Some are long because they involve calling out the recipients of gifts in a potlatch. Sung in chorus, but never in parts, they are accompanied by drumming. No·kwi·s are potlatch-entry songs accompanied by drumming; they are also known as marching or canoe songs, because they are sung while travelling to or arriving at the place of the ceremony. Chi·chi·sa songs are used with the women's sway dancing in ceremonial displays. The ts'i·qa· song was sung by the giver of a potlatch to boast of his wealth or tell what kind of dance display would follow while the dancers were getting ready. There were special *ts'i·qa·* songs for the Wolf Ritual accompanied by the drum and bird-shaped rattle. *Tsitsiḫink* were very solemn chants accompanied by the bird rattle and tremolo beating with sticks or drum.

Ya·tya·ta songs were sung when goods were being given away in a potlatch. *Łotsḫa·y'ak*, marriage songs, were also very solemn, using the natural voice at the beginning, then gradually shifting to a high pitch. Only the medicine man, his wife or his helpers sang *tłachity'ak*, the doctoring songs, as he performed his curing. He breathed on the patient as he sang, mumbling the words so that others could not make them out, accompanied by a fast tremolo drum and perhaps a rattle. *ʔAstimxy'ak* lullabies were sung with a soft voice and loving feeling, generally by the mother alone.

We hope that this small sample of the Whaling People's many types of songs indicates the richness of their music. Anyone can sing many of the songs, including practically all gambling songs and most of the informal *t'ama·* and *kwi·kwa·ła* songs. Many others, like all wealth-display songs, are owned hereditary rights (*top·ati*) of high-ranking families. New songs are made up or obtained from spirits, often in dreams. Striking or beautiful places like waterfalls and lakes are good for receiving songs, and some sleep at such spots to dream. Other groups of people on the coast were another source for new compositions. Songs pervade Whaling People's life whether formally in ceremonials or informally. Unfortunately their real nature can hardly be conveyed in words or pictures of the instruments or performers.

MYTHS

As among most peoples without writing and books, oral story telling was a well-developed art among the Whaling People. Many of their stories explained the origins of various family rights and told of their ancestors' encounters with power-giving supernatural beings. Such stories would be told within the family to pass on the historical knowledge to new generations or were recited at ceremonies to publicly validate claims to the associated hereditary rights. There were other stories that might be called popular, being known and enjoyed by all. Some of them are comparatively short, commonly featuring animal characters behaving like humans. Origin myths are often long with a number of episodes. Several characters, notably Raven Boy (*Qoʔishinm'it*) and Mink (Kwatya·t), feature in many tales because of their amusing personalities. Much of the humour was sexual and many tales contained considerable bloody violence. The myths can stand on their own as stories.

Here is small sample of Whaling People's myths, beginning with the continuation (from page 92) of "How Andaokot First Came to This World". In this second part of this Mowachaht version collected by George Hunt (Boas 1916:907-13), the hero becomes Q'anixi·na<u>x</u> and transforms the animal-people into their present forms.

Q'anixi·na<u>x</u> the Transformer

Andaokot then took a long rest; and after that, he told his mother to ask all his people to make a houseful of sharp-pointed arrows. Then all the Mowachaht tribe began to make sharp-pointed arrows, and it did not take them long to fill the house. One fine day Andaokot took his large bow, went out of his father's house, and asked the Mowachaht if they could see the great log (*t'ikip'itkit*) of the heavens; and not one said he could see it. Afterward Snail (*?Inm'i*) said that he could see the great log that lay across the doorway of heaven. And then Thunderbird (*?Awati*) said to Snail, "Please let me have your eyes to see the great log up in heaven!" for Thunderbird was blind at that time. And the foolish Snail took his eyes out and gave them to him.

Then Thunderbird put Snail's eyes on and looked up, and he saw the log. He kept Snail's eyes, and now he can see everything; but Snail has been blind from that day until now, for he was foolish and lent his eyes to Thunderbird.

Now, Andaokot took his great yew bow and began to shoot at the log with the first arrow; and the second arrow he shot was at the nock of the first arrow; and so on until a chain of arrows reached to the ground from the great log of heaven. Then Andaokot told his mother that he was going to see his father in heaven: so he began to climb on the long string of arrows, and it did not take him long to go up to heaven. As soon as he reached the great log, he went to the doorway; and as soon as he passed through to the upper world, he saw two blind women. They seemed to be very old; and Andaokot went toward them and took up their clover root, for they were digging it; and he stood near them for a while, to see what they would say about their brown clover root. Very soon one of them began feeling round for her clover root, but she could not find it. Then Andaokot asked her if she was blind; and she said, "We are blind, Andaokot, we can not see the face of the earth."

Then he told them that he was going to see his father, and that he would tell him about the things that needed to be put right all round the world, and that he might be sent down again by his father to put the world right hereafter.

"Then I will open your eyes," he said.

Now, these two old blind women were the Mallard Ducks. Then they

thanked him for what he had said to them; and they also said to him,
"Andaokot, which road will you take to go to your father's house? There
are two roads. One of them is a broad road, and there are many dangerous
animals on it; but on the narrow road there is only one dangerous woman.
Her name is Hoksimaqas. If she sees you, she will call you into her house,
and she will feed you on brown clover root. Now, if she calls you in to eat
that clover root, do not eat it, but take some of our clover root and hide it;
and when she offers you her clover root, pretend to eat it, throw it away
without her seeing you do so, and eat some of what I give you. Then,
when you finish eating, walk out of her house and toward your father's
house. Then you will be safe."

After the two old blind Duck Women had given instructions, he found
and followed the narrow road. He had not gone far, when he saw a small
house. A woman was standing at the door; and when he came near, the
woman called him. When he was in, she told him to sit down on a mat.
Then she took some brown clover root and put it on red-hot stones, and
steamed it. After it was cooked, she placed it on a small mat, put it down
in front of him, and said,

"You had better eat it."

Then she went out of the house. He ate the brown clover root that was
given to him by the old women, but the clover root on the mat he threw
into the corner of the house. After he had finished eating, he walked out
of the house and went along the road. Then he saw a house, a long way
ahead. He walked up to it, and then went in. There he saw his father on a
seat at the rear of the house.

His father said to him, "I am glad to see you. Come here, my son for I
see that there are many things that need to be changed in the lower world.
I see there are people there who look like men, but they are not men:
they have the souls of animals. So I want you to go down again and put
all of them to rights. Now and hereafter your name shall be Q'anixinax̱w.
I want you to go down again; and now I will give you this blanket that
carries the herring (tɫosmit) and all the different kinds of salmon in it; and
whenever you come to a river that you think should have some salmon in
it, take two of the fishes only and put them into the river, one female and
one male; and do likewise with the eulachon. Now, that is all I can say at
this time. Put this blanket on and go down again."

Then Q'anixinax̱w came down to Dza·wadi·, on Knight's Inlet, and
there he saw that Dza·wadi· was a good river for the eulachon, so he took
all the eulachon from his blanket and put them into the river. He also
took one pair of silver salmon and one pair of spring salmon, one pair of
dog salmon and a pair of steelhead salmon, from his blanket, and he put
them into the river, and that is why all kinds of salmon go up Dza·wadi·

River. Now, he did not keep any eulachon in his blanket for the other rivers, but he put them all into this river. That is why there is no eulachon in any river except that of Dza·wadi·.

After he had put all these different kinds of fish into the river, he went on. Then he saw a house on the right-hand side of the river, and at the door stood the daughter of the owner of the house. She seemed to be very pretty, and he was the same in her sight. As soon as she saw him, she called out to him to come to her, and he went. As soon as he came up to her, she said to him,

"Come in, and you shall be my husband!" for he was really a handsome man, and she was pretty. So he went into the house with her. And now he was married to the chief's daughter, and they lived together a long while and were very happy. The woman kept telling her husband to take care, for her father was always bad to whomever she had married before him; he always found some way of killing them. And Q'anixinaxw said, "Don't trouble about me, for he will never hurt me!"

Next morning the chief said to him, "My son-in-law, get ready and let us go to split a log in two, for I am going to make a canoe!"

And Q'anixinaxw said, "I shall be ready soon."

Then he went into his bedroom with his wife, and she told him that that log had been the death of her former husbands. "Now take care!" she said to him, "for he will throw his stone hammer into the crack of the log, and he will tell you to get it for him; but when you go inside of the crack, he will take out the wedge and kill you, as he did my former husbands. Now, goodbye, my husband!"

He walked out of the bedroom and down to the canoe. He went aboard, as did the chief, and he paddled away toward a river. They went ashore in a cove. The old man led the way up, and Q'anixinaxw followed. Then they came to a large log with a crack in one end of it, and the old man took his wedges and put them into the crack. Then he began to drive his wedges with a stone hammer; and when the crack was wide enough for a man to enter, he threw the stone hammer into it.

Then he said, "Ah, my son-in-law! My stone hammer fell in. Will you go in and get it for me? I will put in a spreading-stick to keep the crack open while you are inside." And he took a round stick and put it across the crack of the great log.

After he had finished, Q'anixinaxw went into it. When he was inside, the old man struck off the spreading-stick, and the crack closed on Q'anixinaxw. But as soon as he saw his father-in-law strike off the spreading-stick, he turned himself into mucus, and it ran through the crack of the log. After the mucus had all run through, he turned himself into a man again; and he saw under the log many bones and skulls of men who had been killed in the same way as it was intended he should be killed. He also heard his father-in-law say, "Now I am glad that I killed you, for you have brought shame on me by marrying my daughter."

He was saying this as he picked up his wedge and was leaving for home. As he neared his canoe, Q'anixinaxw picked up the stone hammer and ran after him, and said, "My father-in-law, how is it that you left me behind when you sent me to get your stone hammer? Here it is!" said he, as he gave it to him.

The old man took it, and said, "I was going to get some help to get you out of the crack after the spreading-stick jumped out."

Then Q'anixinaxw went ahead of the old man to the canoe; and on the way he picked up some pieces of wood and hid them under his arm-pits. Then he jumped into the bow of his canoe and lay on his back, and began to carve the pieces of wood into dolphins. He made four of them. Then the old man went into the stern of the canoe and paddled away.

After they were halfway across the head of the inlet, Q'anixinaxw whispered to the carved dolphins, "When I throw you into the water, you must turn into dolphins and go away for awhile; then you must come and jump on my father-in-law, and keep on jumping until he is dead."

This he said to the carved pieces of wood as he put them secretly over-board. As soon as he let them go, they all turned into fishes and began to jump away from the canoe. They went away for awhile; then they came to where the canoe was, and began to jump close to the stern. Suddenly they all jumped at the old man and killed him.

Then Q'anixinaxw went home to his wife, who said to her husband, "Where is my father?"

He answered, "Your father has gone to the place where he wanted to send me; for he tried to kill me with that log, and I made him die instead of me. I will go now and do what I have to do."

So he left her; and the first man he saw was Land Otter (*Wa·xni·m'it*). He was hard at work sharpening his spear. Then Q'anixinaxw asked him what he was doing, and he said, "Who are you and where did you come from? You are the only one who doesn't seem to know that Q'anixinaxw is coming to do mischief to the people of the world. Now, all are getting their fighting-spears and knives ready to fight him with."

And Q'anixinaxw said, "How will you fight him with that thing?" And he said, "I will spear him with it."

And Q'anixinaxw said, "If I were you, I would put that spear behind me, and I would fall on him backward with my full weight."

Then Land Otter said, "Take it and show me how you would put it on!"

So Q'anixinaxw took the spear, and said, "Turn your rump this way!" and Land Otter turned his rump to him.

Then Q'anixina̱xw stuck the spear into it, and slapped on each side of it with each hand, and said, "Hereafter you shall be a land otter."

Land Otter walked off for a little way. Now and then he would look back at Q'anixina̱xw. Then he went into the woods, and Q'anixina̱xw walked ahead for a while.

Then he saw Raccoon Man (*Tlapisim*), who was also sharpening his spear; and Q'anixina̱xw asked him what he was doing. Raccoon said, "I am sharpening my fighting-spear to have it ready to fight Q'anixina̱xw when he comes to do mischief to the world."

This he said as he rubbed a painted round stick on a rough stone. Q'amxina̱xw said, "Let me see your spear!" and Raccoon gave the spear to him. And then he took it and said, "Turn your rump this way!" And the foolish Raccoon turned his rump toward him.

"I will put this spear on your rump, for it is always best to fight backward," said he, as he stuck the spear on Raccoon's rump, and slapped on each side of it, and said, "Now, you shall be a raccoon hereafter!"

Raccoon walked away slowly, and went into the woods.

Q'anixina̱xw walked along, and he saw a man with a big belly sharpening a broad flat stone. This man was Beaver Man (*ʔAt'oˑ*). Q'anixina̱xw asked him what he was doing. And the man said, "How is it that you are the only man who does not know that Q'anixina̱xw is come to do harm to the world? I am sharpening this stone to fight him with it."

Then Q'anixina̱xw said, "Let me see your great spear, so that I may make one like it!"

Then Beaver gave the spear to him, and Q'anixina̱xw took it and looked at it for a while. Then he looked at Beaver, and saw that he seemed to be foolish, and did not look as if he were ready to fight. Then Q'anixina̱xw walked behind him and put the great flat spear on his rump, and slapped each side of it, and said, "I am Q'anixina̱xw, who came down to put everything right in the world. Hereafter you shall be a beaver."

And Beaver walked away very slowly. He would look back at Q'anixina̱xw and stared at him. Then he went into the woods.

Again Q'anixina̱xw walked on. He had not gone far, when he saw a small man sharpening his little spear. This little man was Marten (*Tl'itl'iḥiˑt*), and he seemed to be very quick in his movements.

Q'anixina̱xw asked him what he was doing, and Marten said to him, "Where have you come from? You must be a stranger, for you are the only man who does not know what I am sharpening my war-spear for. Don't you know that Q'anixina̱xw is coming to this world to do harm to all who are living in this place? Now, I shall get my spear ready to defend myself against him whenever he comes," said Marten.

And Q'anixina̱xw said to him, "Will you let me see your war-spear, so that I may make one just like it, and be ready to fight him when he comes?"

The little man Marten looked at him for a long while. Then he gave his spear to him. And Q'anixinax̱w took the little spear, and said, "Now I will look at it, and I will make one to fight against Q'anixinax̱w when he comes; but I shall try to put it on you in the place I think best for it, that I may put mine there too. Now, turn your rump this way!"

Marten obeyed him, and then he stuck the spear into his rump and slapped on each side of it, and said to him, "I am Q'anixinax̱w. Hereafter you shall he a marten: so stay in the woods and live on whatever food comes your way!"

And poor Marten walked away slowly, and went into the woods.

Then Q'anixinax̱w walked on again; and he saw another man, very stout. He was sharpening something that look like a black stone, and his look was very angry. Q'anixinax̱w went up to him, and said, "Man, what are you doing?" and the angry-faced man said, "Don't you know that there is a man coming, whose name is Q'anixinax̱w, to do mischief to us all? The two stone hammers I am making are to fight him with."

And Q'anixinax̱w said, "Let me see them, so that I myself may also make two of them."

And the man gave the two black stone hammers to him, and then Q'anixinax̱w took them and said, "Let me try them on your hands!" And he stuck them on the angry-faced man, and said to him, "Now hereafter you shall be a bear (*chims*)". And the Black Bear walked away into the woods.

Q'anixinax̱w kept on doing this to all the other animals until he came to Yuquot, the place where we are living. Then he saw Deer. He went up to him, and he saw that man also hard at work sharpening two shell knives; and Q'anixinax̱w asked him what he was doing; and Deer said, "Where have you come from, that you do not know what is known all round the world? Don't you know that Q'anixinax̱w is coming to do mischief to us all? These two war-knives are to fight him with."

Then Q'anixinax̱w said, "How will you fight him with those two knives?" And he replied, "I will carry one of these knives in each hand, and stab him when he comes near me."

And Q'anixinax̱w said, "Do you think you can fight him in that way? You ought at least to have one hand empty; but I think if you had both hands empty, and had those two knives tied on the top of your head, you could fight him better by catching hold of him with both hands and butting at him with the two knives on your head."

Then Deer looked at him, and asked him where he came from and who he was; and Q'anixinax̱w said, "I am only trying to find some one to make friends with." For at that time Deer was thinking that it was

Q'anixina<u>x</u>w who was speaking to him.

Then he began to rub his two large mussel-shell knives on the sandstone. Then Q'anixina<u>x</u>w spoke to him, and said, "Deer, let me see your knives!" Deer looking up, said in an angry way, "I don't want you to have them, for I know that your name is Q'anixina<u>x</u>w."

But Q'anixina<u>x</u>w only laughed, and said, "I just want to see your knives, so that I may make two of the same kind for myself to fight him with whenever he comes."

And Deer looked at him once more. Then he handed his knives to him; and as soon as Deer had given the two knives to him, he lost his power. Then Q'anixina<u>x</u>w said to him, "Now, put your head down, and let me show you the right way to put on these two knives; then you can fight Q'anixina<u>x</u>w or anything whenever they come to fight."

This he said as he put the two mussel-shell knives on Deer's head; and he slapped him on each side. After they were on, he said, "Hereafter you shall be a deer!"

Deer looked at him, shook his head, and walked away for a little distance; then he stopped and looked back and stared at Q'anixina<u>x</u>w; then he walked into the woods.

Then Q'anixina<u>x</u>w walked on southward, and he had not gone far, when he saw Mink (*Tł'itłi·ḥiyo·ḥ*) sharpening a short spear. And he went up to him and asked him what he was doing, and Mink said, "Why, don't you know the news about Q'anixina<u>x</u>w coming to do mischief to us all in this world? I am making this spear to defend myself against him."

Then Q'anixina<u>x</u>w said, "Let me have your spear, for I want to see how it is made!"

Mink gave the spear to him; and as soon as Q'anixina<u>x</u>w took the spear, he said, "Turn your rump this way, so that I may fix it for you."

And right away the foolish Mink obeyed, turning his rump towards Q'anixina<u>x</u>w. Then the latter stuck the spear on his rump, and it was made into a tail instead of a spear. Then Q'anixina<u>x</u>w slapped on each side of it, and said to him, "I am Q'anixina<u>x</u>w. Turn into a mink for the generations to come! "

And the little mink ran away into the woods without turning round to look at Q'anixina<u>x</u>w.

Then Q'anixina<u>x</u>w walked again, and he saw a man and woman with their private parts on their foreheads; and he went up to then, and asked them if they could breed as they were. Then the man said, "I have tried to make her pregnant, but without success." Then Q'anixina<u>x</u>w said, "I know that the people in the world will be all gone if no change is made." So he put the man's privates in the place where they are now, and he put the woman's secret parts also in the right place. After he had finished, he told the man to try to make his wife pregnant, and she immediately became so. Then Q'anixina̱xw left them.

Then he came to a place where he thought that he had better make man. He took from the beach a piece of wood and carved from it a man's and a woman's image. After he had finished carving them, he spat on them, one man said, and another man said he breathed on them, and brought them to life. After he gave the life, he told them how to live, and then he went on southward. This is all that is said about him. This story ends now.

The repetition of the same statements and actions for each animal that the Transformer meets was far from boring for the Whaling People listeners. Each animal was well known and meaningful to them. Children would never have grown tired of hearing how each creature was tricked in turn by the Transformer into having its weapon stuck on to become part of the animal. The part about redesigning a couple may seem out of place, but George Hunt was a very capable ethnographer and there is no reason to doubt that this was part of the Mowachaht's Transformer myth.

The next story, also recorded by Hunt (Boas 1916:933-35), features that favourite comic character of the North Pacific area, the tricky, greedy Raven (*Qoʔishinm'it*). The ball of quartz mentioned is the supernatural crystal, <u>Hin</u>'a, regarded as a valuable possession full of mysterious power and displayed in ceremonials like the Wolf Ritual. A Raven story, set in their most important ceremonial event, was very funny for the Whaling People.

How the Raven was in the Woods for a *Tło·kwa·na* Dance at Yuquot

Once upon a time there lived a man whose name was Raven (*Qoʔishin-m'it*), of a tribe belonging to the Ts'aw·n'at<u>h</u>, one of the brother tribes of the Mowachaht at Yuquot. Raven had a wife whose name was Sea Egg (*Pa·sh<u>h</u>ak*). It was in the wintertime, and the Mowachaht tribe were talking about having a *Tło·kwa·na* dance. After they had stopped talking about the *Tło·kwa·na* dance – how they would appear in the village – a number of young men went at night into the woods to howl like wolves, to give notice to the people that the *Tło·kwa·na* was coming to bring the dance to the people. Now, this notice has to be howled, as wolves howl, three different nights, so as to get everybody ready for the fourth night, for the wolves come to the door of the *Tło·kwa·na* dancing-house and throw in the ball of *Tło·kwa·na*, the dance-giver, or in Kwakwala the "ball of quartz." This ball is said to strike whatever girl (or boy) is going to dance the *Tło·kwa·na*. Then she pretends to be dead until all the people come to sing their secret songs. Then she comes to life again.

But as soon as Raven heard the wolves howl the first notice of the dance, he disappeared, and his people did not like it, for he was always doing something that did not please them; and, of course, his disappearance on the first notice of the winter dance made them feel very bad. Then all the people were called into a house, and also one of the speakers of Chief Woodpecker.

After all the people had come in, he said, "We are not pleased with what Raven has done in breaking the rules of our old custom regarding the *Tło·kwa·na* dance, for he disappeared before the fourth night of the wolves' howling, and he ought also to have given notice to all the chief men of what he had done. Now, we shall leave this village, and go to Deep Bay *(Ko·pti)* to have our *Tło·kwa·na* dance."

All the people were pleased with what their chief said. The first thing they did was to push their canoes *(ch'apats)* into the salt water, and to take whatever things they wanted. Then they all left the village and went to · Deep Bay; and then they had to give the second notice of the *Tło·kwa·na* dance on coming there.

On the fourth day Raven thought that he had been in the woods long enough, so he came out at the west corner of Yuquot, and began to sing this song: "All you, my friends, listen to me, for I will call you all to come and get me out of the woods. I have seen enough of the *Tło·kwa·na* dance, and I am truly hungry."

While he was singing, he was standing on a rock, naked. The only thing he had on was a wreath of hemlock branches round his neck and head. He had a piece of ice about two feet long and a foot wide.

This piece of ice was supposed to be quartz. When his wife heard him singing, she went out of the house and said to him, "Don't sing any more! You had better come home, for there is no one in the village to go and bring you out of the woods. They have all gone to Deep Bay to have their *Tło·kwa·na* dance there."

After she had finished speaking, he started home; and the first thing he said to his wife was that he was hungry.

Then she fed him, and when he had finished eating, he said to his wife, "Don't you think it is best for us to go to Deep Bay and join our friends?"

His wife said, "No, for it was you who made them leave this place, because you disappeared before the fourth notice was given by the wolves, and that is why Chief Woodpecker called our people into his house and told them to go and leave you here."

Raven said, "You may say whatever you like, and you can stay here, but I am going to Deep Bay and join my friends." And he picked up a paddle and went out of the house, down to the beach, where his canoe was.

Then he pushed the canoe down to the salt water; and when he got it into the water, Sea Egg saw that her husband meant to go where his friends were; so she took what things she thought she would want, and went down to the canoe to her husband. In a very short time they arrived at Deep Bay, for it is not far from Yuquot.

After Raven had arrived at Deep Bay, a man went to all the houses to call every man by name to go into his house to eat steamed salmon (so·ẖa), but Raven's name was not called, and it made him feel very bad. He said to himself, "I will say that I am a great shaman." And when all the people had gone into the feasting-house, he took hemlock branches and made one wreath for his head, and one for his neck. Then he put them on and began to sing his shaman's secret song, and these are the words of it:

"I am a shaman now, to heal the sick people, instead of Wolf Dancer. And whenever I dance, I can go under the floor, where no one can go, and I will show it to you all."

He left his house, singing, as he went to the feasting-house; and of course all the people became frightened, for they believed that he was really a shaman and could kill anyone whenever he liked.

. As soon as they heard him coming towards the feasting-house, each took a baton to beat time, for now they were waiting for the salmon to get cooked on the red-hot stones in the middle of the house, and it was all covered with mats to keep the steam in. Just before it was uncovered, Raven came into the house singing, and all the people began to beat time. Just before he went round the heap of cooking salmon, he disappeared and went through the floor. He had not been down long, when he appeared on one side of the heap of cooking salmon. In a short time he went down a second time, and again came up and went round the heap once more. He then disappeared the third time; and again he came up, but only showed himself. He went down the fourth time. This time he stayed down longer than usual; and when he came up, he was singing. Then he went out of the house; and after he went out, all the feasting people said, "Let us uncover the mats, for the salmon is cooked now!"

When they uncovered the mats, they found that all the salmon had been eaten by Raven, and that he had put many sticks to keep the mats up in the shape of the cooking salmon; and all the people were very angry with Raven, for he had got the best of them once more.

All the people had to go out of their feasting-house hungry. That ends the story.

The other Whaling People's trickster, Kwatya·t, appears in the next two stories. In the first he has the lowly social position of slave to Chief Wood-pecker. Involved at the beginning is Woodpecker's wife, Sparrow-daughter (ʔA·wi·pẕi·kwas), a bird who creates salmonberries by singing their name, "*qawi·*". There are four Thunderbirds in the story, the oldest called Thundering-now-and-then (*Toto·tsh*). This story also has some interesting details, like the ancient hoop-spearing game played by hunters the world over and the diving canoes of the Whales. This Whaling People's tale like many others was also known among the Kwakwa̲ka'wakw. The present version was collected from the Tseshaht (Sapir and Swadesh 1939:51, 53, 55).

Red-headed Woodpecker and the Thunderbirds

The Thunderbirds were going to play the hoop game and went to M'a?aqo·?a, where Woodpecker lived. They came from H̲och'oqtlis. Woodpecker invited those who were to play the hoop game to a feast. Woodpecker's wife took out her salmonberry dish. And then Sparrow-daughter (*?A·wi·p̲?i·kwas*) prepared salmonberries. "*Qawi· qawi· qawi· qawi·*," said she, and the berry dish filled up. The hoop-players were looking at her. And then the oldest Thunderbird fell in love with the woman. She passed him where he was eating salmonberries, and he squeezed her ankle.

After eating, they got ready – the Thunderbirds got ready to start the hoop game and their men gathered together. Black Bear, who was their hoop-thrower, was their first man to play. And Crane too was of those first on the level ground, he who was the best marksman in spearing. And also Woodpecker had his man who was best of all in marksmanship. And he had Kingfisher for spearing, and his hoop-thrower was Kwatya·t. They were finished taking their places and got ready for the hoop game.

The Thunder people were the first to throw the hoop; it was Black Bear, the strong one, who threw the hoop. And at the same time that he threw the hoop, the Thunderbirds made hail and made lightning, so that the hoop was lost to sight. The only one who could see it was Kingfisher, the sharp-eyed one. He speared, and his spear-point came off and stuck in the hoop. Then it was the turn of Woodpecker's hoop-thrower. Kwatya·t, the one of many tricks, set the hoop going. And then he said, blowing into his hoop to give it power, "Get small, get small!" and the hoop became small at once.

Crane, the marksman, missed his aim. Black Bear in his turn set the hoop going again, and Kwatya·t again blew magic into it. "Grow big, grow big," said he, and the hoop got big.

Again Kingfisher's spear remained stuck in it. Four times they rolled the hoop on each side. Kingfisher's spear never missed. The Thunderbird people were beaten. They finished.

And then Thundering-now-and-then (*Toto·tsh*) was angry and he made a great hail and lightning.

Woodpecker did not know that his wife was being taken away. Thunder took her along with him as he flew back to his home.

Woodpecker could not find his wife. He took his slave, Kwatya·t, and they deliberated. "Now! You will look for my wife, whom I have lost."

He went to the ones who had come to play the hoop game, Kwatya·t went to them. "I want you to be green salmonberry shoots," said Woodpecker to him, so Kwatya·t turned into green salmonberry shoots.

The former wife of Woodpecker went out to gather young salmonberry bushes. She discovered the shoots and recognized them as Kwatya·t, the one to do all kinds of tricks. She was afraid of him.

Kwatya·t returned to the place that he had come from. "She was afraid of me." he said.

"Go back!" he was told again. "You shall turn into a salmonberry. Be small!"

Again he went where he was sent. The woman who had been run away with went out again to look for salmonberries. The salmonberry too was noticed; it was very big. Again she recognized that it was Kwatya·t and again she was afraid of him. Once more he returned home and told this chief. "She is afraid of me," said he. Kwatya·t was made to stop going.

It became the time for the run of salmon, and Woodpecker himself went off to where there was the salmon trap of he who had deprived him of his wife. Woodpecker was a nice little young spring salmon in the trap. Thunderbird went to see his trap. He had his wife along in his canoe. He got there, and discovered the little spring salmon. He threw it, giving it to his wife, and she took it.

The little young spring salmon spoke. "It is I, your husband Woodpecker. Eat me all alone, won't you? And then you shall throw my left-over bones into the water," said he.

Thunderbird, who had come to see about this trap, turned back home and they arrived at their home. She roasted the little spring salmon on a spit. Her salmon was roasted and she ate it all by herself.

She finished eating and threw the bones into the water just as she had been told to throw them. She kept walking out farther and farther into the water.

"Say! Stop going and putting them so far out in the water," said those who were sitting on the beach and watching her. She had got far out in the water and she went right in. Woodpecker took her along with him. He had got her and returned home.

"Now!" said he. "Go and borrow Whale's diver." This was told to Kwatya·t. He borrowed it. "I shall have my revenge," said Woodpecker, "on the one by whom I was deprived of my wife." He went out to sea and got into the diver. He took along his slave, and off they went to where lived the Thunderbird people. It was early in the morning when they arrived. The whale came up out of the water.

The people who were sitting and looking saw him.

"Go, some of you, and wake up Catching-such-whales-as-come-out-once-in-a-while, so he may seize the whale in his claws."

He approached to get hold of the whale but he was unable to lift him. Goes-out-once-to-sea came under to help his older brother, but they could not lift him up. There was in the canoe-whale the one who knew many tricks, Kwatya·t.

"Get heavy, get heavy," said Kwatya·t.

And the whale grew heavy. The two of them could not lift him up. Between their talons they were all cut up into slits by Woodpecker.

Now came the time to help the next to youngest Thunderbird, too. He too took hold of the whale but, like them, he could not do much with his claws. Thundering-now-and-then went to help his younger brothers, but one spoke, "Don't you go! You alone shall remain alive. There is something wrong with us, it appears. We are as though our limbs were dying."

"Get heavy, get heavy! Get big, get big!"

And the whale grew heavy. All the brothers together sank into the water. All died. The oldest, Thundering-now-and-then, was the only one to remain alive. Woodpecker had his revenge on them, who had wronged him in taking away his wife. Woodpecker returned home, bringing back Whale's diver. This is how he had his revenge, and it is for this reason that only one Thunderbird is left alive.

In the second story about Kwatya·t, he and his brother avenge the death of their mother (Sapir and Swadesh 1939:38–39).

"Kwatya·t's Mother Moved, It is Said"

Kwatya·t's mother moved, it is said, in her canoe and arrived at Bluff-standing-big-in-the-water [a part of Alberni Canal now known as Hell's Gate]. And then she was swallowed, together with her canoe, by he who was fond of eating movers, a sea monster.

Now then, Kwatya·t found out that his mother had been swallowed, so he went out to pray for power to rescue his mother who had been swallowed. Then he made a box for boiling, poured in water, and built a fire on which stones were heated; then he put out the fire, dropped the stones into the box, and the water started to boil. And then Kwatya·t jumped into the box, of which the water was as hot as was the inside of Canoe-swallower. Once again he got into the boiling-box. His brother, T'i·xt'iyapixin, came near and said, "Let me straddle your hips!"

He stayed inside a little longer this time, and came out of the box again. The water was as hot in the box as was the inside of Canoe-swallower. He was finished. Then he made a spear in order to rescue his mother who had been swallowed. Now he got ready. He had many mussel-shell knives, which were to be used for cutting up the inside parts of the monster, when he was to be inside his body, besides these he had a sharp-pointed wooden spear of young fir, so that he might cause it to be stuck in his throat when he was to be swallowed down – a stick such as is used to lay across two canoes.

Now the two brothers paddled off in their canoe. They went to where their mother had been swallowed down. There they arrived and started to sing, "Come up out of the water, you who are wont to swallow those that move past in a canoe, who have your intestines curled up behind you! Ha ha, guts! Ha ha, guts!"

Both brothers danced as they sang, taking turns in dancing and beating time. The monster did not come up out of the water.

When they started in to sing again, the surface of the water was calm, but now bubbles began to come up out of the water and, as they bobbed up, grew bigger and bigger, and the water began to stir upward in waves. They began to circle around in their canoe, and Kwatya·t said, "Paddle so as to keep it straight!"

Now the sea ran in a current, the waves grew bigger and bigger, the water whirled about like a whirlpool. As it turned out, they were moved around, and it was the spirit that was fond of devouring those who moved past in a canoe that caused them to do thus. The sea ran in a current and was now about to open up – Kwatya·t and his brother were about to be swallowed down. The monster came up out of the water with his mouth wide open; they were swallowed now and went right down his throat clean down to his stomach. Then he settled down under the water.

Then Kwatya·t began to move around; he took his knife and started to cut inside of the monster, and cut off his heart. T'i·xt'iyapixin moved around too, and cut up all the insides; it was because of his mother who had been lost that he did this. Whatever was inside of him was all cut to pieces, they cut him all up. Kwatya·t heard how he moved around; while he was inside of the monster, he moved up out of the water, twice he moved up out of the water. Then he drifted ashore on the beach at Long Beach.

The Chiton was the first to get to the beach, with his round back up along side the stranded monster on the beach. All kinds of animals heard about it, and everybody came. Then they began to cut his intestines, which they were bent on getting; the Chiton was the first to get intestines. All kinds of animals came to get intestines. Then Kwatya·t spoke, "Look out lest you cut us without seeing what you're doing!"

All ran off frightened; those who were cutting were filled with terror. Kwatya·t and T'i·xt'iyapixin came out from inside.

"Bald headed, sure enough, is T'i·xt'iyapixin! Ahahaha!" said Kwatya·t, laughing at his younger brother. "Bald headed, sure enough, is T'i·xt'iyapixin! Ahahaha!"

He was bald headed too, but did not know that he was. They became bald headed for this reason, that they had not bathed their heads in hot water when training in the cooking-box.

This story also explains how the animal-people acquired intestines: they had none of their own before getting the intestines of the sea monster; since Chiton was first, he has the longest intestines (Sapir and Swadesh 1939:218).

The next story is a fantasy about a dispute between the Lice people and the Wolf people over deer (Sapir and Swadesh 1939·85, 87, 89).

A Fight Between the Chiefs of the Lice and the Wolves About Hunting Grounds

The Chief of the Lice people was a stalker and hunter of deer. Louse had a certain place where he always did his stalking and this place was well stocked with deer. Louse would always bring two out of the woods on his back. The Chief of the Wolf people likewise used to go stalking, but he did not find anything. The chief of the Wolf people, who was called T'it'i·chaqyo, did not get any deer. Louse would go stalking, and he would bring two deer on his back.

T'it'i·chaqyo would bring nothing out of the woods. T'it'i·chaqyo started spying to see where Louse was always getting many deer. He saw him going along there again with two deer on his back. So he started out early. He went where Louse had come from and actually got two deer. Louse again went stalking in his hunting place and caught nothing. T'it'i·chaqyo hunted again and once more got two. He would start out early while it was still night. He would be the first to start out. Louse would start out last and for that reason always found no deer at his hunting ground, though it was well stocked. Louse ceased to get deer because T'it'i·chaqyo got ahead of him each time. He returned empty-handed when he hunted; only T'it'i·chaqyo brought two deer out of the woods.

Louse found out that only T'it'i·chaqyo was bringing two deer out of the woods. He was angry. He said to himself that he would kill T'it'i·chaqyo. He started out early while it was still night. He lay in wait and did not have to be there long. T'it'i·chaqyo appeared with two deer on his back. At once Louse shot and hit him under the armpit. The Chief died. He died instantly. Louse dug in the ground and buried his victim after first cutting off his tail. He covered him up. He took upon his back the two deer that he had got by violence. He came out of the woods. Then he feasted his commoners.

T'it'i·chaqyo did not come out of the woods. Another day came and still he had not come out of the woods. The Wolf people began searching for their chief. They were excited. The keen-scented band went about smelling, but did not find him. The Chief Louse tied about his head the tail that had belonged to T'it'i·chaqyo. He went about with it tied around his head.

"Damn it, I say! Louse is wearing about his head the former tail of the one talked about as dead; he is wearing around his head the former tail of T'it'i·chaqyo," the people, the neighbours of Louse, began saying.

The tribe began talking of Louse having been seen wearing T'it'i·chaqyo's tail tied about his head. The Wolf people found out that Louse had tied about his head the tail of the one whom they were unable to find, their former chief. They got excited. They gathered the tribe together to consider how they would take revenge.

"Well, let's attack," said the warriors of the Wolf people.

The Louse people heard that they were to be attacked by the Wolf people. Louse also gave a feast and collected his commoners. The chief spoke and said, "Well, let us dance into the house of those who are about to attack us, let us anticipate them."

"Very well, let us do so," said the commoners.

"Let us each carry a bow and arrow," said the chief.

Then the chief began making a song and deciding what his entrance song would say. The Wolf people, in turn, heard that they were going to come dancing to their house. The Wolf warriors, the Fond-of-bones band, likewise assembled and sharpened their teeth. The Wolf people gathered in one house, they went to the house of their former chief.

"O warriors, stand at the door," they said.

The Louse people came to a decision and started off. All were ready, holding bow and arrows. The Louse people would whoop, "*Wa·· yi··, wa·· yi·· hi··*," the Louse people said, whooping. They whooped again in front of the house. "*Ha·· yi··*," they said. Those Lice rascals started their song. "*Haha* T'it'i·chaqyo *hiyhiy*, whom I have come for, *hiyhiy*, come for." said their song. Louse pretended to come for the one whom he had killed. The Louse people started dancing into the house; they all had their bows bent and pointed their arrows in the faces of the ones in the house.

The Wolf people were angry at what was being said about their former chief in the song. The chief of the Louse people was in the middle as they filed dancing into the house. He entered the house and there he was, sure enough, with T'it'i·chaqyo's tail around his head. And now the Wolf people were angrier than ever, because they saw that it really was T'it'i·chaqyo's tail that the chief of the Louse people had around his head. The Wolves were standing packed close all around the house.

All the Louse people came dancing into the house and the chief, with the tail around his head, reached the rear of the house. There, too, he continued dancing.

"Comrades, let us now bite them!" said the Wolf people.

Each singling out the one before him, they bit at them on the floor. The wolves were just as though they had collapsed, because they bent forward to bite at them on the floor. They bit nothing, but got their mouths full of dirt because they only bit into the dirt floor. The Louse people turned into lice and jumped through the spaces between the teeth. None was even grazed from biting.

"Ah ah ah," said the Wolf people who were choked with dust, each with his mouth full of dirt.

"*Ha· yi·, ha· yi· hi·*," said the Louse people.

"I have pity for you. I would have set you all on end if I had wanted to. I would have bitten into your hearts," said one of the Lice and, having said that, they left.

They yelled and went home.

"We really cannot get the better of them. Let us just let it go," said one of the Wolves.

It seems fitting to end the book with a whaling story. This tale is about an amorous Humpback Whale (after Sapir et al. 2004:141-5). It happens at a village called P'omp'oma?a ("Lots of Moss on the Rocks"), on the southeast side of the mouth of Alberni Inlet on the point between San Mateo and Ritherdon bays. Figuring in the plot is the nature of the whale, physical and psychological, as known to the Whaling People.

The Whale Sweetheart

There was a girl from P'omp'oma?a called Watsswo·?otł being courted by a young man of the P'omp'oma?atḥ who was just starting to prepare to be a whaler. But Watsswo·?otł refused the young man who was trying to get her for a wife. Watsswo·?otł went down the beach to defecate, and while she was down there heard what sounded like a Humpback Whale going along the middle of the beach, blowing as it went along.

"Oh, I wish I were the wife of the one making that sound!" said Watsswo·?otł as she heard the Humpback coming up from time to time.

The ones who were along with her started to laugh.

"That poor girl's always exaggerating. Look at the size of what she wants to marry!" they were all saying, laughing at her. "Would you be able to throw that around as you make love if the one that's making that sound became your husband?"

Said Watsswo·?otł, "Anyways, I would still like to be married to it."

The Whale heard what was being said about him. The girls went up the beach as they had finished. Those who had gone along with her were still saying that Watsswo·ʔotł wished she could be married to the Humpback Whale who was making those noises as he kept blowing.

"So you only want to marry the ugly one, while rejecting the others who are asking to marry you?" those living in the house said to her.

The whole village went to bed and were soon asleep. As she slept Watsswo·ʔotł was startled to feel someone push her.

"Wake up. It is I, the one you said you wish to marry, the one you heard making noises in the water."

That was as far as Watsswo·ʔotł could remember for she went unconscious. Her wish had now come true as the Whale had obeyed her wish to marry the one who was making noises in the dark, the Humpback Whale.

The young man who was courting Watsswo·ʔotł had stopped courting for the time being because all his time was taken up in his efforts at bathing ritually and praying to become a great whaler. When he did it again it was night, and the young man went to ask Watsswo·ʔotł if he could sleep with her. It was the full moon, just when it became full. He entered the house where Watsswo·ʔotł lived and stealthily went to the back end, the young man. Meanwhile the Humpback was already lying down with Watsswo·ʔotł. He was in the middle of the house when he became aware of a noise that sounded like a man going along the floor. It sounded as if it was going by behind him, feet thumping along as it went out. He looked back to see a man just as he stooped and went out of the house.

Right away the young man turned around and ran back outside. He saw a man walking along looking as if he was naked. He was not big but kind of fat and chunky. The young man, who was going to sneak into bed with Watsswo·ʔotł, now started walking after the other man. Then the young man saw that the man had his hair tied in front, on his forehead. He followed along at a respectful distance. He could see him clearly, for the full moon was shining down on a clear night. The man went for the other side of the hill at P'omp'omaʔa. The young man was following close behind as they went over the hill and down the other side. The man went down the beach, and the young man stopped as he saw that there was a Humpback Whale at the head of the bay. He saw that he jumped onto the nose, getting on the Humpback. Then it looked as if the man pulled something to one side behind the dorsal fin of the whale. It seemed that at the moment he lifted something he disappeared into it. All at once the Humpback came to life and thrashed around, causing the bay to become rough with big waves as it backed out. It wasn't long before the Humpback came up and blew as it went straight out of the bay of P'omp'omaʔa.

Watsswo·ʔotł was not aware of the fact that the young man had found

out about her new sweetheart. Next day the young man gathered his crew
together, not in the house but rather at the top of the hill at P'omp'oma?a.
The young man told about what he had seen, what he had found out. The
other young men listened, his crew being made up all of young men.

"You will all try your very best. We will go after it for it's a Humpback
that comes to sleep with Watsswo·?otł, that comes at night. Don't any one
of you go to sleep," he told his crew.

That day they blew up their sealskin floats. The young man got his
sinew line ready and his cedar withe rope. He connected them together
in such a fashion that it would be easy to quickly tie on the sealskin ropes.
When night came again the young man went to sit on top of the hill at
P'omp'oma?a.

As soon as the people of P'omp'oma?a went to sleep, the Humpback
Whale showed up at ?Inma and headed straight to P'omp'oma?a underwater, surfacing and blowing at intervals. While it was still a little ways
offshore it stopped making those noises and did not surface anymore,
the Humpback. Not long afterward it emerged very silently. This time
it went to the mouth of a little dent of a bay this side of the point at
P'omp'oma?a. There it landed on the beach of the little cove where it was
narrow. It looked as if it was forcing itself along in the tight-fitting place.
And then there appeared again a man who seemed to emerge from back
of the fin. He ran to the nose of the Humpback, jumped onto the beach,
and started walking taking the same route as before, straight over the hill.
The young man noticed that he went into the house where he was before,
where Watsswo·?otł lived.

At once the crew gathered round, for they were there in his house all
together. The men got ready for action, putting on the first float after the
harpoon, the next one, then another and another as there were four floats
tied on. The whaling canoe was already on the beach. The crew put their
cedarbark mats into it. The harpoon point was in place on the shaft, the
crew held the sealskin floats, and one them carried a ladder as they went
alongside the houses. Meanwhile the village of P'omp'oma?a slept.

They reached where Watsswo·?otł lived. They were sneaking along
very quietly these men, trying not to make any noise as they stealthily approached the house. Of the two who sat immediately behind the
harpooner in the canoe, the one on the right went onto the roof with
him. Watsswo·?otł was lying down together with her lover, not aware that
he was about to be attacked. Meanwhile the one who sits behind held on
to the float and together with the one he was with on the roof was in line
with where the door is. The young man got ready and tried to place himself in a good position at the edge of the board at the door from which he
would try to spear.

The young man kicked the board, making it squeak loudly. The Whale-man lying with the girl must have suddenly panicked and come to life: the young men heard footsteps pounding on the floor as the man was running out. It's supposed that his hair that was tied at the front was first as he came out the door. As soon as the shoulders appeared the young man speared – really speared him – right between the shoulder blades! So now the bugger started to run, taking the same route, running along the ground dragging the sealskin floats that were being thrown all over the place as he ran. He ran all the way over the hill to where his canoe was. He got to the beach, jumped onto the nose of the whale and went inside in the usual manner. Suddenly the Humpback got into motion, moved backwards out of the bay and took off. The cedar-withe rope did not get tangled up on the ground as it ran out because it was coiled properly. Right away they [the whalers] pulled out their canoe, which was sitting on the beach ready. Hey, out of P'omp'omaʔa they paddled! Now the P'omp'omaʔaʔath were all in an uproar!

"He's trying to capture! He's trying to capture!" they started saying but they did not know where he had speared the thing.

They thought that he had speared the whale at sea. They did not know he had speared him where he was making love. The people were as though they had had a nightmare and just woken up since they had been asleep when all this happened. As soon as the owner of the spear grabbed hold of it the Humpback died. There close to the shore of P'omp'omaʔa it laid its head down on the water and died. That was how those coming on the scene of the action found the ones who went whaling with their whale already dead. All they did then was take the whale in tow. The whalers did not say that they speared it at the house but pretended to have speared in the bay of P'omp'omaʔa. The crew was advised not to say that the young man speared the whale while he went to make love. The Humpback was finally towed in to shore at P'omp'omaʔa and tied up in the moonlight. He hadn't even chased it because it died right away as he had hit the man that's inside the whale. Watsswo·ʔotł was now out of luck. She hadn't had her lover long, and he had died by the hand of the young man she refused.

Next day all the P'omp'omaʔaʔath started butchering the Humpback, cutting it all up. The young man made all the people of P'omp'omaʔa work for the blubber. None of his crew said anything about the fact that he speared the man for taking his girl. They finished butchering the whale that day. All the young man got was the dorsal fin (chakwa·si). He gave each person a piece of blubber, and that night the whole village started cooking. It was as if all the houses were boiling because every household was boiling blubber and skimming off the top. Some were cooking the meat and drinking the broth.

The young man who got the whale now went about looking with the one who sits next to him in the canoe, for the whalers always hang onto this one. They got to where Watsswo·ʔotł lived, those who were looking around. He kept him near because he went bathing ritually with him too. There on the floor was Watsswo·ʔotł, eating blubber.

His sidekick advised him, saying, "'So you are eating your former lover, Watsswo·ʔotł.' Say that."

He said what he was advised to say. And since Watsswo·ʔotł was really enjoying eating the blubber of her whale lover, he added, "How sweet indeed your love was, oh you, Watsswo·ʔotł!"

Suddenly Watsswo·ʔotł fell on her face, dead, the result of what was said to her. Just after that happened, when Watsswo·ʔotł died, he revealed what had really happened, that while the Whale-man was at her house to make love to her he had speared him from the top of the roof, the former Humpback Whale. Watsswo·ʔotł did not regain consciousness. She really died for good.

Spelling Key
for Whaling People's Words

To write the languages spoken by the Whaling People we use a practical orthography with English-like spelling of most of the sounds. A few sounds not found in English have to be represented by letters modified by an underline or by special symbols.

Consonants, Nasals and Semi-vowels

p t k m n w y s ts ch sh h b d l   Pronounced approximately as in English. Ditidaht and Makah use **b** and **d** instead of the nasals **m** and **n** of Nuu-chah-nulth. They also have an English-like **l** plus, rarely, another made farther back in the mouth, represented by **l** (l underlined).

ł   The common **l**-like sound in these languages differs from the English **l** (as in "flap") – it is made with the tongue tip up on the front of the palate at the root of the upper incisors so that the air stream escapes off the sides of the tongue. This lateral sound is "voiceless", being made without vocal-cord vibration.

tł   Like **t** and **ł** run together. Linguists who favour a single symbol use the Greek lambda (**λ**), usually with a lateral bar, for this sound.

q   Like **k**, but made farther back in the mouth.

x x̲   Similar to the German "ich" and "ach", respectively.

kw qw xw x̲w   Said with rounded lips.

248

ẖ   Like **h**, but made with the tongue drawn way back.

? ?   Glottal stops. The first is a silent breath catch, as in "uh-uh", and the second, underlined, is made at the back of the throat, as in Arabic. (Originally, this symbol was a raised hook, which was easy when handwriting. On typewriters it could be made by filing the dot off the question mark. The symbol is not available in the character sets of most typesetting fonts, so we use a normal question mark with the bottom dot.) When a word beginning with a glottal stop is capitalized, the first letter takes the capital.

p' t' tł' ts' ch' sh' k' kw' q' qw' x' xw' x̱' x̱w' m' n' w' y' Glottalized consonants, nasals and semi-vowels pronounced by first withholding then explosively releasing the breath (called "cracked sounds" by some). In the nasals (**m' n'**) and the semi-vowels (**w' y'**) the holding and releasing of breath occurs before the voiced sound. Ideally, the apostrophe appears directly over the letter, as can be readily done in handwriting.

Vowels

i o o̱ a e   Short vowels, close to the sounds in "pit, put, pot, but, bet." Because the lips are thrust forward for **o**, some linguists use **u**, but that does not represent the vowel well. (For **o̱**, which is infrequent as in yells, some linguistics reverse **c** to create another specialized symbol.)

i· o· o̱· a· e·   Long vowels, as in "feed, food, laud, palm, bad". Some writers show lengthened vowels by doubling the letter, quick for typing but often confusing.

i·· o·· o̱·· a·· e··   Extra long vowels.

i··· o··· o̱··· a··· e···   Prolonged vowels as in cries.

ng mg z   Additional sounds made only in singing.

Additional Reading

The following publications provide more detailed information from general to more specific aspects of the history and culture of the Whaling People. All are listed in References.

The Northern and Central Nootkan Tribes by Philip Drucker (1951) is the basic ethnographic work on Nuu-chah-nulth society and culture. Drucker collected information from several northern and central Nuu-chah-nulth consultants in the mid 1930s. Available in major libraries.

Edward Sapir, as head of anthropology at the Geological Survey of Canada from 1910 to 1923, produced a collection of 147 Nuu-chah-nulth texts from Port Alberni and Barkley Sound, with the help of his two chief interpreters, Frank Williams and Alexander Thomas. Texts numbered 1–79 with English translations and explanatory notes were published in two volumes: *Nootka Texts* and *Native Accounts of Nootka Ethnography* (Sapir and Swadesh 1939, 1955). The final four parts have been published in separate volumes as the *Sapir-Thomas Nootka Texts* (Sapir et al. 2000, 2004, 2007, 2009). These volumes amount to an extraordinary record of the Whaling People in their own words.

"The Nootka" in volume 11 of *The North American Indian* by Edward S. Curtis (1916). Reprinted in 1970, this readable account about the Whaling People contains detailed Nuu-chah-nulth narratives and many photographs.

A number of articles in volume 7 of the *Handbook of North American Indians*, edited by Wayne Suttles (1990), provide academic summaries of the history and culture of the Whaling People.

Since the Time of the Transformers: The Ancient Heritage of the Nuu-chah-nulth, Ditidaht and Makah by Alan McMillan (1999) is the most current summary of the history of Whaling People before contact by Europeans.

The Makah Indians: A Study of an Indian Tribe in Modern American Society by Elizabeth Colson (1953) is based on fieldwork that was conducted in the winter of 1941–42.

Out of the Mist: Treasures of the Nuu-chah-nulth Chiefs by Martha Black (1999) is the most comprehensive published record of Nuu-chah-nulth artifacts to date.

Nuu-chah-nulth Voices, Histories, Objects & Journeys, an anthology edited by Alan Hoover (2000), contains both academic and community voices on a wide range of subjects including histories, artifacts, and contemporary art and artists.

Between Ports Alberni and Renfrew: Notes on West Coast Peoples (Arima et al 1991) gives detailed information on the territories and place names of the Barkley Sound groups and those to the southeast of Barkley Sound.

Hunters of the Whale: An Adventure in Northwest Coast Archaeology by Ruth Kirk and Richard D. Daugherty (1974) is a well-illustrated account of excavations at the water-logged site of Ozette, Washington. It describes wonderfully preserved wooden artifacts found in five houses buried by a mud slide five centuries ago.

Three books by George Clutesi (1905–88) describe the culture of the Nuu-chah-nulth people with reference to folk-tales, feasting and ceremonies: *Son of Raven, Son of Deer: Fables of the Tse-shaht People* (1967), *Potlatch* (1969) and *Stand Tall My Son* (1990). In *Stand Tall My Son* he also reflects on issues such as the Canadian education system, progress and citizenship.

As Far As I Know: Reminiscences of an Ahousaht Elder by Peter Webster (1983) is an entertaining and informative memoir about living and working on the west coast of Vancouver Island. The book contains eight traditional narratives and insightful essays on changes brought about by the industrial exploitation of natural resources. The book is illustrated by the well-known Nuu-chah-nulth artist *Kwayatsapalth* (Ron Hamilton, also known as *Ki-ke-in*).

Ahousaht Wild Side Heritage Trail Guidebook by Stanley Sam Sr (1997) illustrates 10 carved and painted wooden markers set up along a heritage trail that skirts the southwestern shore of Flores Island. Each marker relates to a particular historic tradition or contemporary event. The book includes essays on a number of topics including Ahousaht history, social organization, ownership and property, food resources and changes in Clayoquot Sound.

Living on the Edge: Nuu-chah-nulth History From an Ahoushat Chief's Perspective by Chief Earl Maquinna George (2003) is more than just an account of growing up and living in Clayoquot Sound. Chief George (1926–2006), also provides an informed perspective on treaty negotiations between the Nuu-chah-nulth, British Columbia and Canada. In this context he discusses the difficult issues of sovereignty, access to resources, endangered wildlife, and forest management.

Extraordinary Accounts of Native Life on the West Coast: Words from Huu-ay-aht Ancestors by Kathryn Bridge (2004). This account of Huu-ay-aht history is based on information from a number of elders. The chief source was Chief Louie Nookmis, interviewed in 1964 by Eugene Arima.

Queesto: Pacheenaht Chief by Birthright by Chief Charles Jones and Stephen Bosustow (1981) is a first-person narrative touching on episodes in the lives of Chief Charles Jones, his father and grandfather. Jones touches upon many subjects including games, potlatches, slavery, religion, missionaries, the surveying of reserves, hunting and fishing, and the effects of logging on fishing.

The Sayings of Our First People by Debbie Foxcroft (1995) is based on interviews and conversations with members of a Nuu-chah-nulth Elder's Advisory Committee, who met over a period of about 12 years. This book describes the teachings that the elders wanted to pass on to younger people, particularly the customs, practices and beliefs of bringing up a family.

Nuu-chah-nulth Phrase Book and Dictionary: Barkley Sound Dialect by Maggie Paquet (2004) contains maps, place names, lists of phrases organized by category and language dialect, and word lists in two sections. It also features an essay by *Ki-ke-in* on the continuing struggle to maintain the Nuu-chah-nulth language in the face of long-term linguistic and cultural oppression.

Narrative of the Adventures and Sufferings of John R. Jewitt, Only Survivor of the Crew of the Ship Boston ... by John Jewitt (1815). This exciting story also provides a good picture of Nuu-chah-nulth life at the beginning of the 19th century.

Maquinna the Magnificent by Bruce A. McKelvie (1946). This popular biography of the Mowachaht chief who became well known to white visitors to Friendly Cove draws from records left by Cook, Martinez, Meares, Mozino and others.

Scenes and Studies of Savage Life by Gilbert Malcolm Sproat (1868). This excellent description of the Nuu-chah-nulth, made as colonization began at Alberni in 1860, was republished in 1986. Historian Charles Lillard edited and annotated the updated edition.

Two books by ethnobotanist Nancy Turner and co-authors discuss the use of plants by the Whaling People: *Ethnobotany of the Hesquiat Indians of Vancouver Island* (1982) and *Ethnobotany of the Nitinaht Indians of Vancouver Island* (1983). Both of these books are out of print and may be difficult to find. But Turner's more general books on plant usage, written on her own, contain information about the Nuu-chah-nulth and other coastal groups: *Food Plants of Coastal First Peoples* (1995) and *Plant Technology of First Peoples in British Columbia* (1998).

Basketry and Cordage from Hesquiat Harbour by Kathryn Bernick (1998) describes plant-fibre artifacts collected from surface deposits at archaeological sites in Hesquiat Harbour. It also examines the weaving techniques.

First Nations Perspectives Relating to Forest Practices in Clayoquot Sound by the Scientific Panel for Sustainable Forest Practices in Clayoquot Sound (1995) includes an appendix that lists plants and animals significant to the Nuu-chah-nulth.

The Nootkan Indian: A Pictorial by John Sendey (1977) is a collection of early drawings and more recent photographs.

Portrait in Time: Photographs of the Makah by Samuel G. Morse, 1896–1903 by Carolyn Marr (1987) features Morse's photographs and three short essays: "Makah History" by Lloyd Colfax, "Samuel Gay Morse" by Carolyn Marr and "Indian Photography in Washington" by Robert D. Monroe.

Paddling Through Time: A Kayaking Journey Through Clayoquot Sound by Joanna Streetly and Adrian Dorst (2000). In addition to information on the natural history and cultural history of the area, Streetly writes knowledgeably and passionately about the protests against clear-cut logging that culminated in the massive civil disobedience of the late 1980s. The book features beautiful colour photographs by Adrian Dorst.

References

Alexander, Roy. 2003. "Nuu-chah-nulth Loss of Fisheries Access." *Ha-Shilth-Sa* 30:13:4.

Archer, Christon I. 1973. "The Transient Presence: A Reappraisal of Spanish Attitudes Toward the Northwest Coast in the 18th Century." *BC Studies* 18:332.

Arima, Eugene (E.Y.). 1975. "A Report on a West Coast Whaling Canoe Reconstructed at Port Renfrew, B.C." *History and Archaeology* 5. National Historic Parks and Sites Branch, Canada.

———. 1988. "Notes on Nootkan Sea Mammal Hunting." *Arctic Anthropology* 25:1:16-27.

Arima, Eugene and John Dewhirst. 1990. "Nootkans of Vancouver Island." In *Handbook of North American Indians*, vol. 7: *Northwest Coast*, edited by Wayne Suttles. Washington, DC: Smithsonian Institution.

Arima, Eugene, Denis St Claire, Louis Clamhouse, Joshua Edgar, Charles Jones and John Thomas. 1991. *Between Ports Alberni and Renfrew: Notes on West Coast Peoples*. Mercury Series, Canadian Ethnology Service Paper 121. Ottawa: Canadian Museum of Civilization.

Barnett, Homer G. 1968. *The Nature and Function of the Potlatch*. Eugene: University of Oregon.

Beaglehole, J.C., ed. 1967. *The Journals of Captain James Cook on his Voyages of Discovery*, vol. 3: *The Voyage of the Resolution and Discovery, 1776–1780*. Cambridge, UK: The University Press, for the Hakluyt Society.

Bernick, Kathryn. 1988. *Basketry and Cordage from Hesquiat Harbour*. Victoria: Royal BC Museum.

Black, Martha. 1999. *Out of the Mist: Treasures of the Nuu-chah-nulth Chiefs*. Victoria: Royal BC Museum.

———. 2000. "Where The Heart Is: From a Conversation with Tsa-qwa-supp." In *Nuu-chah-nulth Voices, Histories, Objects & Journeys*, edited by Alan L. Hoover. Victoria: Royal BC Museum.

Boas, Franz. 1890. "The Nootka." In *Second General Report on the Indians of British Columbia*. British Association for the Advancement of Science, Report for 1890.

Boas, Franz. 1897. "The Social Organization and the Secret Societies of the Kwakiutl Indians." *Report of the U.S. National Museum for 1895*.

———. 1916. "Myths of the Nootka." Collected by George Hunt. In *Tsimshian Mythology*. Bureau of American Ethnology Annual Report 31.

Bouchard, Randy, and Dorothy Kennedy. 1990. "Clayoquot Sound Indian Land Use: Report Prepared for MacMillan Bloedel, Fletcher Challenge Canada and the BC Ministry of Forests." Unpublished ms. BC Indian Language Project.

Bowechop, Janine. 2004. "Contemporary Makah Whaling." In *Coming to Shore: Northwest Coast Ethnology, Traditions and Visions*, edited by Marie Mauzé, Michael E. Harkin and Sergei Kan. Lincoln: University of Nebraska Press.

Boyd, Robert T. 1990. "Demographic History, 1774–1874." In *Handbook of North American Indians*, vol. 7: *Northwest Coast*, edited by Wayne Suttles. Washington, DC: Smithsonian Institution.

———. 1999. *The Coming of the Spirit of Pestilence: Introduced Infectious Diseases and Population Decline among Northwest Coast Indians, 1774–1874*. Seattle: University of Washington Press.

Brabant, Augustin J. 1926. "Vancouver Island and its Missions, 1900." In *Reminiscences of the West Coast of Vancouver Island* by Charles Moser. Victoria: Acme Press.

———. 1977. *Mission to Nootka: 1874–1900*. Edited by Charles Lillard. Victoria: Gray's Publishing.

Bridge, Kathryn. 2004. *Extraordinary Accounts of Native Life on the West Coast*. Canmore, Alberta: Altitude Publishing.

British Columbia. 2007. BC Treaty Commission *Annual Report 2007*. www.bc-treaty.net/files/pdf_documents/2007_annual_report.pdf

———. 2008. Ministry of Aboriginal Affairs and Reconciliation, Incremental Treaty Agreements. http://www.gov.bc.ca/arr/treaty/incremental_treaty_agreements/default.html

Brown, Steven C. 1998. *Native Visions: Evolution in Northwest Coast Art from the Eighteenth through the Twentieth Century*. Seattle: University of Washington Press.

———. 2000. "Flowing Traditions: The Appearance and Relations of Nuu-chah-nulth Visual Symbolism." In *Nuu-chah-nulth Voices, Histories, Objects & Journeys*, edited by Alan L. Hoover. Victoria: Royal BC Museum.

Buti, Antonio. 2001. "Responding to the Legacy of Canadian Residential Schools." *Murdoch University Electronic Journal of Law* 8:4. http://www.austlii.edu.au/au/journals/MurUEJL/2001/28.html#Introduction_T

Canada. 1916. *Report of the Royal Commission on Indian Affairs for the Province of British Columbia*, 4 vols. Victoria: Acme Press.

Canada. 2007. "Registered Indian Population by Sex and Residence 2006." Department of Indian and Northern Affairs Canada. http://www.ainc-inac.gc.ca/pr/sts/rip/rip06_e.pdf

Carwardine, Mark. 1995. *Whales, Dolphins, and Porpoises*. New York: Dorling Kindersley Publications.

Chittenden, Hiram Martin. 1902. *The American Fur Trade of the Far West*, 2 vols. New York: Francis P. Harper.

Clutesi, George C. 1967. *Son of Raven, Son of Deer; Fables of the Tseshant People.* Sidney, BC: Gray's Publishing.

———. 1969. *Potlatch.* Sidney, BC: Gray's Publishing.

———. 1990. *Stand Tall My Son.* Port Alberni: Clutesi Agencies.

Codlin, Lee. 2011. "Another Win in Fisheries Litigation for Nuu-chah-nulth Nations." *Raven's Eye* 29:3. http://www.ammsa.com/publications/ravens-eye/another-win-fisheries-litigation-nuu-chah-nulth-nations

Colnett, James. 1940. *The Journal of Captain James Colnett Aboard the* Argonaut, edited by F.W. Howay. Toronto: Champlain Society.

Colson, Elizabeth. 1953. *The Makah Indians; A Study of an Indian Tribe in Modern American Society.* Minneapolis: University of Minnesota Press. (Reprinted, 1974. Westport, Conn.: Greenwood Press.)

Cook, Warren L. 1973. *Floodtide of Empire: Spain and the Pacific Northwest, 1543–1819.* New Haven, Conn.: Yale University Press.

Crockford, Cairn. 1996. "Nuu-chah-nulth Labour Relations in the Pelagic Sealing Industry: 1868–1911." M.A. thesis, Dept of History, University of Victoria.

Curtis, Edward S. 1916. "The Nootka." In *The North American Indian*, vol. 11. Norwood, Illinois: Norwood Publishing. (Reprinted, 1970. New York: Johnson Reprint Corporation.)

Dart, Jennifer. 2008. "Esowista Reserve Expansion Still Needs Federal Sign Off." *Westerly News* http://www.canada/westerly/

de la Pena Saravia, Fray Tomas. 1891. "Diario. Documents from the Sutro Collection." *Publication of the Historical Society of Southern California* 2:1:83-143.

Densmore, Frances. 1939. "Nootka and Quileute Music." *Bureau of American Ethnology, Bulletin* 124, Smithsonian Institution.

Dewhirst, John. 1978. "Nootka Sound: A 4,000 year Perspective." *Sound Heritage* 7:2:1-29.

Drucker, Philip. 1939. "Rank, Wealth, and Kinship in Northwest Coast Society." *American Anthropologist* 41:55-65.

Drucker, Philip. 1951. *The Northern and Central Nootkan Tribes.* Bureau of American Ethnology Bulletin 144, Smithsonian Institution.

———. 1955. *Indians of the Northwest Coast.* New York: McGraw Hill. (Reprinted, 1963. Garden City, NY: Natural History Press.)

———. n.d. Field Notes. Smithsonian Institution, National Anthropological Archives, Photocopies, 1935–55. MS-0870, Box 2, Part 23, Vols 1-10, 12-15. BC Archives, Victoria.

Drucker, Philip, and Robert F. Heizer. 1967. *To Make My Name Good: A Re-examination of the Southern Kwakiutl Potlatch.* Berkeley and Los Angeles: University of California Press.

Duff, Wilson. 1965. *The Indian History of British Columbia: The Impact of the White Man.* Reprinted (new format), 1997. Victoria: Royal BC Museum.

Duffek, Karen. 2000 "*Tla-kish-wha-to-ah*, Stands with his Chiefs: From a Conversation with Joe David." In *Nuu-chah-nulth Voices, Histories, Objects & Journeys*, edited by Alan L. Hoover. Victoria: Royal BC Museum.

Dyler, Harry. 1981. "Mabel Taylor – West Coast Basket Maker." *American Indian*

Basketry Magazine 1:4:12-22.

Ellis, David W., and Luke Swan. 1981. *Teachings of the Tides: Uses of Marine Invertebrates by the Manhousat People.* Nanaimo, BC: Theytus Books.

First Nations Fisheries Council. 2009. "Nuu-chah-nulth Celebrate Fisheries Decision." Press Release, November 3. http://fnfisheriescouncil.ca/index.php/fish-in-the-news-/528-press-release-nuu-chah-nulth-celebrate-fisheries-decision-nov-309

Fisher, Robin. 1977. *Contact and Conflict, Indian-European Relations in British Columbia, 1774–1890.* Vancouver: University of British Columbia Press.

Fladmark, Knut R. 1975. "A Palaeoecological Model for Northwest Coast Prehistory." *Archaeological Survey of Canada Paper,* Mercury Series, no. 43, National Museum of Man.

Flucke, Archibald F., and A.E. Pickford. 1966. *Nootka.* British Columbia Department of Education Heritage Series 1:5.

Folan, William J. 1972. "The Community, Settlement and Subsistence Pattern of the Nootka Sound Area: a Diachronic Model." PhD dissertation, Southern Illinois University, Carbondale.

Foxcroft, Debbie, ed. 1995. *The Sayings of Our First People.* Nuu-chah-nulth Community Health Services. Penticton: Theytus Books.

George, Chief Earl Maquinna. 2003. *Living on the Edge: Nuu-Chah-Nulth History from an Ahousaht Chief's Perspective.* Winlaw, BC: Sono Nis Press.

Gogol, J.M. 1981 "Nootka/Makah Twined Fancy Baskets." *American Indian Basketry Magazine* 1:4:4-11.

Growlings Aboriginal Law Practice Group. 2011. "BC Court of Apeal Affirms Nuu-chah-nulth Right to Commercial Fishery." http://www.gowlings.com/KnowledgeCentre/enewsletters/Aboriginal/HtmFiles/specialBulletin_20110613.en.html

Gunther, Erna, ed. 1942 "Reminiscences of a Whaler's Wife." *Pacific Northwest Quarterly* 33:65-69.

———. 1960. "A Re-evaluation of the Cultural Position of the Nootka." *International Congress of the Anthropological and Ethnological Sciences,* Acts, 5: 270-276.

———. 1972. *Indian Life on the Northwest Coast of North America as Seen by the Early Explorers and Fur Traders During the Last Decades of the Eighteenth Century.* Chicago and London: University of Chicago Press.

Haggarty, Jim, and Gay Boehm. 1974. "The Hesquiat Project." *Midden* 6:3:212.

Haggarty, Jim, and Neal Crozier. 1975. "A report on Archaeological Investigations at Hesquiat, BC, Summer 1974." Unpublished ms, Royal BC Museum.

Hajda, Yvonne. 1990 "Southwestern Coast Salish." In *Handbook of the North American Indians,* vol. 7: *Northwest Coast,* edited by Wayne Suttles. Washington, DC: Smithsonian Institution.

Ha-Shilth-Sa. 1978–2008. Various articles cited by year, volume, issue, pages.

Happynook, Tom Mexsis. 2008. Quoted in "Important Fishing Case Involving Aboriginals Returns to BC Court." Canadian Press, February 2, http://cnews.canoe.ca

Harris, Douglas C. 2001. *Fish, Law and Colonialism: The Legal Capture of Salmon in*

British Columbia. Toronto: University of Toronto Press.

Hoover, Alan L., ed. 2000. *Nuu-chah-nulth Voices, Histories, Objects & Journeys.* Victoria: Royal BC Museum.

Howay, F. W. 1925 "Indian Attacks Upon Maritime Traders of the Northwest Coast, 1785–1805." *Canadian Historical Review* 6:287-309.

Irving, Washington. 1836. *Astoria: or Enterprise Beyond the Rocky Mountains.* Paris: Baudry's European Library.

Jewitt, John Rodgers. 1807. *A Journal Kept at Nootka Sound, by John R. Jewitt. One of the Surviving Crew of the Ship* Boston, *of Boston; John Slater, Commander Who Was Massacred on 22d of March, 1803. Interspersed with Some Account of the Natives, Their Manners and Customs.* Boston: Early Canadiana Online http://www.canadiana.org/. Original in BC Archives.

————. 1815. *Narrative of the Adventures of John R. Jewitt;, Only survivor of the Crew of the Ship* Boston, *During a Captivity of Nearly Three Years Among the Savages of Nootka Sound: With An Account of the Manners, Mode of Living, and Religious Opinions of the Natives.* Middleton, Conn.: Loomis and Richards.

Jonaitis, Aldona, and Richard Inglis. 1999. *The Yuquot Whaler's Shrine.* Seattle: University of Washington Press.

Jones, Chief Charles, and Stephen Bosustow. 1981. *Queesto [Kwi:sto͟x], Pacheenaht Chief By Birthright.* Nanaimo: Theytus Books.

Kennedy, Bob. 2004. "News and Comments." Turtle Island Native Network, http://www.turtleisland.org/communities/Tla-o-qui-aht.htm.

Kenyon, Susan M. 1973. "The Indians of the West Coast of Vancouver Island (The Nootka)." Unpublished report, Canadian Ethnology Service, National Museum of Man, Ottawa.

————. 1975. "Rank and Property Among the Nootka: Ethnographic Research on the West Coast of Vancouver Island." Unpublished report, Canadian Ethnology Service, National Museum of Man, Ottawa.

Kirk, Ruth, and Richard D. Daugherty. 1974. *Hunters of the Whale: An Adventure in Northwest Coast Archaeology.* New York: William Morrow.

Klokeid, Terry J. 1972. "Introduction to the West Coast Languages of Vancouver Island." Unpublished report, Canadian Ethnology Service, National Museum of Man, Ottawa.

————. 1975. "The Nitinaht Feature System: A Reference Paper." *Lektos,* August: 81-95.

Koppert, Vincent A. 1930a. "Contributions to Clayoquot Ethnology." *Catholic University of America, Anthropological Series* 1: 11-30.

————. 1930b. "The Nootka Family." *Primitive Man* 3:49-55.

LaBudde, Nathan. 1998. "IWC debates Whaling Proposals." *Earth Island Journal* 13:1:8.

Laforet, Andrea. 2000. "Ellen Curley's Hat." In *Nuu-chah-nulth Voices, Histories, Objects & Journeys,* edited by Alan L. Hoover. Victoria: Royal BC Museum.

Lok, Michael. 1906. "Lok's Account of Fuca's Voyage, 1592." In "Hakluytus Postomus", or "Purchas His Pilgrimes", by Samuel Purchas. Hakluyt Society, *Works,* ex. ser. 14:415-21. (Reprinted in Cook 1973 (above).)

Lavoie, Judith. 2007. "Ahousaht: Get Clean or Get Out." Victoria *Times-Colonist*, July 10.

———. 2008. "Land, Cash Pave the Way for Treaty." Victoria *Times-Colonist*, November 14.

Macnair, Peter L. 1986. "From Kwakiutl to Kwakwaka'wakw." In *Native Peoples: The Canadian Experience*, edited by R. Bruce Morrison and C. Roderick Wilson. Toronto: McClelland and Stewart.

———. 2000. "Tim Paul: The Homeward Journey." In *Nuu-chah-nulth Voices, Histories, Objects & Journeys*, edited by Alan L. Hoover. Victoria: Royal BC Museum.

Macnair, Peter L., Alan L. Hoover and Kevin Neary. 1984. *The Legacy: Tradition and Innovation in Northwest Coast Indian Art*. Vancouver: Douglas and McIntyre. Reprinted 2007, Victoria: Royal BC Museum.

Marine Mammal Centre. n.d. "Gray Whale." http://www.marinemammalcenter. org/learning/education/whales/gray.asp

Marr, Carolyn. 1987. *Portrait in Time: Photographs of the Makah by Samuel G. Morse, 1896–1903*. Neah Bay: Makah Cultural and Research Center.

McDowell, Jim. 1997. *Hamatsa: The Enigma of Cannibalism on the Pacific Northwest Coast*. Vancouver: Ronsdale Press.

McKelvie, Bruce A. 1946. *Maquinna the Magnificent*. Vancouver: *Daily Province*.

McMillan, Alan. 1999. *Since the Time of the Transformers: The Ancient Heritage of the Nuu-chah-nulth, Ditidaht and Makah*. Vancouver: UBC Press.

———. 2000. "Early Nuu-chah-nulth Art and Adornment: Glimpses from the Archaeological Record." In *Nuu-chah-nulth Voices, Histories, Objects & Journeys*, edited by Alan L. Hoover. Victoria: Royal BC Museum.

McMillan, Alan, and Denis St Claire. 1982. *Alberni Prehistory: Archaeological and Ethnographic Investigations on Western Vancouver Island*. Penticton: Theytus Books.

Meares, John. 1967. *Voyages Made in the Years 1788 and 1789 from China to the North West Coast of America*. Amsterdam & New York: Bibliotheca Australiana #22, N. Israel, Da Capo Press.

Menzies, Archibald. 1923. *Menzie's Journal of Vancouver's Voyage April to October, 1792*, edited by C.F. Newcombe. Memoir 5 (8). Victoria: BC Archives.

Moogk, Susan. 1980. "The Wolf Masks of the Nootka Wolf Ritual: A Statement of Transformation." M.A. thesis, Dept of Anthropology and Sociology, University of British Columbia.

Morrow, Shayne. 2008. "Nuu-chah-nulth Fisheries Trial Resumes." *Alberni Times*, February 4.

———. 2009. "First Nations Land Deal Historic, Strahl Says." Victoria *Times-Colonist*, April 10.

Moser, Charles. 1926. *Reminiscences of the West Coast of Vancouver Island*. Victoria: Acme Press.

Mowachaht-Muchalaht First Nations. 2000. "Yuquot Agenda Paper." In *Nuu-chah-nulth Voices, Histories, Objects & Journeys*, edited by Alan L. Hoover. Victoria: Royal BC Museum.

Mozino, J.M. 1970. *Noticias de Nutka; An Account of Nootka Sound in 1792*.

Translated and edited by I.H. Wilson. Toronto: McClelland and Stewart.

Murray, Peter. 1988. *The Vagabond Fleet: A Chronicle of the North Pacific Sealing Schooner Trade.* Victoria: Sono Nis Press.

Newcombe, C.F. 1907. "Petroglyphs in British Columbia." *Victoria Daily Times,* September 7.

Newman, Philip L. 1957. "An Intergroup Collectivity Among the Nootka." M.A. thesis in Anthropology, University of Washington, Seattle.

Nuu-chah-nulth Tribal Council. 1996. *Indian Residential Schools: The Nuu-chah-nulth Experience.* Report of the Nuu-chah-nulth Tribal Council Indian residential school study, 1992–94. Port Alberni: Nuu-chah-nulth Tribal Council.

Nuytten, Phil. 1993. "Money From the Sea." *National Geographic* 183:1:109–114.

Ogilvie, Ruth. 2008. "Incremental Treaty Deal Under Fire." *Westcoaster.ca.* http:// www.westcoaster.ca/modules/AMS/article.php?storyid=5505.

Okerlund, Lana. 2007a. "Too Many Sea Otters?" *The Tyee.ca,* October 4.

——. 2007b. "Taking Aim at Otters." *The Tyee.ca,* October 5.

Olson, Ronald L. 1936 "The Quinault Indians." University of Washington *Publications in Anthropology* 6:1.

Paquet, Maggie. 2004. *Nuu-chah-nulth Phrase Book and Dictionary: Barkley Sound Dialect.* Port Alberni: Barkley Sound Dialect Working Group.

Peterson, Melissa, and the Makah Cultural and Research Center. 2002. "Makah." In *Native Peoples of the Olympic Penninsula: Who We Are,* edited by Jacilee Wray. Norman: University of Oklahoma Press.

Phipps, The Right Reverend Bill. 1998. "To Former Students of United Church Indian Residential Schools, and to their Families and Communities." http:// www.uccan.org/airs/981027ap.htm

Pitt-Brooke, David. 2004. *Chasing Clayoquot: A Wilderness Almanac.* Vancouver: Raincoast Books.

Powell, James V. 1990. "Quileute." In *Handbook of the North American Indians,* vol. 7: *Northwest Coast,* edited by Wayne Suttles. Washington, DC: Smithsonian Institution.

Renker, Ann. n.d. "The Makah Tribe: People of the Sea and Forest." http://content.lib.washington.edu/aipnw/renker.html

Riley, Carroll L. 1968. "The Makah Indians: A Study of Political and Economic Organization." *Ethnohistory* 15:57-95.

Roberts, Helen H., and Morris Swadesh. 1955. "Songs of the Nootka Indians of Western Vancouver Island." *American Philosophical Society Transactions* 45:199-327.

Rosman, Abraham, and Paula Rubel. 1971. *Feasting with Mine Enemy: Rank and Exchange among Northwest Coast Societies.* New York: Columbia University Press.

Ross, Alexander. 1849. *Adventures of the First Settlers on the Oregon or Columbia River: Being a Narrative of the Expedition Fitted Out by John Jacob Astor, to Establish the Pacific Fur Company; with an Account of Some Indian tribes on the Coast of the Pacific.* (Reprinted 1969.) London: Smith, Elder.

Ruyle, Eugene E. 1973. "Slavery, Surplus and Stratification on the Northwest Coast: The Ethnoenergetics of an Incipient Stratification System." *Current Anthropology* 14:603-631.

St Claire, Denis E. 1976. "Report of the Archaeological Survey of the Barkley Sound Area." Unpublished report, Archaeological Sites Advisory Board, Sheshaht Band, Opetchesaht Band, Alberni Valley Museum, Port Alberni and Victoria.

———. 1977. "Ts'ishauth Fieldnotes." Unpublished ms (with Eugene Arima).

Sam, Stanley, Sr. 1997. *Ahousaht Wild Side Heritage Trail Guidebook.* Vancouver: Western Wilderness Committee.

Sapir, Edward. 1911. "Some Aspects of Nootka language and Culture." *American Anthropologist* 13:15-28.

———. 1912. "Nootka Notes" (1910–12). Unpublished ms 1237: 1, 5, 6, 17, Canadian Ethnology Service, National Museum of Man, Ottawa.

———. 1913. "A Girl's Puberty Ceremony Among the Nootka Indians." *Royal Society of Canada Transactions* (third series) 7:67-80.

———. 1915. "The Social Organization of the West Coast Tribes." *Royal Society of Canada Transactions* (third series) 9:355-374.

———. 1919. "A Flood Legend of the Nootka Indians." *Journal of American Folk Lore* 32:351-355.

———. 1921. "The Life of a Nootka Indian." *Queen's Quarterly* 28:232-243, 351-367. (Reprinted, 1925, as "Sayach'apis, a Nootka Trader", in *American Indian Life*, edited by Elsie C. Parsons. Lincoln: University of Nebraska Press.)

———. 1924. "The Rival Whalers, a Nitinat Story." *International Journal of American Linguistics* 3:76-102.

———. 1949. *Selected Writings of Edward Sapir in Language, Culture and Personality,* edited by David G. Mandelbaum. Berkeley: University of California Press.

Sapir, Edward, and Morris Swadesh. 1939. *Nootka Texts: Tales and Ethnological Narratives with Grammatical Notes and Lexical Materials.* Philadelphia: Linguistic Society of America.

———. 1955. "Native Accounts of Nootka Ethnography." *International Journal of American Linguistics* 21:4, part 2. Reprinted 1978 by AMS Press.

Sapir, Edward, Morris Swadesh, Alexander Thomas, John Thomas and Frank Williams. 2000. *The Whaling Indians: Tales of Extraordinary Experience.* Part 10 of *Sapir-Thomas Nootka Texts.* Mercury Series, Canadian Ethnology Service Paper 134. Hull, Quebec: Canadian Museum of Civilization.

———. 2004. *The Whaling Indians: Legendary Hunters.* Part 9 of *Sapir-Thomas Nootka Texts.* Mercury Series, Canadian Ethnology Service Paper 139. Gatineau, Quebec: Canadian Museum of Civilization.

———. 2007. *The Whaling Indians: The Origin of the Wolf Ritual.* Part 12 of *Sapir-Thomas Nootka Texts.* Mercury Series, Canadian Ethnology Service Paper 144. Gatineau, Quebec: Canadian Museum of Civilization.

———. 2009. *Family Origin Histories.* Part 11 of *Sapir-Thomas Nootka Texts.* Mercury Series, Canadian Ethnology Service Paper 145. Gatineau, Quebec: Canadian Museum of Civilization.

Savard, Dan. 2010. *Images from the Likeness House.* Victoria: Royal BC Museum.

Scammon, Charles M. 1968. *The Marine Mammals of the Northwestern Coast of North America.* New York: Dover.

Schultz, C.D., and Company. 1971. "Study to Determine the Effect of the Pacific Rim National Park Upon the Several Indian Reserves Located Within the Proposed Boundaries." Unpublished report, Parks Canada, Dept of Indian and Northern Affairs, Ottawa.

Scientific Panel for Sustainable Forest Practices in Clayoquot Sound, The. 1995. "Inventory of Plants and Animals Culturally Significant to the Nuu-chah-nulth of Clayoquot Sound." In *First Nations Perspectives Relating to Forest Practices in Clayoquot Sound*. Victoria: Crown Publications.

Sendey, John. 1977. *The Nootkan Indian, A Pictorial*. Port Alberni, BC: Alberni Valley Museum.

Shoop, Gregg Brian. 1972. "The Participation of the Ohiaht Indians in the Commercial Fisheries of the Bamfield Barkley Sound Area of British Columbia." M.A. thesis in Anthropology, University of Victoria.

Shukovsky, Paul, and Mike Barber. 2001. "Resident Gray Whales Now Fair Game for Makah." *Seattle PI* http://seattlepi.nwsource.com/local/31319_makah14.shtml

Sproat, Gilbert Malcolm. 1868. *Scenes and Studies of Savage Life*. London: Smith, Elder. Reprinted, 1986 as *The Nootka: Scenes and Studies of Savage Life*, edited and annotated by Charles Lillard. Victoria: Sono Nis Press.

Steel, Deborah. 2008a. "Comments 'despicable', says NTC's Happynook." *Ha-Shilth-Sa* 35:6:1,4.

———. 2008b. "Tla-o-qui-aht Quits Main Nuu-chah-nulth Table." *Ha-Shilth-Sa* 35:18:1,7.

Streetly, Joanna, and Adrian Dorst. 2000. *Paddling Through Time: A Kayaking Journey Through Clayoquot Sound*. Vancouver: Raincoast Books.

Sullivan, Robert. 2000. *A Whale Hunt*. New York: Scribner.

Suttles, Wayne, ed. 1990. *Handbook of North American Indians*, vol. 7: *Northwest Coast*. Washington, DC: Smithsonian Institution.

Strange, James. 1928. *James Strange's Journal and Narrative of the Commercial Expedition from Bombay to the Northwest Coast of America*. Madras: Government Press.

Swadesh, Mary Haas, and Morris Swadesh. 1933. "A Visit to the Other World, a Nitinat Text." *International Journal of American Linguistics* 7:195–208.

Swadesh, Morris. 1948. "Motivations in Nootka Warfare." *Southwestern Journal of Anthropology* 4:7–93.

Swan, James G. 1870. *The Indians of Cape Flattery, at the Entrance to the Straits of Fuca, Washington Territory*. Smithsonian Contributions to Knowledge 16:8.

Swanton, John R. 1910. "Nootka." In *Handbook of American Indians North of Mexico*, edited by Frederick Web Hodge. *Bureau of American Ethnology Bulletin* 30:2:82.

Tenant, Paul 1990 *Aboriginal Peoples and Politics: The Indian Land Question in British Columbia, 1849–1889*. Vancouver: University of British Columbia Press.

Times-Colonist. 2007. "Band's Supreme Court Petition Continues". Victoria *Times-Colonist* July 27, p. D2.

Titian, Denise. 2008. "Hesquiaht Family Honours Ancestor Unjustly Hanged." *Ha-Shilth-Sa* 35:14:1,3–4.

Touchie, Bernice. 1977. "Report on the Settlement of Whyack Village, Vancouver Island, British Columbia." Unpublished report, National Historic Parks and Sites, Parks Canada, Calgary.

Townsend-Gault, Charlotte. 2000. "A Conversation with *Ki-ke-in*." In *Nuu-chah-nulth Voices, Histories, Objects & Journeys*, edited by Alan L. Hoover. Victoria: Royal BC Museum.

Turner, Nancy. 1995. *Food Plants of Coastal First Peoples.* Victoria: Royal BC Museum.

———. 1998. *Plant Technology of First Peoples in British Columbia.* Victoria: Royal BC Museum

Turner, Nancy J., and Barbara S. Efrat. 1982. *Ethnobotany of the Hesquiat Indians of Vancouver Island.* Cultural Recovery Paper 2. Victoria: British Columbia Provincial Museum.

Turner, Nancy J., John Thomas, Barry F. Carlson and Robert T. Ogilvie. 1983. *Ethnobotany of the Nitinaht Indians of Vancouver Island.* Occasional Paper 24. Victoria: British Columbia Provincial Museum.

Waterman, Thomas T. 1920. "The Whaling Equipment of the Makah Indians." University of Washington *Publications in Anthropology* 1:2.

Webster, Peter. 1983. *As Far as I Know: Reminiscences of an Ahoushat Elder.* Campbell River, BC: Campbell River Museum.

Whitner, Peter L. 1981 "Makah Commercial Sealing, 1860–1897: A Study in Acculturation and Conflict." Unpublished paper, Fourth North American Fur Trade Conference, October 1-4.

Wike, Joyce. 1958. "Social Stratification Among the Nootka." *Ethnohistory* 5: 219-41.

Wiwchar, David 2003a "Nuu-chah-nulth Leaders Concerned about Maa-nulth A.I.P." *Ha-Shilth-Sa* 30:15:3.

———. 2003b "Maa-nulth Counters Claims." *Ha-Shilth-Sa* 30:15:3.

Index

The Authors

Eugene Arima is an ethnologist specializing in Arctic and Northwest Coast culture areas. After graduating from the University of Toronto in 1959, he began working as an ethnologist in the Human History Branch of the National Museum of Canada. He first studied Arctic ethnology, particularly Inuit skin boats and myths, but in the mid 1960s overlapped this work with Northwest Coast cultures, with watercraft and traditions continuing in the forefront of his interest. In the 1970s, Arima left the museum, completed a long deferred doctoral dissertation on the Caribou Inuit kayak, and the reconstruction of a west-coast whaling canoe for National Historic Parks and Sites. The canoe construction led to a position as an ethnohistorian with NHPS in Ottawa., which he held for 31 years, retiring in 2007. From his home in Ottawa, he has written, edited and contributed to several books on the whaling people, including the orginal edition of this book, *The West Coast (Nootka) People* (RBCM 1983).

Alan Hoover was educated at Simon Fraser University and worked for 33 years as a curator and manager at the Royal BC Museum, until he retired in 2001. He has written extensively on the material culture and art of Northwest Coast peoples, including articles and essays on the works of Charles Edenshaw, Bill Reid, Robert Davidson and the history of the Dundas Collection of Tsimshian art. He is a co-author of *The Legacy: Tradition and Innovation in Northwest Coast Indian Art* (RBCM 1984) and *The Magic Leaves: A History of Haida Argillite Carving* (RBCM 2002), and editor of the anthology *Nuu-chah-nulth Voices, Histories, Objects & Journeys* (RBCM 2000).

Royal British Columbia Museum

The Royal British Columbia Museum explores the province's human history and natural history, advances new knowledge and understanding of British Columbia, and provides a dynamic forum for discussion and a place for reflection. Situated in the heart of Victoria, British Columbia's capital city, the Royal BC Museum serves all citizens in all parts of the province.

It celebrates culture and history by telling the stories of British Columbia in ways that enlighten, stimulate and inspire. The stories are based on the millions of artifacts, specimens and documents in its collections. The museum produces publications, exhibitions and public programs about these collections, bringing the history and nature of this province to life in exciting, innovative and personal ways.

Looking to the future, by 2017 the Royal British Columbia Museum will be a refreshed, modern museum, extending its reach far beyond Victoria as a world-class cultural venue and repository of digital treasures.

Find out more at: royalbcmuseum.bc.ca